THIS BOOK IS FOR Y

- You are a person who has suffered domestic abuse—be it physical, financial, emotional and/or mental.
- You are a person who has been ashamed of your childhood and upbringing.
- You are a person stuck in the pain of incest and you want to break free and spread your wings to fly again.
- You are a person who has been a victim of your insecurities, low self-esteem, and lack of self-confidence.
- You are a person who wants a good read on resilience, hope, courage, and how to get unstuck in your life.
- You are a person who desires to be encouraged to get up one last time and push through the birth canal of your circumstances.
- You are a person who wants inner growth and personal power.
- You are a person who is tired of playing small based on your past experiences.
- You are a person who wants to start your *Purposewalk*.

WHAT PEOPLE SAY ABOUT THE BOOK

"Wow! What a life! It is such an intimate account I feel I've known you for twenty years . . . I had heart pangs in places throughout your story. I'm sure you've shed a quiet tear every time you are on the plane leaving Jamaica. Much love."

Matthew Binns
Producer: *2fast2furious*

"It is difficult to imagine the levels of determination in the mind of Dr. Ava Eagle Brown as 'The Mango Girl' recounts a brutal upbringing only the strongest would survive. Her strength of mind and resilience finally results in success against the longest of odds; a unique and compelling story."

David Ball, Wales, United Kingdom
Movie Line Producer

"'The Mango Girl' recaptures the vividly brutal youth of Dr. Ava Eagle Brown and her journey to find self-respect and esteem. The book is littered with the spectrum of emotions as Ava sets about finding who she is and who she is determined to become; a must read!"

Diana Mae Fernandez
Design Thinking Business Coach—New York

"It's hard to imagine my mum being abused by her father and held up and abused at gun point in front of me, her then three-year-old daughter. But I didn't have to imagine; I witnessed it. Yet, mum's struggle for survival in her native Jamaica reveals a terrifying tale experienced by a few. Driven by instinct and 'nous', Mum overcomes ongoing spousal abuse by starting a new life against the odds in the UK; a life demanding total dedication, guts, and vision . . . to succeed."

Chardonae Stephenson (Jasmine)
Author and Music Student

"It was heartening to hear my student say that he stayed up almost the whole night reading. This followed Ava's book reading session at my University in Jamaica.

When I inquired what kept my student up, he said the book by Ava Brown was so riveting that even he, a non-reader, was compelled to read on into the night.

This is the nature of the autobiography of my friend whose story of courage, resilience and triumph is an inspiration to many. Ava was not hesitant to be vulnerable as it is clear that her intention is to impact lives and generate change for [the] better. I believe she was successful in this regard and for that I applaud her. God has certainly given Ava "beauty for ashes."

Dr. Garfield Young
University of Technology, Jamaica

THE MANGO GIRL

AVA BROWN

Published by Authors Place Press
9885 Wyecliff Drive, Suite 200
Highlands Ranch, CO 80126
AuthorsPlace.com

Copyright 2020 © by Ava Brown
All Rights Reserved

No part of this book may be reproduced or transmitted in any form by any means: graphic, electronic, or mechanical, including photocopying, recording, taping or by any information storage or retrieval system without permission, in writing, from the authors, except for the inclusion of brief quotations in a review, article, book, or academic paper. The authors and publisher of this book and the associated materials have used their best efforts in preparing this material. The authors and publisher make no representations or warranties with respect to accuracy, applicability, fitness or completeness of the contents of this material. They disclaim any warranties expressed or implied, merchantability, or fitness for any particular purpose. The authors and publisher shall in no event be held liable for any loss or other damages, including but not limited to special, incidental, consequential, or other damages. If you have any questions or concerns, the advice of a competent professional should be sought.

Manufactured in the United States of America.

ISBN: 978-1-62865-721-0

CONTENTS

This Book Is For You If..1

What People Say About The Book 2

About The Author..9

Dedication 11

Acknowledgements 12

Bonus 14

Disclaimer 16

Mango Muse 17

Chapter 1: The Birth Canal 18

Chapter 2: The Dark...32

Chapter 3: The Real Dad Stands Up 52

Chapter 4: Comfort Zone..66

Chapter 5: New Life Appears...................................79

Chapter 6: Broken 88

Chapter 7: Pushing Forward....................................97

Chapter 8: Your Gut 118

Chapter 9: Your Gut 130

Chapter 10: The Unknown.................................... 137

Chapter 11: Deep End.. 144

Chapter 12: Transition 151

Chapter 13: Readjustments 163

Chapter 14: Weapon 171
Chapter 15: Prison 180
Chapter 16: Unbroken 183
Chapter 17: Temporary Breakdowns 188
Chapter 18: Fierce 195
Chapter 19: Penalty 200
Chapter 20: Permanence 209
Chapter 21: Reputations 221
Chapter 22: The Crumble 231
Chapter 23: Weakness 240
Chapter 24: Letting Go 248
Chapter 25: Home At Last 261
Chapter 26: Landlady Drama 268
Chapter 27: Heading Back To London 278
Chapter 28: Displaced In London In December 286
Chapter 29: Homebound 294
Chapter 30: The Journey Of An Unknown Visa Girl 303
Chapter 31: The Woman Made Of Steel And Stone 312
Chapter 32: Why This Caged Bird Sang 320
Chapter 33: My Full Circle 326

ABOUT THE AUTHOR

Dr. Ava Eagle Brown was born and brought up in Saint Elizabeth, Jamaica. She trained as a secondary teacher at the Sam Sharpe Teacher's College in Montego Bay, Jamaica, followed later by an MBA in Business Administration from the University of Wales. Ava now holds an honorary doctorate degree, which was given to her for her philanthropy work in women's empowerment, homelessness, and people transformation.

Ava lives in London and is the mother of two children, who she calls her life. She is a transformational coach, international motivational speaker, and author. She is the CEO of The Mango Girl CIC - a non for profit that focusses on helping women to be their best selves as well. She is also the owner of Chakai, a hair and skin business born out of her pain to purpose story. See more at www.chakai.co.uk. Ava is someone who makes it a mandate to remind everyone good things are possible.

The Mango Girl is an updated version of her first book, *Bamboo and Fern*, from which she is set to launch a movie campaign. Ava hopes to see this book on the Hollywood stage. She is currently working on part two of *The Mango Girl*, to be called *Steel and Stone*. She has written and published several books. Her original autobiography, *Bamboo and Fern*, has sold in more than forty-five countries.

Ava's vision is to help other people tap into their full potential by eradicating self-limiting beliefs. For them to ultimately live the lives they want, need, and desire; essentially, a life of abundance and purpose.

Ava has been featured on BBC, The Financial Times, The Telegraph, and the Huffington Post, just to name a few of the press that have sought after her. She was awarded:

- 2017-Business Woman of The Year—Citibank sponsored award
- Radio W.O.R.K.S. World Author Awards, 2017

- 2016-Author of the Year Award
- Powerhouse Woman Award 2017
- We Are The City Award—Entrepreneurship, 2017
- Inspirational Role Model Award, 2015
- Motivational Woman of 2015—Black African Women Rock
- 2015-Nominated for a BEFFTA Award
- 2015-Nominated for London Leadership Peace Award

Her life has not been an easy one, having gone through numerous storms, namely: domestic violence, child abuse, single parenting, divorce, financial deprivation, marital deception, molestation, and gun violence. And yet she survived and thrived. Ava uses her experiences to help other people. She is on a mission to do that globally, by helping women work through trauma and understand that nothing is impossible. Her motto is the very word *impossible;* it says, "I'm Possible." This is the way she has been able to survive.

She can be contacted via:

www.avaeaglebrown.com

www.themangogirlcic.com

www.chakai.co.uk

info@avabrown.org

DEDICATION

This is dedicated with all my love to my mum and my children. You have given me a reason to go on despite the storms. Because of you three, I understand unconditional love.

Thank you, Mama, for choosing to bring a child into the world when you were just a child yourself. This could not have been an easy decision, especially when your parents had put you out on the streets; so you had to grow up fast. Until recently, I did not understand your inability to show love emotionally or physically, but I knew you loved us when you sacrificed your last $100 and bought a "tups" of salted fish to ensure we had food to eat. You gave your children the most and remained hungry at times; you fussed over us and made us feel like royalty . . . Mama, I love you.

My daughter, Chardonae (Jasmine) Elizabeth. Jasmine, as a child you had to grow up so fast and saw some of your mum's struggles. It's my hope that they strengthened you and made you a warrior of a woman, but with the heart of an angel. You have been the best daughter I could have asked for, especially as I have had the privilege of seeing you turn 21. You are an amazing young lady, full of grace, compassion and wisdom and I would not change anything about you. I am thankful that the challenges have not broken us, but made us a stronger mother and daughter team, and most importantly, friends. All my love, Mum xxx

My son, Mikhel Kai. You came into my life long before this was written, but you are such a sweet son who has added joy daily, whether it is with your smile or just asking for a cuddle. Little did you know that you were adding to my life in a significant way, especially at times when writing, proofreading, or editing *The Mango Girl* was just a difficult thing to do. Those cuddles helped me push through the birth canal to give birth to this book. With all my love, Mum xxx.

ACKNOWLEDGEMENTS

Auntie Norma Knight, I love you. Thanks for the love through the years and the belief in me. More importantly, thank you for the trip to London that changed the direction of my story.

Jean Marie Thompson, my confidante and friend, thanks for all your support over the years. Without even knowing, you gave me the name for my book in an email, and you helped me through some of the tough times.

You are such a caring soul, someone who took me into her arms despite the risk. Thanks for the late night chats, the running up of your phone bills, and even sending me money when I was stone-broke. Jean you were my sanctuary. When I needed to offload, you just sat and took it all in. I always felt better walking away after my sessions with you.

Buju Leonard Brooks, my stepfather, the man who fed me when my own father didn't care to. The man who would give me the last piece of meat on his plate and ensured that, regardless of how little, we had food. Thanks for everything.

Uncle Ken Brown, my real daddy. Thanks for being my daddy, and thanks for showing me how a dad should love his child. You didn't have to but took it on yourself.

Dario Pirjak, the stranger who believed in me and became one of my motivators and my life coach. Your counsel, belief, wisdom, and, most importantly, consistent listening ears, are totally appreciated. I admire your zeal for success that's rubbing off on me.

Audreia Josephs, my new mum, sister, and friend. The day we met was an amazing design by the Creator. Thanks for being there as the secret witness. Your additions to this book from a bird's-eye view help to solidify that the later part of my journey wasn't just seen by you but experienced in parts. We love you for simply being you.

Sonia Poleon, my ride-or-die chick. Girl, the times you have held me down, chatted on the phone late at night, and even helped with childcare. Your friendship and sisterhood, I will cherish always. Xxx

Angels who gave me wings over the years:

The Honourable Ambassador Burchell Whiteman, you gave me my first real chance. May you continue to always be a believer in young people.

Mavis Taylor and Mrs. Johnson, my former teachers at Saint Elizabeth Technical High School. You mothered me and moulded the little ability I possessed at the time.

Mrs. Taylor, you fed me when I was hungry, sometimes without even knowing. I thank God for you all, three women who inspired my drive through their belief in me.

BONUS

To see pictures of my childhood and get a special video of aspects of my life not included in the book, and to see more about what I have been up to, click these links:

http://www.avaeaglebrown.com

http://bit.ly/2rHtMjB

"We are scared of the dark, light is comforting as it helps us see shapes and forms. Light helps with recognition and shows what lies ahead of us. We yearn for the comfort of light as it provides silhouettes and form, allowing us to recognise and define what's before us. Are we afraid of the darkness, or is it the truth hiding behind it?"

—***Dr. Ava Eagle Brown***

DISCLAIMER

I do not remember all of the exact words said in all of the stressful situations I have endured, but I do remember the gist of what was said, and what I felt and experienced. I have attempted, to the best of my ability, to recreate the extreme stress and anxiety of those situations.

MANGO MUSE

Having failed English in high school and spoke "patios" the local vernacular all my life, I had no intention of writing a book. However, as my experiences and challenges grew, my makeshift diary became a large handwritten book.

Fast forward to London. The vicissitude I endured meant I knew that there had to be others who were enduring similar issues. I wanted to share my journey to heal not just myself, but to free others and make it permissible for others to share.

CHAPTER 1: THE BIRTH CANAL

Birth is a special time for any mother; she forgets all her struggles and latches onto the bundle of joy she is gifted with.

To understand the woman I am today, you'll have to first learn the story of my beginnings.

I was born in an old post office in a poor district near George's Valley, St. Elizabeth, Jamaica. My mother, who was only sixteen at the time and far too young to be a mum, was almost as much of a stranger in that district as I was.

She had been put out by her parents with "good riddance" for the trouble she (and I) represented. I've been told that she had chosen that district, which adjoined her own, because that was where my father was from. Of course, she had gone straight to his parent's home, which was one of the community's largest and most impressive, hoping to find shelter. Yet, when she turned up on their doorstep to say that she was pregnant with their son's child, his mother furiously chased my mum away. She answered my mother's request for support and food by mockingly suggesting that she start collecting dirt to make Milo (a chocolaty drink that most children loved) for her bastard spawn.

Shortly after my birth, the young man who was said to be my dad absconded. In my childish mind, I imagined him as a scared young man, fleeing the massive responsibility that was to come with a child, hoping to live out the rest of his youth in the carefree manner that all young men seem to crave. It was only as an adult that I began to understand the implications of the rumours that had always circulated around me; whispers that my father's parents' response could be based on the fact that he felt I wasn't his child.

Alone and pregnant in that new town, my mother switched her efforts to finding a new boyfriend as a breadwinner. She quickly found Jack, who was employed at the nearby rice factory, and that was the familial situation into which I was born. Despite Jack making scarcely enough to feed himself, I don't remember my mother ever having a proper job. It was painfully clear to me, even as a young child, that our family was extremely poor. By the time I was seven, the hunger in my belly had already ignited the flame that would propel me out of our one-room house, which by then was bursting at its seams with me, my stepfather, mother, and three siblings. Though I had no idea of how I would escape the misery within its walls, I had a fire in my blood that would have burned that little one-room shack down.

Inside the house, a sheet was used to separate us children, with the adults on one side and the four children on the other. There was never enough bed space when sleeping four to a bed. And it was not unusual that someone would wet the bed, so we often slept soaked in urine. We awoke each day with the sun kissing our faces despite many daily chores that awaited us. Some of these included taking care of the goats, fetching the water from the only pipe that served our entire community, collecting wood for the fire, and washing clothes. Sometimes, we even had to cook the family meals. Being the eldest, babysitting was something I was expected to do from an early age. We were expected to clean the floor of our room every day using a dye called "red oak," which turned the concrete floor a deep red, then polish it to a high shine. We weren't allowed to stop until my mother could see her reflection glaring up at her from below.

It always seemed to be my duty to clean our side of the room, but I had to let my frustrations at that unfairness bubble inside of me in silence. If I didn't, a stone, machete, or any solid item within my mum's reach would come hurtling towards me, of course, flung from my mother's strong arm.

Chapter 1: The Birth Canal

I had been born with a streak of rebellion, and my mother, who was keenly aware of that, was always ready to squash it out of me.

One night I had been overly tired from the day in the sun and refused to finish my chores, knowing very well this wouldn't go down with mom. Instead of laying low, I was moving my weary feet to follow my siblings inside. But that rebellion had not escaped my mother's attention, and she had already come up with her own plans to show me who was boss.

I was at the end of the line filing in the door, and when everyone else had made it inside, my mother rapidly slammed the door shut in my face and locked it. She answered my surprised cries by jerking it open again, saying, "You want to come in? Then come in now." Of course, I thought she was serious, and I immediately moved into the doorway. Her strong grip, as she grabbed me and gave me a good beating, left me in such shock that I was startled to find myself being pushed right back outside. Hearing the sound of the lock shutting me out was her final punishment, and it almost felt as though she enjoyed it..

That was my first taste of my mother's penalty meted out on those who dared to disobey her. The darkness around me seemed darker than ever; my only light was the inconsistent flickering of the fireflies we call *peanie wallies*. The realization that I was alone, left to the elements, filled my heart with a wild fear. All of the ghost stories we were told came rushing back. I could feel every dead person we had ever spoken about floating around me.

I crouched into a tight ball, the night's silence nearly smothering me. It was more than two hours later when my brother opened the door to let me in. That was no heroic or chivalrous effort on my brother's part; my mum had allowed that kindness. I guess that she knew I had learnt my lesson.

My mum told me a story of when she'd taught me another lesson as a child. She stated that I'd refused to hold one of my infant siblings so she could perform in a concert. She said she got mad and tore off all my clothes as we travelled from the concert venue to our house. I was only about ten years old at the time. She had a very volatile temper and she scarred one of my sisters for life. My sister had gone to a shop on an errand for my mum, but when she didn't come back on time, my mum went in search of her. On finding her in a boy's home, she gave her a beating that was a notice to all of us girls to never venture out of her reign again.

The rule in our house was that as soon as children rose out of bed in the morning, they were set to work and then ushered outside. We were forbidden to go back into the house until the sun was setting and we were ready to go to bed. If we lingered in the morning, we would be drenched in cold water, a definite out-of-bed strategy that worked every time. However, that was rare, as the bed was normally so full of people that we were either jostled awake or pushed out by the smell and feel of urine. Before we came back in the evenings, we would have to fill up pans with water, to wash ourselves the next morning. Our house didn't have a bathroom, so everyone bathed outside, boys and girls alike. Privacy wasn't a word I knew when I was growing up in our home. It wasn't until I started "feathering" (growing pubic hair) that the adults decided it was time to grant me some privacy to that routine. So they built a washroom out of some salvaged corrugated zinc sheets.

On the evenings that my mother cooked dinner, we would all gather around the old makeshift kitchen outside, which stood near where we bathed. After we were served our dinner, we would each find a somewhat comfortable stone to sit on and eat. There were always dogs around, so our mealtime was filled with a mixture of dog breath and food. As soon as we got our meal, we would try to eat as quickly as possible, with the hope that someone else would *buss* (be full) so that we could help them finish their meal. There was no TV to watch after dinner, so we stayed outside, sitting on the stones and making jokes with one another, or taking turns making up ghost stories. Since we had no electricity, we bottled up the *peanie wallie* to chase the blackness away. Finally, when we were too tired to stay up any longer, we would retreat to the dank and cramped bed. I was always among the last to stay up, simply because I despised the sleeping arrangements.

We each had a sparse wardrobe and the few pieces we had were all hand-me-downs. Each of us had one pair of good shoes. This was the pair we would wear only to church; school was attended barefoot.

There was also only one uniform for each of us, which was the required outfit for primary school, so we had to wash the white blouse every day. We attended the local public school where our classrooms were always overcrowded. I can remember attending my fourth-grade studies alongside more than fifty other pupils crammed into the overcrowded and boisterous room. I'm sure the teachers did their best in these situations, but they always moved the lessons along according to the brightest students' progress, meaning the slower students, like me, were often left behind. Even so, I did my best to keep up. We walked to school like all children in the district. It was only the ones who attended school outside of our area that were driven. For us, lunch usually consisted of a fried egg and bread, which had been placed in a brown paper bag along with our drink - a mixture of sugar, water, and lime. Unfortunately, by the time lunch rolled around at mid-day, the egg would have begun to smell really unpleasant. Sometimes, I would hide my lunch in the bushes near the school and use an object to mark its spot so that I could find it at lunchtime. It never occurred to me there might be mongoose or rats in the bushes. If I had known then what I know now about all the vicious, hungry creatures living around us, I would never have done such a thing!

There were times when there was no food in our house to pack for lunch, and I was left with two choices: go without or stay home. I always chose the go-without option, trying instead to ward off the eventual hunger by eating as hefty a breakfast as possible, although that strategy was a challenge and sometimes completely unfeasible. Occasionally, we could come home for a lunch of overnight-roasted dumplings. These dumplings were a traditional, simple food in Jamaica, made from a paste of flour, water, and salt that has been rolled into a spherical shape and then fried or boiled. The ones we ate had been boiled and then left overnight and cooked on a coal fire; the end result was a roasted dumpling that had absorbed most of the charcoal it had been cooked on. My mother would serve these roasted dumplings with mint tea. We would rush through the meal, drink some water, and run back to school so that we wouldn't miss the afternoon classes.

Truth be told, by the time I reached school, I was already hungry again. That was a little life lesson: no matter how much effort I put in, very little of my hunger for a better life would be satisfied while I remained reliant on someone else. At the end of each school day we would rush home, not because we were excited to play evening games with one another, but because we had a pile of chores waiting for us. We did, however, entertain ourselves along the walk home, usually by playing cricket, or catch with sour oranges. Sometimes, we would steal some precious minutes to play a game called "stuck," in which two of us would stand at opposite ends of a street facing each other, with a third in the middle trying to "site" (dodge) a ball, or whatever object we could find for throwing between the first two. We always played these games in the middle of the road, with passing cars blowing their horns and sending us scattering out of the way. Thankfully, none of us was ever hurt!

It was customary for the children from our school to gather in little groups to walk home together. I yearned to find that perfect group to fit in, but I was always on the periphery of any group that I tried to join. Mostly, I was pushed aside by teasing remarks about how I was always getting good grades at school, in subjects such as Food & Nutrition and Home economics; the non-numeric subjects. That was just the start, though. At times, some of the meaner girls would wait for me and inflict some type of physical torment. It was an easy escape if they only intended to pull my hair or spit on me, but things got more challenging when they decided to gang up and wallop me with their punching fists and kicking feet. Despite all the times they had beaten me up, I never tattled. I would just hobble home and pretend to my mother that I'd had a hard fall or something equally clumsy.

I gave these self-deprecating excuses for my dirty uniform because I didn't want her to get into quarrels with anyone in the district. These types of raucous spats between neighbours were common, and boy, did I hate them! Since I was not a tattletale, the bullying went on for a few years. It worsened when I reached grade five and I became more serious about my schoolwork.

As kids, we would roam the entire district and no place was out of bounds for us. We would go searching for fruits, like mangoes, and climb any tree that promised a good view, regardless of how tall it might be. I was a tomboy and had no interest in dolls. I was much more engrossed in all of the energetic things the boys were doing, possibly because my closest sibling was a boy only eighteen months younger, and we went almost everywhere together. We would often hang out with his friends, who were mainly boys. We would go fishing and hunting for birds; just about anything that was an outdoor adventure, we engaged in them. There were no limits, as long as we stayed out of trouble.

My brother and I had daily outdoor adventures because we had to hunt for food to snack on if we got hungry between meals. That was our only means to quell the hunger pangs. Today, when I see children who are never far away from a filled refrigerator, who go around laden with the latest technological gadgets, I am shocked to consider how humble our lives were.

We made most of our own toys from whatever we could find. We used to collect sour oranges that were unfit to eat to make wheels for play trucks. We would gather empty drink cartons that served as the people in the trucks. By attaching strings to the front of these makeshift vehicles, we could pull our "cars filled with people" up and down the road. We also made a trap called a *calaban*. It was a rectangular box made from wicker that we had woven from whatever pliable wood we could find, and we used it to catch birds. We would prop it upside down on a stick to hold it up and scatter seeds to bait the birds, leading into the trap. We would hide nearby and watch the unsuspecting bird follow the trail, pecking away and steadily walking forward until it was under the *calaban*. Before it realized what was happening, we would pull the stick out and trap the bird. I'm sorry to say that in most cases, that bird would then become our snack. We would eat it on the spot after quickly roasting it on a wood fire.

When I was around eight years old, I became curious about who my father was. I wondered why my surname was different from my siblings. They all shared my stepdad's surname. To make matters worse, I had my mother's surname. This pointed discrepancy made me feel awkward, more so because I didn't understand the reasoning behind it.

In my family, there was hardly any verbal communication, and without being told, I knew there were questions I shouldn't ask. It all came to the surface one day as I was out with my brother and his group of friends playing our regular bird-hunting game. One of the boys suddenly asked me if I knew that my dad was a man named Dave, who lived only two minutes walk from my house. What was he talking about? I wondered. How could a man who lived so close to me, who acted like such a stranger, be my father? My brother, who was protective of me, was furious with that sort of talk going on and wound up starting a fight with the other boy.

When we went home that evening, I casually mentioned that strange comment to my mum. I was hoping to have her spill the secret as to whether it was true or not. She immediately grew enraged, throwing stones, ashes, pots, pans, and anything else at me. I was completely confused as to what I had done to trigger her outburst, but I learned that I had better kill that curiosity. Afterward, life continued as usual and the subject never came up again. When I was out and about, however, I would see that man who was supposed to be my father. I dared not approach him, and he never showed any special interest in me except to say a regular "hello" or ask me to run to the local shop. I was treated no differently than the multitude of children who wandered past his house.

I always complied with his request without question because we were taught to respect our elders. He always gave a little token for our efforts, so I wasn't about to complain.

At age ten and a half, our family situation changed drastically when my stepdad lost his job at the rice factory. My mother had recently given birth to two more babies, which meant I was expected to acquire a more adult role as a partial breadwinner for the family. It became my responsibility each day to go to a privately owned property nearby, where there grew an abundance of mango trees. I would pick as many of the mangoes as I could to sell throughout the day. I was anxious about the prospect because that property was where airplanes would land in the wee hours of the night to collect the illegal marijuana grown in that region. I would be venturing into dangerous territory to complete my new task. Until then, I had been relatively fearless, but on those inky black mornings when I had to sneak around in the mango bush, fear came at me from every direction. I feared being shot because I was trespassing, I feared being taken captive if I wandered into a marijuana operation, or that the police might have caught me. But that task was not optional, we were hungry, and I had to do it to help keep my family alive. So, it came to be that most mornings while the community slept, I joined the other children of neighbouring families, sneaking around with torches in the darkness to find the mangoes. We were often still there when the sun rose so daylight came and gave us better sight to pick the best fruits on the tree and those that fell on the ground. We collected the fruit in baskets carried on our heads, which sat atop a *catah*, fashioned from a piece of folded cloth, normally old clothes, to help cushion our heads against the load when the basket became heavy.

I hated my life at that stage. I wished that I were the baby of the family, so I could still be sleeping that early in the morning. Most mornings, we would try to get back from the mango walk before sunrise; after sunrise we could sort and wash the mangoes. Only the most bruised and unpleasantly soft fruits were kept for ourselves. As soon as the sorting was done, I would be sent anywhere that the mangoes might sell best that day. The location changed frequently. Most days I couldn't make it to school because the need to sell every mango so my family could eat ranked above my desire to sit in a classroom.

Even with my contributions, our family's diet dwindled. We would eat rice or chicken back and turned cornmeal, a dish similar to the Nigerian *ebba* or *gari,* or the Ghanaian's *banku.* The only cereal we knew was plain cornflakes, and someone would have had to acquire a barrel sent from overseas in order for us to get a small portion.

More regularly, we had oats. They were not the most flavourful food, but they were filling. My stepdad had cows, so he would milk them every morning for us. Milk was about the most consistent thing in our diets.

I guess that's where my love for cornmeal porridge came from. Whatever we had for breakfast would have to last my family the whole day, until I came home with money from the mango sales. On numerous occasions, I was only able to make enough to buy myself a snack for energy to continue the selling, and to pay for my transportation back to our home when the market was far away. I knew Mum would not be very amused if I returned home without money, so I pushed myself to ensure I sold as many mangoes as I could. I didn't know it at the time, but it was here my resilience, courage under fire and tenacity started taking root.

Sometimes, when the day's sales were slow, I would have to lower the price per dozen just to get rid of them and make some money. After all, any amount I made was good, since we didn't pay for the mangoes in the first place. Again negotiations skills were being taught by the simple need to survive.

Myself and others from my community would sell mangoes anywhere we thought there might be a demand. On the train rails, in the park, in the shopping plaza, and at any temporary attractions where people were gathering. If there was a fete, fair, or sports day, I tried to be right in the thick of it, we were hung-rrrr-yyyy. There were days when we would be selling mangoes in the same region where my school was located and the kids from my class would recognize me in passing.

They rarely missed a chance to greet me with a mocking shout, saying, "Mango gal! You are so poor, you *skull* (skip) school to sell mangoes."

At times, I felt like running away and abandoning my basket of mangoes. But I would force myself to sit there and endure their chants because I knew the consequences that I would be met with at home if I ever did such a thing. Back then, I would have been in grades four or five, when the students were preparing for the Scholastic Aptitude Tests (SAT). Since I attended school so irregularly, I didn't want to fall behind, so I asked my teachers for the books that were used in the classes to study on my own. I was told I would have to buy them, but our family couldn't afford the books. As a result, my education had a roadblock.

I had heard about a man called Spike, who would have been my uncle if Dave was really my dad. Up to this stage, no one had acknowledged me as Dave's daughter, especially not Dave, although the word was out in our entire district about this possibility. It was close to Christmas that year and I boldly sent a message to my supposed uncle to ask if he could buy me the books for the SATs. I explained that the exams were to be held in the summer and I needed to study. I was stunned when he did not just reply, but he replied and sent the books. It was the first time anyone outside of my family had shown me any outward love or kindness. And it was from a total stranger, not my mum and stepdad who I saw every day. Although I knew they loved me, they never seemed able to show it.

When I look back on that situation, myself a parent now, I am resolved to do everything in my power to ensure that my children know that I love them. Love for me is not just by saying it (which I do often) but by showing them as well. As a child, I lived with the idea that my mum hated me and depended on me too much. Every interaction we had left me feeling unloved and unwanted. I still carry traces of that painful emotion even now, as an adult, living far away from that small Jamaican village. I carried traces of that painful emotion and released it in 2019 when I did course of emptying and realised that was the story I told myself. Mum actually loved me, she just showed it in her own way.

After I received the SAT books, I was inspired to rush through my chores each day so that I could sit under the trees to study them. Unfortunately, on my first glimpse of book one, I was completely bewildered. I realized that task was going to be incredibly challenging; even more than my daily task of gathering and selling the stolen mangoes on the trains across the length and breadth of Jamaica.

My eleventh birthday was approaching, and I saw no end in sight to my daily routine. Little did I know that very soon my life would again take another turn, and one that none of us could have seen.

Dave, the man I believed to be my father, had begun living with a pretty woman named Sarah. Not only was she the most beautiful woman I had ever seen in my life, she was also kind and gentle to me and it felt good. One day, she invited me to her house. She was the first adult who had ever sought me out and spoken to me like I mattered. I was thrilled to accept her invitation, and before long, I was at her house all the time. It was wonderful! She would comb my hair and feed me. Boy did I feel loved, especially as mum had a few of us to share her own love with. Here I felt this love was not diluted so I actually leaned into it readily. We would attend the community's clothes washing day together. In those days, we would hand wash our clothes in the river and then hang them on the bushes to dry in the sunshine. Usually, the children would just swim and wait for the adults to finish. During one of these excursions, while Sarah and I sat side-by-side, washing in private, she helped me answer the one question that mattered to me at that stage, that Dave was indeed my father. I was thrilled to finally hear that validation, as the rumour had been flying all over the community for years. There, in that quiet moment, that beautiful woman had given me the answer to the very question my own mother was afraid to address. I felt resentment and had to contain it, as it would serve no one. I am of the opinion Dave knew about the time I spent with Sarah or gave her permission to acknowledge the truth of the rumour.

Over the next few weeks, Sarah and I grew closer. I began to spend less and less time at my own house. Mind you, I still did all the household chores that my mother expected me to, and I made certain that I did them well, as I would have gotten a good beating if I didn't. But I loved being in my dad's house, especially because it was an actual house with two bedrooms, a living room, an indoor bathroom, and a veranda. To top it off, they also had a car. Their life seemed so luxurious to me, but my only comparison was the ever-more cramped one-room shack I lived in, where I still slept in a urine-soaked bed.

Although Sarah had confirmed that Dave was my father, he rarely spoke to me and he kept our interactions on the level of sending me to the shop. I felt hurt by the lack of recognition on his part, but I preferred that small bit of familiarity to none at all. After a few weeks, Sarah told me that she and my dad were going to be moving to the community where she had come from originally and she wanted me to go with them! I was thrilled beyond words but was equally anxious about what my mother would say. When I approached her with the careful request, my mum surprised me by immediately agreeing. I would have thought that since I was now the main breadwinner of the family, my value would have been higher. But just like that, I was being hurried out of her front door. I think this was my first time of feeling neglected and unwanted…how could mum just ship me off?

I didn't have much to take with me. I had very few personal belongings. When I arrived at my dad's home, Sarah, my would-be stepmom expressed that the items I had really weren't worth taking with us. She set them aside and told me that she would replace them with new ones once we settled in at the new home. I had never had any "new" clothes before. I thought to myself that if the way she dressed was any indicator, I was going to live out a dream. In my mind, I was entering the happiest time in my life.

> ***Changes can sometimes be laced with hidden journeys we would rather not have encountered.***

CHAPTER 2: THE DARK

We are scared of the dark. Light is comforting as it helps us see shapes and forms. Light helps with recognition and shows what lies ahead of us. We yearn for the comfort of light as it provides silhouettes and form, allowing us to recognize and define what's before us. Are we afraid of the darkness, or is it the truth hiding behind it?

Sarah and I got into her car. The drive to her old neighbourhood was filled with excitement and apprehension. I didn't know what to expect, and at times, I felt panicked and wanted to ask Sarah to turn the car around to take me back home. I wanted to be back with mum; somehow fear suddenly came over me. We had turned off the main road and were travelling along a winding road that seemed to go on forever. In my angst, the journey felt like it was taking an eternity. My mother's home was close to the main road, but now we were going farther and farther away from anything familiar to me and deeper into the hills. A meandering journey that seemed endless. I felt like we were leaving civilisation behind and I didn't like it. I remember feeling the panic rising as I silently questioned myself, *what have I done? Why would anyone choose to live so far away from lights and civilisation?*

The roads continued to go round and round, climbing up into the mountains. It was meandering, indeed. When we turned from one road to another, I would look down and see the road we just came off.. I had never been so high up and it was scary. It felt as though the car was going to fall and it made my stomach nervous. The mix of emotions I felt at leaving my mother's home for that unknown place made my anxiety about the height so poignant; it became a lifelong fear. We eventually arrived at Sarah's house. She introduced me to her own father, daughter, and son. He was about two years older than me, and her daughter two years younger than I was. I must say they seemed rather happy to have me there. I felt like I belonged. My father was not there at the time. He was splitting his time living here and at his main home back in the district I had just left. I was surprised to find such a ready-made family unit and I felt like the odd one out. I was unaware that Sarah even had children. She took me inside and showed me the room I would be sharing with her daughter. That house wasn't nearly as crowded as the one I had just come from, and there was an inside bathroom and plenty of outdoor yard space. They had an outside kitchen and attached to it was a "butchery," which was like a spare room that farm produce was kept in.

My life settled into a routine quickly, but soon I began to realise that I was becoming a sort of housekeeper. I washed the clothes for everyone and cooked the family's meals. Sarah did register me at the local school, and I started grade six. All of these changes, the new school, a new home, and new family, were quite overwhelming. I had no way of communicating with my mother's family, as there was no phone. As the days passed, I started to get a bit lonely and missed my old way of life. The walk to my new school was long. It felt like about two hours in a child's eyes, but I was conscious it was about 45 minutes to an hour each way - made harder by the fact that I was still making the journey without any shoes. Clothing was not a problem, though, as Sarah had given me some new ones. I also found it challenging to adjust to my new classmates. These kids were brighter, and some of them much wealthier than the children who had attended my old school. I decided that my best tactic was to keep quiet and not draw any attention to myself, but being the new girl, everyone noticed me right away.

Every day after lunch, the teachers would expect us to recite our timestables. I remember the head teacher clearly and her ever-present cane that she carried as she walked down each row of students seated at their desks.

She would randomly stop in front of a desk, point the cane at a student, and bark out the quiz question: "What is seven times seven?" That would go on for quite some time, with mixed up variations of the numbers. The students who had not yet memorized their times-tables completely, me included, would just mumble some guessed answer or an ashamed admission that they didn't know. I used to sit in dread of being called on, even when I knew the answer, because I was still trying to stay invisible among my new classmates. You see, here kids would be beaten if they did not know the answers to questions being asked.

I think the teacher recognised my apprehension, because I was thankfully spared questioning for the first few weeks, but eventually my turn came. To me, it seemed to happen almost in slow motion. I saw her turn towards me, and the world seemed to stop spinning as she walked towards my desk, raised the cane at me, and asked, "What is nine times six?"

I can't remember if I didn't know the answer or if I was just smothered by the fear of having all eyes on me, but I do remember my tongue remained absolutely still. Out of the corner of my eye, I could see a multitude of hands popping up and the smirking grins on the faces of the kids who knew the answer. I was so angry with myself as I dutifully stretched out my hand to receive my caning.

The pain was far worse than I had imagined. Extremely sharp and nothing like the smacks my mum used to give me. When the first whack sent a jolt of agony rushing from my knuckles through my hand and up my arm, I nearly wet myself! The second one on my arm was even worse. I know for a fact that was a severe punishment because the scar is still on my arm. When I arrived home, I didn't tell anyone about that cruel experience. I was afraid that their concern over my silliness would be a source of a new problem for them. I needn't have worried though. No one paid any attention to my nursing the unsightly wound, nor did they inquire about it when it turned into a scar. As the pain began to subside,

I promised myself that I would never again get caned for not knowing something in school.

I reminded myself, as I had many times before, that some things were best endured and left unsaid. I applied myself completely to the task of learning my times-tables. In every waking minute, while I ate, washed, cleaned, cooked, and bathed, I had the times-tables running through my mind. Time progressed and I learnt them perfectly and was able to recite them in class without a hitch. With that, I began to settle in more comfortably at school and, finally, I felt like I was getting on with my life. Dave came around and was now more involved in my life, and I was now blending in with Sarah's children.

There were times I could steal away from school during lunchtime. I would go to the mango market spots to look for anyone from my old district that could pass along a message of greeting to my mum and siblings, as this was near my new school. I was very keen to know how they were doing. Sometimes I would recognize my mum among the crowd, but she always disappeared before I reached her. Those close encounters always left me wondering how she could come so close to my new school but not look for me. However, these meetings with old neighbours became fewer and farther between, and I heard less and less about my mother and her family. The fact that I had chosen to leave them to join a new family in search of a better life weighed heavily on me, and I constantly carried the longing for my mum's love in my heart.

Towards the end of my sixth-grade year, Sarah gave birth to a baby boy, my brother Chad, with whom I would cultivate a beautiful relationship. To me, it seemed like my dad worshipped that new little life. The attention he poured on the baby made me a bit jealous, though he still split his time living both at his old house and Sarah's. I yearned for Dave to give me just one-tenth of the gentle attention the baby received. After all, he had missed out on the first twelve years of my life and I felt due some level of affection. During that time, I was preparing to take my SAT exams. I was also anxious about the possibility of getting to sit for an extra post-SAT preparatory test called the Twenty Percent. That test was given to a select group of students chosen by the head teacher according to the expectation of their success on the SATs. I was crushed to find out that I wasn't chosen, but looking back, I should have realized that my chances were slim. I had no parent advocating for me either at school or in the home. To this day, Dave does not know my books came from his brother Spike.

Although my new home afforded me clean clothing, daily meals, and even lunch money, it did not provide anyone who parented me. There was no one journeying to my school to discuss my progress or prospects for the future of my education. This seemed a familiar pattern with the two women who had parented me so far. I was acutely aware that many of my classmates who were chosen to sit for the extra placement exam were no smarter than me, but they had parents who would deliver coffee and yams to the teachers. At that time, it was well known that many teachers could be cajoled to show an extra bit of interest in your child if you "greased their palms." I took mental notes on the importance of social standing and once again told myself I was going to overcome that challenge.

I knew that I had to pass my SAT exam to further my education and better my life, and this only served to motivate me to study harder. When the day came to sit for the exam, I gave it everything I had, barefoot and all. I left the test feeling confident that my studying would pay off with a passing score. In the weeks leading up to the delivery of the results, I saved up my lunch money every day, refusing to buy anything to eat because I planned to celebrate passing that hurdle. The day the results came out, I was eager to get into town and see my score. As I passed the local police station and turned towards the town square, I saw a friend of my new family who was a policeman. His name was Mutty Scot. He shouted out at me, "Girl, I told you I had faith in you!" That was all the proof I needed to know that I had received passing marks that were my ticket to a better future; that I would now be admitted to a good high school. I did not care about what percentage score I got, all I wanted to know was that my score would get me in the door of a good school, which meant I stood a chance of a better life.

I threw myself in the middle of the road and started a *piece a bawling* (very loud crying), as it's called in Jamaica. Inside me, I felt that something great was beginning to take shape in my life, and I reveled in the fact that I could do anything I set my mind to . . . How naïve I was. I was so ecstatic that I didn't even hear the car horns honking at me. Two policemen came out and escorted me out of the road. As soon as I came to my senses, I turned tail and ran home, delirious with excitement to share my news.

When I arrived at Sarah's house, I found that they all had already heard and had planned a little celebration with homemade cake and lemonade. They were so proud of me, and it was the first time I had heard such adulations aimed towards me. In that moment I felt cared for and loved. It was a great new feeling and one I could get used to. I was starting to feel like I belonged there. Though I missed my old home, and more so my siblings, this new life was starting to grow on me.

On the following Monday, I went back to school with a strut like a peacock in my step. I was so happy to find that my passing marks had brought me a level of respect from some of my teachers who had previously looked straight through me. Generally, only about thirty percent of students would pass this test, so I was elated to be among them. I also found out that my scores allowed for entrance into the DeCarteret College in Mandeville, which was in the neighbouring parish and over an hour's drive away. We were assigned schools, so I didn't have a say in the matter. It also didn't bother me that I was now among the "bright kids." But my excitement over my passing score was tempered by the very realistic concern about how I would afford to go to that new school. There were school fees, books to be purchased, and the cost of transportation to and from school. I was now deflated over these necessary costs, as I could not fathom how they would be paid for.

My life back at Sarah's house was starting to change too. I had not been paying much attention to the changes occurring in my twelve-year-old pubescent body, but others certainly had. In particular Sarah's son started trying to fondle me and make advances towards me, but he was not the only one. We attended the same primary school, so we would walk to school together, though thankfully he didn't pass the test for my new school and I only had to tolerate him at home. I thought his friendliness was his way of welcoming and trying to integrate me into the family. I guess I was wrong about that. I told Sarah, who spoke to him and really made him understand that he should see me as a sister, but also that his behavior was inappropriate. It happened less frequently and eventually Dave stepped in and got him to stop all together. I felt like my father was my hero at this stage. He saved me from the vultures.

Sarah had gotten involved with politics, and as a result she was away frequently. Her father was an old man and could barely help himself, so after dinner he would be fast asleep. In some ways he was the adult they kept there for safety, but he was always on autopilot, never really present. If the house had burnt, he would have been the last one to know.

Thankfully, Dave was often home, as he was then generally unemployed. One day, he did something that made me keenly aware of the fact that I needed to be more mindful of myself when I was alone with men. Even ones I thought I should have been able to trust implicitly. It was so unexpected when he started a real conversation with me that I had no misgivings when he led me back into his room to continue the talk. In fact, my heart soared with happiness over the attention I had so long yearned for. While he was speaking, though, he took my hands and pulled me close to him, only to lift my blouse and put my very small breast in his mouth. No one had ever spoken to me be about intimacy, sex, or even puberty, and I wasn't certain what he was doing. But I knew that whatever it was, it didn't feel right. I immediately pulled away and sprinted out of the house. I gasped in the fresh air outside and tried to dispel the sense of suffocation and the feeling of nausea that rose in my throat. Even today I still dislike that breast and can feel his horrible touch with a cringe on my skin.

My mind was racing. That wasn't what I had expected a father-daughter relationship to be. I could hear him yelling behind me, calling for me to come back. I felt so dirty and his voice had turned angry. He bellowed out, "I didn't do anything to you!" When I returned to the living room, he came at me and spoke in a quiet but stern voice. He told me that if I told anyone what had happened, they wouldn't understand or believe me and that I would be sent back to live at my mother's. I made the promise not to tell anyone. That was a promise that I would keep simply because I was far too afraid of leaving the home I had now become accustomed to. Also, I feared the truth in what he said—that no one would believe me. So I went through life with these feelings:

* It was my fault

* Become Mute

* Trust no one especially men.

It wasn't until I was nineteen that I dared to tell anyone, sharing it with my first husband, Tobore.

As an adult, I still saw my dad from time to time when I make the journey across the pond to visit Jamaica, but I have never been able to broach this subject with him. Unfortunately he has since died and I had to learn to forgive his actions. I only recently gathered the courage to tell my mum during one of her visits to London where I now live, and I could tell that she found it hard to conceptualise.

If I had the courage to face Dave, I would want to tell him that that single event altered my perspective on humanity, and caused me to lose the ability to trust those who were supposed to love me the most. More importantly, it has negatively affected the relationships I've had with the opposite sex. After all, he was the first man who was suppose to show me how a man should treat me and instead he defiled me.

Instead, I went through life after that being merely civil with him. If someone were to ask me if I loved my father, I would not be able to give a simple answer. I do care for his general well being at the time when he was alive, but otherwise, there is only indifference. Keeping this dirty secret made me feel dirty each time I saw Dave, and I even became uncomfortable around even my stepfather, who prior to this felt very safe. Like I said, it taught me three things: trust no one; it was my fault; and it is easier to become mute in some respects. I avoided being in the same place with men or boys alone. I found every excuse not to walk home alone. I constantly felt that someone was following me and would drag me into the bushes. I felt Dave everywhere I went like a shadow over me. I had constant nightmares that he would strangle me if I told anyone. I even started to wonder if he had troubled any of the girls in my old district, as well as Sarah's daughter, but I dared not broach the subject.

That event was to have an impact on my entire adult life, but at the time it had little impact on my daily life at home. Certainly, I was more careful around all men, and I had to fight off the desire to run away to my mum's home every time I found myself alone in the house with my dad. But my being scared of him, even when others were around, was something I kept hidden from everyone. Our lives just went on as usual, as if nothing had happened. Thankfully that was the only time he approached me in that manner. I think he was fearful I would speak or hurt him physically. Needless to say, I was never certain that he *wouldn't* do it again, given an opportunity. So, I walked around with a lump in my throat each time I saw him and found every excuse not to be in the same room with him and Sarah. Sadly, she didn't even realise the change in my behavior. She was either too busy with politics or didn't care.

Life continued in this new existence, Sarah engrossed in politics, and me walking around being cautious of what this new idea of having a father in my life truly meant. It was an uncomfortable new life. I would have given anything to go back to the wet urine-infested mattress with my mum. Somehow it felt like I was crippled, and I couldn't function.

My new school in Mandeville was too far away to walk to, so I had to start taking the bus to attend my classes. The cost of my bus fare soon became an irritating issue for Sarah. In addition, the bus I had to take left very early in the morning. That meant that it was nearly impossible for me to complete my chores before I left for school. The grades from my first term were not very good, and I started to sense that going to high school wasn't going to work out as well as I had hoped. I was very aware of Sarah's annoyance with me as she was now faced with additional expenses because of my new educational pursuit. This made me very nervous and edgy when I was at home. When the first term ended, I was informed that Sarah and Dave had decided not to send me back for the next term because they couldn't afford it. I received no further explanation of their decision, even though our financial situation seemed very stable. I wondered who had been paying for my bus fare and now felt the cost was unreasonable. Was it my mother, who Sarah demanded money from weekly or whenever she had it? I gathered that mother had started to do some domestic work in addition to our mango-selling tradition.

Or was it my father, who pitched in a little something every now and again? It didn't matter, as whoever it was they had decided they were going to stop.

That summer, I received my first life lesson in puberty. I was home one afternoon, wearing one of my old school uniforms and playing in the yard with the other children. We were climbing up and sliding down the columns on the veranda. As I came down one of the columns, one of the boys told me that I was bleeding. I was frantic but couldn't see a cut anywhere on my legs or hands. I quickly turned my lavender skirt around and was met with the shocking sight of a bright red stain! I ran crying to Sarah. She quickly shushed me into silence and ushered me back into the house to give me the lecture on the basics of puberty. One bit of the information she gave me that stood out was that I could now get pregnant. She explained that I needed to be careful, but at the time she didn't shed any light on how anyone actually got pregnant.

As the summer progressed, I wondered where I would be attending school when the new school year finally started. My inquiry, however, led to the suggestion that I should look around on my own and find a school that was nearer to our home. I was shocked by that answer. I quickly started considering getting a transfer to a school in my own parish. This would be a better cost option for us all given the circumstances.

I was only a child, but there it was, revealing a deeper truth about my situation. That at twelve years old I was expected to assume responsibility for myself. I came up with a plan. I asked for bus fare to travel to my mum's to seek help in my new school transfer quest. When I reached mum's house, I requested the fare to go to one of the high schools in my parish to get registered for a transfer. At only twelve years old, I had made the first step into adulthood. I had to take responsibility for obtaining my own education. I guess the one good thing in this new scenario was that the fare to school was less expensive and I got to pass my mum's home daily.

I realised that even if I got accepted into the school, I would need to pay school fees and purchase the school's uniform. By the time the acceptance letter arrived, I had eight weeks to come up with the money and uniform. Sarah was not able to help, citing the initial money problems that precluded my attendance at school in Mandeville.

The idea of selling mangoes cropped up at this point, but it just wouldn't work as the mangoes were in my mother's district and not where Sarah lived. If I were going to do that, it would make more sense to move back in with mum, as she lived closer to the school I had in mind.

My father was a potential source of aid and although he had done me wrong, I wanted to stay in his good graces, so I passed on asking him. I went to my aunts, uncles, and everyone I knew to ask for money to help fund my second year of high school, but nothing came of it. I even tried to get help from a member of Parliament who lived in our area, but that, too, produced nothing.

It turned out to be my mum who was finally able to find the money for me. She was a domestic helper and also a mango seller by this time. Just like Mandeville, my new school in Santa Cruz was a long bus ride from our house, but at least the fees were cheaper, as it was a more frequent route and it was in my parish, and I was living with Sarah and her family. Every day was a challenge, but I was determined to stick with my decision to go back to school.

By the end of year nine, when I was about thirteen or fourteen years old, I started to notice the cute boys in my class. It was only a flirtatious interest and nothing more, especially because my mum had told me that if she got any inkling that I was having sex, she would rub scotch bonnet pepper in my private parts! That threat was enough to scare me into staying absolutely chaste.

While at secondary school in Santa Cruz, I struggled to eat, as food was scarce. I recall loving practical lessons, where I would get food in abundance.

So early in year nine I decided that I would study food and nutrition, mainly because I already knew how to cook, but also because I would get to eat whatever was prepared that day. My home economics teacher and my home management teachers were like my away-from-home mothers. They made me love going to school, and I appreciated their care. There were aspects of how I was schooled that I wished my kids had experienced, such as teachers who acted as parents in absentia.

I volunteered at the home economics block where they sold baked goods, for two reasons. First, it allowed me to get some food to eat, and second, I would steal some of the money to help me pay for my bus fare to travel to and from school. I hated stealing but I felt I had no choice. It was either that or stay at home.

By then, my dad and Sarah had a falling out of sorts and there was no longer any consideration to assist me. In addition, due to her own needs, my mum was not consistent with her help towards me. I supposed that if I was living with mum and was present and in her face, she would have no choice.

High school was an uphill battle for me. It seemed it was always a toss-up between staying home, sitting on the roadside gambling (this is what most young people my age did; they didn't bother with the stress of trying to get to school—they gave in to the life they were dealt), stealing from school, begging my member of Parliament to help with my education, or simply going to school hungry, provided I even got a ride. In spite of all that, I made it through.

I had only one uniform for school, as I simply couldn't afford more. It was a navy-blue tunic with four gores (panels). We ironed with a sad iron, which we heated in a wood fire. There was no ironing board; ironing was done on the bed. We would stupidly hold the iron near our faces to feel the heat to see how hot it was. It was our way of testing the temperature, but it shows how irresponsible we were at that age. One evening, when attempting to iron, I didn't bother to test. I just slapped it on my only tunic and "bang, slap, damn," it left its shape burnt into my tunic on the front panel. I was left with a permanent sad iron imprint on my only tunic.

As a child in my mum's community, I had always hated when the adult and teenage men would bathe at the community pipe. They would stand there in their briefs when we passed. Many would be disgusting enough to try to get our attention to look at their manhood, and when we refused, they would inform us that we were old enough to go on the "cutting table" (ready to lose our virginity).

It was revolting. I would cross the road and turn my face to the bushes to the disadvantage of "bucking" (stubbing) my toes. When that failed, I would tell them to "suck their mums" which were the worst swear words you could tell a Jamaican man. Mums were revered.

One of my first crushes in high school was a boy who lived in my district. That, however, wore off rather quickly, and I then began to like his brother. Looking back, I realise I was trying to see if a boy would be interested in me. I had very low self-esteem and felt ugly and unlovable. I paid close attention in my guidance classes. The teacher explained that our class was at the age when kissing would become a point of interest, and I was no exception. I started looking forward to my first kiss and began planning how to get it. Soon, I had my first boyfriend and it felt wonderful when we were together. The two of us would walk the two-mile journey from our homes to the bus stop together. Sometimes we would walk back together in the evenings as well. However, whenever we got onto the bus, he would stop talking to me, and that general disregard would continue at school. I reasoned that I must be really ugly, and he was embarrassed to be seen with me in public places. The truth is that I was merely too naïve to realize was that he already had a real girlfriend. I was only a target for the sex he wasn't getting from that other girl. Thankfully, I never gave in to his requests and our "affair" only consisted of a few kisses.

The next crush I fell for was nothing like that previous boy. In fact, he was a man. I was absolutely smitten by his age and his drop-dead gorgeous, mature look. His name was James, and he was about twenty-five at the time. The fact that he was from the capital city, Kingston, which was far away from my rural community in Saint Elizabeth, made him all the more alluring to me. I told my stepmother, Sarah (who by the way didn't get married to Dave), about him and I was delighted that subject seemed to pique her interest in me and my life. Looking back, I realised what the source of that interest really was. I was still very young and naïve, and at the time I didn't wonder why an older woman was suddenly so interested in the stories of a lovesick girl. By the time I realised what was really going on, it was too late, and I just wound up feeling like a fool.

Every summer the people in my stepmom's district would hold a summer party, and I loved to go. That particular summer I went with James as my date. When the festivities wound down, we stood close and he whispered a tantalizing promise that he would keep in touch with me, as he was going back home to Kingston. In the weeks after the party, my dad and Sarah began arguing frequently. I would hear her yelling about all the men she could have chosen instead of him, men who had a great deal more money than he did. In their last big argument, she called him a worthless swine, and soon after he moved away to Kingston to find better work. Things calmed down in our house, and Sarah started visiting Kingston on the weekends. I naturally assumed that she was going to visit my father there. She would return and pass along a greeting to me from James. I wondered about that, but told myself that she must have just run into the object of my affection when she was visiting my father. Over time, the greetings became fewer and farther between. I wanted to ask if she knew if he had a new girlfriend, but as a child who was barely coping with her own life, I had learnt to keep my silly questions to myself and not bother the adults.

Time passed and so did the crush. Christmas came and there was a celebration on Christmas Eve, called the Grand Market. It was a huge street festival that gave us kids the chance to stay out really late; it was such a lovely celebration. I loved it when everyone was in a festive mood and the streets were laced with all the items for Christmas. I felt like a child in a candy shop with a bit of freedom at last. It was my favourite night of the year, when I reveled in my freedom from chores and the watchful eyes of the adults. The evening of the Grand Market, I noticed a car in our drive that wasn't my dad's. When I peeked closer, I realised that it was James's and I thought he had come to see me. Yes, I know, stupid girl, but I was fourteen.

Without a word, my stepmom ushered him into her bedroom and asked that I get his bags. Although it wasn't said, it was obvious that they were together. I think that was my second heartbreak after what my dad did to me.

I dutifully brought inside the bags of the man I had been so crazy about. Sarah then told us all to quickly get ourselves ready so that we could go to the Grand Market. She hurried us out of the house with a pocketful of money from "Daddy James." She didn't even give us a curfew. I was, however, given the task of being responsible for my younger brother, Chad, while all of us kids went on our merry freedom ride. I was to be the responsible one in charge of our little group as I was the oldest, I suppose. With nothing else left to do, we headed off for the Grand Market and got caught up in the festivities until midnight. I finally gathered the younger ones and we started the walk back home. A short way into the walk, a car pulled up beside us, and my dad's head popped out of the driver's side window. He was astonished to see us all by ourselves and quickly asked about my stepmother. The young ones answered in a chorus that she was at home, but my voice was a bit more timid because I knew that there was a showdown in the making. My father said to get into the car and drove us home in silence. Even the young ones started to feel the tension of the situation, although they didn't understand it.

When we arrived, all of us quickly scampered out of the way, while dad stood at the front door trying his key in the lock. We could hear him angrily jiggling the key with no success. He called out to my stepmom, but there was no answer. She must have known that he had seen the strange car in the driveway and deduced what was going on. At that point, my dad was more than angered and was trying to kick the door down. Sarah shouted at him to leave because she was through with him and that she had told him this long ago! Things escalated into a screaming match between the two. It was interesting, as the entire argument happened through the door as James stayed silent and allowed Sarah to defend the territory. They caused such a ruckus that they woke up the entire community, and all the neighbours started coming out to witness the hullabaloo. It was so embarrassing. My dad broke some of the windows in the house, all the while screaming like a madman. Finally, his energy left him, and he got in his car and sped away. He had not paid any attention to me or Chad, and there was no invitation for us to go with him. Yet another abandonment and rejection in my life. You could just feel the tension in the air. The humiliation Dave felt as he left was evident in his posture. His manhood was now publicly humiliated, and I knew based on who he was that this was the point of no return for them.

I could never have anticipated how that break of a love affair between two people would have such a profound impact on my life. But Sarah immediately saw the consequence and told me that I would have to leave as soon as possible. I thought that if I worked harder, she would be convinced of my worth to her family and let me stay on, so I worked harder. Little did I know, I was about to be expected to work in a way that no girl or woman should ever have to resort to.

Following my father's departure, our money got tighter and tighter. James did not stick around. Looking back at our situation now, I saw how my position in the family at that time was more that of a dutiful slave than of a daughter.

I was at the end of year nine in school, with all of my focus being on the excitement of what year ten was going to bring. I was certainly interested in boys, but I wasn't self-aware enough to appreciate the womanly figure I was developing. Our house at the time didn't have any electricity and Sarah decided it was high time that we got some. She found a man to wire the house, but his cost was beyond anything she could afford in our current situation. But she was crafty and knew of other ways to get the things in life that she needed.

Sarah had a male friend who would come over to the house occasionally. He was a tall, strapping man, about forty years old. He seemed like an old man to me. But that man had money, and she needed money to pay for the house to be wired, and he was obviously interested in me. I would catch him eyeing me during his visits. In her mind, it must have seemed like an easy trade-off. The man started coming around more frequently, and each time I would be released from my chores and sent out to the veranda to entertain him. Sarah would always pick out my shortest shorts, telling me to wear them because they would keep me coolest in the heat. I hated those days when he came to visit. I would try to stall or even hide. When his visits became regular, I started coming home late from school so that I could at least limit the time I would have to endure his company. Each visit followed the same routine. He would sit on the veranda, and Sarah would lock all the doors leading to the rest of the house. Thinking back, I believe that was her feeble way of protecting everyone else from having to deal with the fact that a lamb was being put to slaughter. Certainly, no one would have wanted to hear me constantly pleading with that man to not touch me in places I wasn't comfortable with. But my pleas fell on deaf ears. He would fondle me, touch my breasts, and grope me. Every time, I felt sick. She allowed that man to fondle me in exchange for the money she needed. I was the currency that was used to pay for the wiring of the house. It wouldn't be my last time being a currency, I came to learn later in my adult life.

I was naïve, yes, but I was not stupid. Although it was never openly discussed that he was abusing me, I quickly realized the role my stepmother was playing, and our relationship became strained. One day I just couldn't take it anymore, so I sent a message from school back to Sarah's house to say that I would be staying over at a friend's home. My friend's family understood my situation and did not have any problem with me staying there. I didn't even have a change of clothes with me, but my friend kindly offered me some of her own. The next day, when I returned to the house that had become my prison, I was flogged severely. I took the beating with dignity though, because in truth, it felt better than being fondled all evening. At least I wasn't being squeezed and probed by some old man's disgusting hands.

Luckily my virginity was still intact, despite all the sexual abuse I encountered up to this point, and I was determined to keep it that way. The situation had become unbearable and I made a plan to escape back to my mum's house. Although her home was not as lavish as Sarah's, it was safer and devoid of that lecherous old man. By that time, my friends from school knew what was happening at my home, but there was nothing they could do to help. Jamaica did not have any proper social services to deal with such situations, so one just had to get on with life.

I surreptitiously packed a bag and hid it in the bushes outside. I didn't even feel guilty when I tucked in all the nice clothes Sarah had given me to replace the raggedy ones I had arrived with.

I was sure my plan would work, but I was sadly mistaken. Someone had obviously figured out my intent, because when I set off into the night to collect the bag with my things, I discovered it was gone. That didn't deter me, though, and I took off anyway. I headed towards my mum's place. I made it there without any obstructions.

My mum was surprised to see me, but instead of greeting me with tears of joy and relief, she insisted that I go back to where I came from. Her mind was not changed, even after I tried to explain what had happened that had made me so desperate to leave. In her mind, my stepmother's home was still a better place for me. Through my mum's eyes, I looked healthier and better taken care of than any of the girls in my old district, and she wanted me to stay that way. I wound up leaving her house to travel to another friend's house, located in Southfield, Saint Elizabeth, about twenty-five miles from my mum's place. I was very relieved when my friend's family welcomed me in and allowed me to stay for a few days. I knew it was not a permanent solution to my situation and I couldn't stay there forever. I was still attending school every day, and came up with the idea of trying to live secretly on the school compound. It's no surprise that plan didn't work out at all. After sleeping there for a few nights, the caretaker found out and talked me out of how dangerous it was.

Eventually, I wound up at the house of one of my aunts on my mum's side. She lived in a single-room house, which was about one hundred thirty square feet and was already filled with five people. I was in grade ten at the time, and I remember one night when I wet the bed because I was feeling so stressed. I felt embarrassed, but my aunt was extremely understanding about the situation. I stayed there for about two weeks until her husband started behaving inappropriately towards me. Thankfully, my aunt listened when I came to her with my concerns about her husband, and she decided that her home was not a safe place for me anymore. Once again, I was let out into the world. I thought things couldn't get any worse, but boy, was I wrong.

Even without recognition, in the coldest part of us, fear has burnt from conception.

CHAPTER 3: THE REAL DAD STANDS UP

True identity at times is hard to recognize, leading to questioning of characters and traits, and for some even leads to questions about one's existence.

During those last days at my aunt's house, fate challenged me yet again. One day when I was in class, a message came for me that a man had come to the school to see me. I was perplexed and asked what he looked like, trying to place who could possibly be interested in visiting me midday. From the description, however, I had no idea who he could be and the girls delivering the message made it sound as if the man was mentally ill. They told me that he was waiting at the front of the school and loudly refusing to leave. Apparently, he was convinced I was his child! I was torn as to what to do, but the situation was turning into a ruckus, and the longer I dawdled in indecision, the more embarrassment I was causing myself and the school.

At the front of the school, I found a short, dishevelled man walking in agitated circles. I was with some friends for support, and we had decided to gingerly walk by him to first check out the situation, but as soon as we neared him, he immediately rushed towards me. His story came pouring forth, like he was in urgent need of claiming his stake as my father. He told me his name was Ralf and he was certain that I was his child. He was even able to provide me with quite a convincing history to support his claim. "Hello, Teacher, I need to talk to my daughter. Why won't anyone believe me? That little girl there, yes that one, is my daughter," he said. "All I want to do is talk to my daughter." He was so gentle and all he seemed to want was just an acknowledgement of what he held as fact.

By the time he finished speaking and fell into an expectant silence, my thoughts were swayed, and I began to think that man could really be my father. Parts of me just wanted to reach out and talk with him, run into his arms and feel safe with a father regardless of his mental state, but I was too embarrassed to try.

In fact, I still carry a suspicion that man did plant the seed from which I grew, but time consumed my chances of finding out the truth, and with both men now dead, I will let sleeping dogs lie for now. This new father, for a few minutes, represented a world of promising possibilities. Namely, that I had a whole other family that could love me and treat me with respect, and just maybe not abuse me in any shape or form. But, in a hunt for a father, I was too afraid to venture into the unknown yet again, after what happened with the last.

I had never received that in Sarah's house, and my disgusting experience with Dave overshadowed everything. I allowed my mind to go into a whole new world of what it could or might be like if he were my father instead of Dave.

But I decided I didn't want another father to cope with. I could survive without one! When I went home that evening, I relayed the experience to my aunt. As our community was relatively small, she knew exactly who Ralf was. My aunt surprised me by confiding that she had long thought he was my real father. That was all too much for me at the time, and I simply put the thought aside and never explored the possibility in earnest. That was the last time I saw him until I heard long after that he had died. I had more pressing issues to worry about at the time. My days of safety in my aunt's home were dwindling and I needed to take my meager belongings—a few pieces of clothing and my single school uniform—and find a place to live. My schoolwork was suffering, and it was evident in my grades. I was failing at Maths, and many other subjects, yet I kept going, as school was my safe haven.

Chapter 3: The Real Dad Stands Up

As my aunt and I had feared, her husband's inappropriate behaviour continued to escalate in both frequency and aggressiveness. My aunt suggested that I travel the short distance to one of my uncles on my father's side—meaning Dave's side (a new uncle, not Spike this time around), as he had played the role of father to me for much longer than Ralf. I was terrified at the thought of having to put my life in the hands of yet another man, but what choice did I really have?. On the day of my departure, she helped me pack my belongings into a small plastic bag and assured me that man could help me. Despite the awkward nature of the situation in her own house, I could hear the sincerity in her voice and began to let my guard down to trust my aunt's judgment.

My aunt made the walk with me to a nearby garage where my uncle frequently took his work vehicles for maintenance. It was a Saturday morning and the garage was buzzing with activity, all of which only served to make me pull further into my shell; it was packed with M-E-N. We waited for about twenty minutes until he arrived. My aunt approached him first, alone. After speaking to him briefly, she beckoned for me to come and meet him.

I remember that my heart was filled with such trepidation. I had to force myself to move forward. Due to my previous experiences with the older men in my life—all of whom were supposed to be my protectors—I had developed a general mistrust of the opposite sex.

As I moved one foot in front of the other, my mind was racing with the question of what I was getting myself into this time. But what other choice did I have? I had nowhere to go and I had to rely on myself for protection. Hopefully, he would not be an enemy and another attacker from which I would have to flee.

My aunt introduced me to Gregory, but using the simple familiar term "uncle," which I was to call him by. I was only slightly relieved to find that he had a very gentle and polite manner. In front of me, he agreed to assume responsibility of me, and I felt a greater sense of relief that I was finally in the presence of two people who might actually care for my well being. Needless to say, I was quite surprised when my aunt suddenly turned and left, without even a parting word or offering to come along with me to his house to settle me in. I had thought she would at least want to see the home where he would be taking me so that if anything happened, she would know where to find me. It was as if a business transaction had been completed. An inanimate object had been delivered and there was nothing left to do but head home.

Not knowing what else to do, I waited quietly until my uncle finished his evening work at the garage. We carried out the trip to his home in awkward silence. It was a nerve-wracking experience. I was only fifteen years old and on my way to my fifth home. Gregory actually tried to make small talk with me as we travelled, but I was too busy making mental notes of where we were going, in case I needed to retrace my steps. I was slightly comforted by the fact that the distance from his home to my aunt's did not seem to be too great. I could make it on foot if necessary.

We arrived at a tidy two-bedroom house that could have passed for a cottage. Although it was smaller than Sarah's house, it was still bigger than my mother's, and I was in no position to be picky. When we entered, the house was still and quiet. He showed me to the room next to his and said that it would be mine. The room appeared to be set up for one person, but I couldn't sense that anyone else was living in it. My heart skipped a beat when I realized that I was going to have a room of my own for the first time in my life! However, my excitement was tempered by the nagging curiosity about where this man's family was. Where was the wife, or girlfriend, or even boyfriend, for that matter?

Panic began to rise in me, but I held silent as my mind raced frantically to find a trace anywhere in the house of anyone who might be his partner. There was a faint glimmer of hope when he said that a lady washed for him, but it was dashed when I found out that she only worked there in the daytime. At night, it would just be the two of us. He told me that his brother (this one was not my uncle) and family lived next door and that they had two daughters. I focused all of my attention on that fact to calm myself down (I was too afraid of men, so I built a relationship initially with just those girls).

The tour ended, and he retired to his room and I to mine. I slept fitfully, but the morning came, and my fears had gone unrealized. More importantly, though, my trust in the opposite sex was starting to gradually be restored.

I quickly befriended the two young girls next door, and in no time, I trusted them. I pretended to be afraid of the dark so that they could come and sleep in the house with me at night. Soon, it became a regular thing for them to sleep over—the three of us sharing a room and my sleeping soundly with their presence as protection. After being there for a few weeks, I realised that my uncle was prepared to be the father I never had. I became more relaxed about my living situation. Uncle started to teach me how to drive and trained me in the accounting practice so that I could help out with his business. He was concerned about my education, provided me with food, and gave me my first room by myself. Even though he was now the breadwinner for two, he never showed that he begrudged the financial assistance he gave to me. Because I handled his accounting, I knew that he wasn't hiding anything from me in regard to his money, and I flourished, having someone trust me so completely.

In many ways, that time in my life was like a dream. The two of us established a daughter-father relationship that I had never thought possible, and it was one that everyone admired. I was finally content with life and able to have the childhood I had been denied for so long. Eating full meals, going to school, and sleeping with ease. As with all things in life, though, that time was only temporary. For all of his responsible actions, my uncle was still a bachelor and wanted a partner to share his life with. An introduction to a young woman named Clementine brought that to fruition. Unfortunately, it also ushered in the end of our harmonious times.

Clementine wanted to become more involved in every aspect of his life, as new lovers often do. Soon, she started campaigning to take over the accounting from me and quickly grew more courageous in her interrogations. She constantly questioned me about the real reason I was doing his accounts, hoping to discover that I was collecting money from his business for my personal benefit. I was extremely uncomfortable in her presence and started staying at my friend's house in the same district. Even though my uncle wasn't happy with me staying away so much, I needed to escape the intense atmosphere that Clementine was creating at his house.

I was no longer comfortable sitting in the living room to watch TV with my uncle. She would now do everything with him, and I was sidelined. She would only speak to me if I spoke with my uncle. My uncle had been more than good to me, but by now I was so used to moving, I was running at the earliest sign of trouble.

Eventually, I made the move to my friend's house permanent. I knew that broke my uncle's heart, but I felt it was for the best. I felt that I needed to be somewhere more stable, and Clementine was securing her position even more firmly in my uncle's home, which did not promise to go well for me. I found out later that the relationship between my uncle and Clementine broke down irretrievably and that he moved to the Cayman Islands to find better work. That revelation helped to ease my conscience, since I knew that his situation would be better.

Meanwhile, I finished high school and started to plan for getting into college. The only person who came to mind to help me on that ambitious venture was my father, Dave. He owed me that much. I had heard from a friend that he was still living in Kingston, having made his residence there since Sarah had kicked him out of the house that fateful Christmas.

I made the journey to Kingston by bus in search of Dave, with the hope that he would want to take any opportunity to make right the father-daughter relationship that he had treated so carelessly. Once there, I was surprised to find that he lived in a ghetto. He resided in a small hovel with his new partner and a whole new set of children. The conditions were dreadful!

I felt awkward telling him my reason for coming to see him. I had finished high school and was there to seek his help to start college. I braved it anyway. After all, what did I have to lose by asking? His advice was to find a man who could look after me and send me to school. In his opinion, having a "sugar daddy" was my only option. He had no sense of obligation to me. He felt he had done enough for me in my younger years.

Night had fallen by the time we finished talking and it was too late for me to return home to Saint Elizabeth. I ended up sleeping at his house on the filthy floor, atop a dirty mattress covered by a thin sheet. The pungent smell of feces and stagnant water wafted in from the street outside through all the cracks in the doors and windows. The smell was so strong that you could taste it, and I wondered how the rest of the family could breathe that putrid air every day.

While I slept that night, I dreamt that I went to the Ministry of Education, and when I told them my plight, they helped me. I woke the next morning with full recollection of my dream, and a burning excitement about the possibility in my belly. I left the house unbathed and still in my clothes from the day before. My old, yellow, rayon challis trousers and shirt were crushed like a spinach leaf, but I didn't let my dishevelled look deter me from my mission to go to the Ministry of Education. I was in Kingston, and I was a sixteen-year-old girl with no fear of failure in her head. When I am in Kingston today, I am a scared wimp, even though I have the life experiences of thirty-three years behind me. But at sixteen, I was courageous. I quickly boarded a bus to make my way to downtown Kingston with determination in my soul.

Chapter 3: The Real Dad Stands Up

As I boarded, I took one last look back in the direction of the pathetic ghetto where my father was living and thought, *Well, Dad, that was your last chance to be in my life and fuck you! You blew it!*

The bus arrived in front of the Ministry at seven thirty a.m., far too early for a governmental office to be open. I posted myself in front of the Minister's office to wait for him to arrive. Every time the security guard passed me, he would give me a strange look. The intensity of my determination must have made me seem as if I were crazy, but he never harassed me. The Ministry's staff was beginning to trickle in, and they were not happy with my loitering. They tried every trick in the book to get me to leave, but I refused to budge, telling them that I had an urgent matter to discuss with Minister Burchell Whiteman.

It wasn't until about four in the afternoon that the staff finally realised I was not going to leave without seeing the Minister, who apparently was in his office all day, as they have secure entrances for such important individuals. A lady came out and told me that he had made time for me to come in and speak to him. I could see him in about half an hour. I began to consider my dishevelled physical state. Man, my mouth stank! I could smell it each time I breathed out.

I hadn't eaten since the day before, and there was nothing around that I could use to wash it out or clear it of that bad smell. I bucked up and reminded myself that I had come that far and had no time for embarrassment over something as silly as my outward appearance. Soon enough, Minister Whiteman stepped out into the hallway where I was sitting and kindly invited me to take a seat in his clean and comfy office.

I remember his calm voice putting me at ease as he expressed his admiration of my intense resilience. He said that he was intrigued to hear what I had to say that had given me the patience to wait so long while he finished the urgent duties of his post. I started to tell him my whole life story, leading up to what caused me to travel the long distance to Kingston and even how my dad had received me and what advice he had given me.

Chapter 3: The Real Dad Stands Up

I ended my plea by expressing my desire to become a lawyer, and how it was necessary for me to go to college to make my dream come true, so that I could help others who were in my situation. He listened attentively and then gently told me the unfortunate news that their office couldn't provide any help for that particular desire of mine, but that he could offer me training to enter the career of teaching.

I was not interested in that field and began to reiterate my initial intended career path in law, but he quickly pointed out to me that I was not in a bargaining position. Instead of getting mad or asking me to leave his office, he briefly outlined the positive aspects of his offer and the reality of my situation. His words were not unkind when he told me that I could either take or leave the offer. Well, I was stubborn, but I was not stupid.

I grabbed at it! Since it was my hope to start my life anew and attend school in a different parish from the one I currently resided in, I asked if he could recommend me for matriculation at a Teacher's College in Montego Bay, Saint James, a co-educational residential college.

To my utter delight, he agreed! I left his office with his promise that I would be going to college in September; we were in June so not long left to wait. My heart was so full of gratitude towards that kind man. A man who was asking nothing of me in return except my promise to live a full and productive life. The relief accompanying that momentous occasion in my life erupted in big, wet tears. I had seen what perseverance could accomplish and I set it as my life's guiding light.

I went back to Saint Elizabeth to give the great news to my uncle and the rest of my family. They were over the moon for me. Many people in the district said they knew I would amount to something. Another example and confirmation that not all men were bad and abusive.

Since I would be living on campus, I asked different members of my family to help me procure each item I was going to need for my time there. That was just before my uncle left for Cayman, and he was kind enough to contact someone he knew at the local bank, Jamaica National, to secure a job for me. Beneath it all, he was skeptical of the Minister's promise and only wanted me to have something more secure so that I could make a living if everything fell through. I was touched by his continued show of genuine care for me, but I was certain that my dream was going to come true and I declined the job offer when it came through. Certainly, that path could have provided me a salary and some prestige among our largely unemployed community, but I wanted an education and greater stability. I wanted my passport out of poverty... education.

I readied myself for the long trip to the Teacher's College to put in my formal application. It was a testament to how eager I was, that I had already collected everything that I would need for attending the college before I had even applied! On arrival in Montego Bay, I went directly to the admissions office of the college and again started the waiting game.

A secretary finally asked me what my purpose was and became furious when I told her that I had arrived to complete an application for the upcoming semester. She asked loudly, "Who do you think you are? Everyone applied back in April. You are two months too late." Her tone with those last words was final and she was set to walk away from me, but I wasn't about to let that rude and unpleasant woman push me aside and hinder me from reaching my goal. I trailed behind her, apologised profusely, and did not respond in anger to her insults. She laughed mockingly, stating that even if she allowed me to fill out the form, my application would only wind up in the waste bin. I offered her my reasoning that trying was all I could do, and explained that it was really only her conscience that she would be dealing with if she chose to put my application in the trash. She relented and gave the form to me with a flick of her wrist.

I summoned my courage yet again to bravely ask for a pen, which she provided with an audible murmur. She told me not to make a mistake with this form as she was not going to give me another, and you can be sure as hell I did just that. Suddenly, the enormity of what I was undertaking hit me. I became extremely nervous, my mind racing with the realisation that I was the first of my mother's children to even apply for college. But I remembered my lesson from the Minister's office about perseverance, and I put the pen to paper.

When I had finished, I handed the document to the secretary and I could tell she was expecting a bunch of rubbish. Instead, I saw a great change come over her hardened face as she read. My stomach somersaulted as her mouth relaxed from its downturned pursing into an easy and calm form. She stood and ushered me from the waiting room into a more formal room, deeper inside the office, and there she helped me fill out new forms this time. It was during that time that I discovered the reason for her attitude change—we were from the same parish, Saint Elizabeth. We finished the application session with her telling me that when I received my end of high school exam results, CXC or GCSE equivalent, I was to take them straight to her. And I promised her I certainly would. God himself was at work in my life here, I thought. When my results finally arrived in the following weeks, I was delighted to see that I had passed enough subjects to support my application for college, even though my English and Math scores were very low. However, when I delivered the results, I was elated to find out that I would be accepted to major in Secondary Education with specialisations in Home Economics and General Science.

The rest of the summer flew by and September came along faster than any other time in my life. On the morning of my departure from Saint Elizabeth to Montego Bay, I woke up with a stomach full of butterflies because I couldn't believe I was actually about to start college. I was full of anticipation for the next chapter of my life, where peers who loved learning and were focused on bettering themselves and the world around them would surround me. Yet, when I arrived, it almost felt like primary school all over again. It was painfully obvious how much I stood out. I felt myself being transformed back into that poverty-stricken, mango-selling girl. Everyone else was dressed in the appropriate college uniform, but I was still wearing my old high school uniform, as the proper clothes were one thing I could not acquire back home before I moved. I looked around the campus on my first day and felt so small and insignificant. But a small voice in my head urged me forward, reminding me to never let such negative feelings overcome my ambitions.

I was relieved to see that the secretary from my previous visit to the college was the one now processing the new students. I quickly jumped into the line to get registered. However, I immediately noticed that everyone was carrying a pink slip that I had never seen before. I quietly asked the girl ahead of me, "What are these slips for?" In response, she loudly announced that it was the payment-of-fees slip and then asked how I could not know that, with an incredulous ring to her voice. Squinting her eyes at me, she asked, "Where is yours?" I mumbled some excuse and she turned her attention away from me. When I reached the top of the line, I spoke to the secretary about that issue, assuming that I would again find understanding and favour in how to rectify that new situation. That day, however, she exercised no tolerance and excused me from the line of students being processed. You see, Minister Whiteman told me he would get me in, so naïvely I assumed that they would just take his name, and all would be okay.

As the day wore on, I stood with my belongings and watched everyone receive the assignment for their rooms and class schedules. I had hung around hoping that after all of the other students had been processed, the staff would find time to be sympathetic to my case and help me get everything resolved. While I waited, I met a girl who, upon realising my plight, offered to keep my luggage for me until I was able to sort out the situation. I accepted and then made my way to the office upstairs to ask if I could make a telephone call. That was before mobile phones—oh, how times have changed! The office staff was busy with registration duties and were not interested in listening to my distracting request.

Whenever a lady became available at one of the service windows, I would ask for the favour of using one of the office phones to make an emergency call. The response I got was a slamming of the glass window in my face. It happened so many times that afternoon that I lost count. As the evening hour approached, I had to change tactics. I went into the village to make the call to Minister Whiteman from a public phone box. The call rang through just as he was about to leave his office for the day. Looking back, I recognized that as just one of the many small miracles that have occurred throughout my life, and I know unmistakably that I should be returning the service back to Christ, who has never failed me. Even though I was crying hysterically into the phone, the Minister's secretary recognised me right away and quickly assured me that I had no need to worry. She told me that I just needed to calm down and take deep breaths.

Even after I quelled the tears, I could not fully let go of the overwhelming fear that my situation was falling apart before my eyes. I was frantic to get her to understand that I had no place to go back to in my district, telling her that the uncle I had lived with had gone to Cayman and I had no place to live. I reiterated that college was my only hope and registration was closing in the next few hours. She reassured me that she was going to call the school immediately and get everything sorted out.

I finally calmed down and went back to the school's registration office. The same rude lady who had slammed her window shut on me multiple times faced me when I returned. As I approached, her phone began to ring, and she again slammed the window shut. I stood in stillness and waited. Eventually, she gently reopened the window and handed the telephone handset through to me. I was afraid to take the phone from her at first, in case she was planning to slam the window down onto my hand in an effort to make me go away once and for all. But instead, she simply handed it over. My timid "hello" was answered by the most important voice I had heard to date. It was Minister Whiteman on the line telling me not to worry and reassuring me that everything would be all right.

The lady at the window beckoned for the handset to be returned and, without any preamble, provided me with a room assignment. I didn't know what Minister Whiteman told the registration staff, but whatever it had landed me in college. I felt as if I had been lifted on the wings of angels. Even more so when I arrived at the door of my room to find my roommate was that very same girl who had earlier taken my bags for safekeeping. Whether that was a mere coincidence or God in action, you decide. I was finally starting college, and it was the most joyous event that had ever occurred in my young life.

Our entry into the world is most often met with laughter and tears of joy. Do we cry because we are fearful, or hopeful?

CHAPTER 4: COMFORT ZONE

Far too often we hide behind that which makes us comfortable, looking for a shelter from the truth of our pain and sadness, as they are too difficult and devastating to confront.

Campus life provided a degree of freedom I hadn't yet known. It was a new environment and I liked it. I felt like I had a place to call home now, with a new family consisting of my classmates and teachers.

All freshmen went through an initiation called "grubbing," a form of hazing that occurred during the first two weeks of college and was headed by the seniors. The senior students would come into the dorm rooms and wake freshmen up at five in the morning. The activities they would have us do varied each day. Sometimes it was running laps; sometimes it was enduring toothpaste being placed on our eyelids. There were all sorts of crazy things they came up with to torture us, but it was all done in good nature and to foster camaraderie between the older students and us. I wound up making friends with several of the seniors, one who even gave me a uniform to wear so that I could immediately start to blend in and understand what it was like to be one of a group.

As the term progressed, I came to realise that the students who had grubbed us at the beginning of the term were the very same ones who were most willing to share their food and their knowledge. They were the ones who were available to give advice on how to cope with exam stress and campus life. Many of us were not accustomed to the workload our teachers were piling on us, or to living away from home.

We were struggling with the new campus routines, missing our families, and generally just living with total strangers in such an environment.

Here it was not like secondary school where teachers spent heaps of time going over unclear subject matters. It was lecture halls and almost like a production line; you had a responsibility to figure it out—be there after the lecture to ask questions, but not hold up the class to explain what it was that you didn't grasp. As for me, I struggled with all that plus how to find the basics to survive, so mine was a double whammy.

All the students were expected to return home at the end of term for a break from the burdens of campus life, but I had no real home to go to and the impending event made me extremely anxious.

When the day finally came, my classmates were all packing their things excitedly. They chattered about whom they were going to see and the home-cooked meals they were going to eat. I stayed quiet and lingered around until I was the last one left. Of course, the housemother noticed, and I had to explain to her that unlike all the other girls, I really had nowhere else to go. I was so relieved when she took pity on me and allowed me to stay in my room during the Christmas break. She warned me that was a one-time thing and I couldn't count on it becoming my regular situation during the term breaks. I didn't care about anything so far in the future at that moment, and I just thanked her profusely for saving me that day.

Despite the grant I received from the Ministry of Education to pay my tuition, which covered living and board, I still had to come up with money for all the miscellaneous things that come along with living on campus and attending classes. Occasionally, my mother would send a small amount of money, but it was so little and infrequent that many times I couldn't even afford sanitary napkins for my monthly flow. I would save up some old pieces of cloth, which I would carefully roll around the crotch of my underwear to catch the blood. These didn't work very well, and it was an embarrassing chore to wash them out at the end of each day so that they could be reused. I was sure everyone knew when I was menstruating, especially because I would only wear my royal blue skirt during those days of bleeding, to hide the stain better if there happened to be a leak. On the occasions when that was the case, I could always feel it before I saw it. So, I would wait until the classroom had emptied and then I would walk by myself to my room, using my books to cover my rear end.

While on campus I made friends quickly and involved myself in all sorts of activities, which helped keep me occupied during my free hours. After all, I didn't have the hours of chores to attend to that I used to have when I was attending secondary or primary school. I found that the social activities served to keep all of my negative thoughts at bay. My closest friend at that time was a girl named Jenn. She quickly proved herself to be someone I could trust and confide in. We were like kindred spirits, as we had come from similar backgrounds. I was shocked and a bit thrilled to find out that she, too, had nowhere to live, so we stayed on campus together that first holiday. She made me feel like I wasn't so alone in my circumstance.

My loneliness was soon to take a turn as I realized that I was now on my own. I had no one to really go to for help anymore. Sarah and that unit were gone, so was my uncle and Clementine, and the harsh reality of being an adult hit me hard. I felt dizzy. I did not like the feeling; it was like being at the edge of a cliff with no restraints to catch you if you fall. My face was awash with sweat, and panic came over me. I went for a walk to get some fresh air. "I needed to find my own family," I suppose was my deeper thought.

One day I was on campus, rushing to get to class, when I met the man who was to become my first husband, though I had no clue of it at the time. His name was Tobore and he was an extremely attractive guy, with freckles and just the most handsome, youthful face I had ever seen.

Soon we were hanging out as friends, and although I thought he was terribly handsome, I did not see him as someone I would have a relationship with. As a matter of fact, I didn't think a guy like that would have any interest in someone like me. At that stage of my life, my self-esteem was non-existent. Jenn, however, was convinced that he liked me from the very start. I had even tried to set him up with one of my other classmates—a pretty girl named Syria—just to prove Jenn wrong. And I was steadfast in my refusal to let anything interfere with my college education, as it was all I could count on to secure my future.

When the summer arrived that year, Jenn and I were literally chased off campus by our housemother. Since neither of us had any need to return to our districts, we rented a single room together in a house owned by a Mr. Brown in Catherine Hall, Montego Bay. Over the next few months, he grew to be a surrogate father to the both of us. He knew that we could not afford the rent or food, but he let us stay and fed us anyway, accepting any amount that we could afford to pay him from the odd jobs we found around the city.

That was how we survived the summer of 1994. At times, we would laugh or cry at the irony of our situation. Here we were, training to educate the next generations of our communities so that they could be successful and live full lives, but we were practically homeless. We would stay up late at night and talk about our dreams and goals, and how we looked forward to the start of our second year. I knew that my grant from the Ministry of Education was limited to my first year, so I had to start applying for grants and tuition assistance. In a short time, I secured a loan from the Students' Loan Bureau. Even though it was not free money and the loan was to be paid back after I graduated, securing it eased my fears about not being able to complete my education.

A few weeks into my second year, my mum contacted me to say that the man I had always claimed as my father, Dave, was petitioning the courts to have a change made on my birth certificate. I immediately assumed that somehow it had to do with him denying me, but instead she told me that he wanted to give me his last name. "What was the need," I wondered? I had always used my mother's last name, the shameful mark of a truly fatherless child that no man wanted to claim as his own flesh and blood. Now, at seventeen years old, I considered the idea with a more rational mind.

I realised that I had survived that long without having a paternal family name or the favours I thought that would have brought. While this gesture was not the cause of any great celebration on my part, I could not bring myself to object to it. Looking back, I suppose I let the change happen for sentimental reasons . . . to respect the child I had once been who would have rejoiced at that moment. My new birth certificate arrived by mail, and I felt nothing when I saw my new name boldly printed on the official document. Ava-Gaye Beckford became Ava-Gaye Brown. I filed the paper away without another thought, having no idea how that change would haunt me in my adult years.

Academically speaking, I was doing well, and my grades were higher than many of my peers. I think my successes in the classroom were largely due to the fact that I stayed on campus over the weekends with nothing else to do but study, while many of the other girls went on trips or travelled home.

One evening, I was completing some coursework in the computer lab when Tobore appeared. I asked why he was not out with our friend Syria. I had arranged a date with her for him and was shocked by his bold reply, "I'm not interested in her. Don't you know that you are the one I am interested in?"

Tobore's confession awoke something inside of me and I almost instantaneously realised that I had feelings for him, too. The fact that we immediately started dating came as no surprise to Jenn. My relationship with Tobore had many unexpected benefits. My whole life seemed to become easier, more pleasurable, and I now saw the sunshine in the sky instead of the clouds, and the flowers covering the ground instead of the weeds. We spent all of our spare time together. He was my escape, my new everything. My friends started teasing me, saying that I was no longer available.

At the beginning, I worried that my newfound relationship might act as a distraction from my studies, but I managed to remain focused. For Tobore's part, he supported me and helped me with my coursework, as he had just finished college himself and was living nearby. He was extremely caring and treated me with the utmost respect. During those times of the month when I would experience chronic pain from uterine cramping during my menstruation—due to a condition I later learned is called dysmenorrhea—he was my nurse. I was so touched by his careful attention to me that I could not help but tell him how much I loved him. That was my first experience of love in any shape or form in my mind. We took our relationship to the next level and I was comfortable and ready. I felt safe, loved, and complete.

It did not escape me that the reason I gravitated towards him and felt so at ease in his presence was because of the healthy affection he showed me, all without expecting anything in return except for my happiness. It was so refreshingly different from the previous concept I'd had of men. He was in no hurry to be involved with me sexually, and I felt such a relief to not have that expectation weighing down our time together. We cultivated a deep and trusting relationship, and I felt secure in the knowledge that he genuinely cared for me.

As any new couple would be, we were curious about one another's history. When he would ask about my family, though, I found it difficult to openly share that information, as it was a source of embarrassment for me. He was also from Saint Elizabeth, and I suppose that fact made me guard my tongue as well. After we had been dating for a few months, we took a long weekend trip back to visit our home parish. During our travels, I plucked up the courage to tell him about my family and my trials growing up among them. I was uncertain of how he would react, but I believed that if he truly loved me, he would not think my past tarnished my present character. He listened intently and was very understanding. Soon after I spilled my guts out to him, instead of him distancing himself from me or treating me awkwardly, he played the song "Somewhere

Out There," by Linda Ronstadt, and we sang along to it at the top of our lungs. It was such a cathartic release, and he fully claimed my heart.

Tobore and I fell into an easy routine after we returned from Saint Elizabeth. He would pick me up after classes, and I would stay some nights at his place. He cooked for the both of us, and we grew closer. I was doing well in school and I was in love with a man who was also in love with me. He would send me roses for no particular reason and there was nothing expected of me in return. I never had to ask him for money. He would somehow know when I needed it and never begrudged helping me. I had finally found comfort and stability in my life and I wanted it to stay that way forever.

My third and final year of college arrived before I knew it. Part of the senior year curriculum included teaching in assigned schools for a term, after which our practical skills would be assessed by an external examiner for certification to obtain employment upon graduation. When the term of the teaching internship came to a close, we threw the traditional celebration that was called "burying the TP" (teaching practice). That event was carried out as a symbolic way to dispose of all the stress from our teaching practice, with the hope that we would all pass the evaluation and successfully move forward into our adult lives.

Tobore had moved to Kingston to find employment in the latter part of my third year. I was dismayed that we weren't able to keep in regular contact, but I was busy enough with my own responsibilities of finishing my education. I was able to visit him in Kingston once or twice during that time, but the fact that he was living at his sister's house was an added strain on our relationship, because it was inappropriate for us to stay there together. When my graduation day came, Tobore was busy at work in Kingston and could not attend. Even though my mum and sister were there to support me, my heart was broken by his absence.

I felt blessed to have my mum there with me and I told her so. She was proud of me, and I could see it on her face. I took the time to reflect on what I had achieved over those past three years and I was even more proud of myself. Graduating from college was the single greatest achievement in my life so far. I had passed my teaching practice, thankfully, and I returned to Saint Elizabeth with my diploma in hand and settled myself back in a new aunt's house. As I reflected on my teacher training experience, I must say I truly enjoyed seeing the eagerness in the faces of those students who thought I was very worldly. Little did they know I was just a child myself.

My relationship with Tobore had begun to see challenges and to deteriorate, but I had to focus my energies on finding a job to support myself. After more than one hundred and twenty applications and one hundred and twenty turndowns or non-replies, I was losing hope. Finally, I applied for a position at the school where my aunt worked and was offered the job (with a little help from my aunt, as we all sometimes do). Someone finally believed that a nineteen-year-old college graduate could be an effective teacher! The job was only for one term, but to me it was better than nothing. My student loan repayments were coming due, and I didn't want to be a burden to my aunt for much longer. She was new in my life and doing me a huge favour, so I was careful to stay on my toes.

The evening before I was to start my first day of work, a call came from the head teacher of the school. Thinking she was calling with last-minute instructions for me, I was shocked to hear her say that the teacher whose position I was going to take had reconsidered quitting and wanted her job back. The bottom line was that there was no opening for me, another rejection in my young life.

How could that be? My heart sank further with every word. The lady apologised but said that there wasn't anything else she could do. I hung up the phone and crumbled into deep cries of despair. I had my loans to repay and wanted desperately to have my own place. After all, hadn't I achieved my qualification to escape that exact situation?

When the tears finally stopped, I began to plan a re-start of my job search to begin immediately in the morning. However, God must have heard my cry, because before the moon came out, I received another phone call. The call was from the head of Food and Nutrition of Ardenne High School in Kingston—Joan Davis Williams. She said that she was looking for someone to fill a teaching position immediately, and that she had heard from my education officer that I was a capable young graduate. The job would be mine if I could make it to Kingston by eight o'clock the next morning. This was over three hours away so to get there by eight a.m. would mean starting my journey at about four a.m.

I owned only one interview suit, which was currently in the wash because, just hours before, I had believed my job hunt was finished. I jumped into action, washed it, and placed it behind the fridge to dry. I didn't know how I was going to be able to make the eight a.m. deadline, but that wasn't about to stop me from trying! I woke before the crack of dawn and by five-thirty a.m. I was on the bus heading to Kingston. I arrived at the school right on time, and my first day was effortless. Joan made it easy by offering support. She told the kids not to use my small stature to judge my teaching abilities. I loved it, and the students were very receptive. I left that day with a smile on my face, knowing I was helping to groom young lives.

Again, the job that was offered was short term, but I took it anyway. I hadn't had time to find somewhere to stay in Kingston. I considered finding Tobore and asking to stay with him, but quickly decided against it. Instead, I remembered another uncle who was living in Portmore, a town near enough to Kingston that I could travel to work every day without much hassle. The minute I arrived at his place I was given approval to stay, but I knew it would not be an enjoyable time. The place was like a matchbox, and humid with a foul smell of a stinking swamp nearby. As I looked around the dilapidated room, I heard a voice telling me "beggars can't be choosers," and I resolved to make the best of my situation. After all, I had lived in worse conditions than this, so I knew I could endure it for a while. I had a job and I would be making my own money.

I worked at Ardenne for only a few days before the same lady who had hired me told me about a new vacancy at a nearby high school. She explained that the job would be "a bit more permanent" than the one I was currently in at her school. I told her that I was interested, and she called to arrange the interview and even drove me there. Her kindness made me wonder if she was an angel sent to guide me. I wound up getting the job at the high school and started immediately. I had felt torn and disloyal accepting the job and leaving the first position, but she encouraged me to look at my long-term future. Today, Joan and I are still great friends. She is a co-author in an anthology I compiled, called *The Single Mother's Diary Volume 1*. I stay at her home on some of my visits back to Jamaica.

The new job would put me in a better position, both financially and in terms of experience.

Tobore and I had reconnected since my arrival in the city, and he helped me look for a place that I could afford on my own. Soon after, I rented a room in a house that was close to my new workplace. My move to Kingston seemed to be a double blessing, as it also helped Tobore and I mend our relationship. Even though we had not officially ended things, we definitely had drifted apart. Over time, he began staying over at my place, and I remembered why I loved being with him, and recognised that I was ready to take our relationship to the next level. Things moved on well for Tobore and me during that time in our young adult lives. I even became friends with the girl who was dating Tobore's older brother. Her name was Constance and she was very kind, funny, principled, and just a genuine girl. We are still friends, almost like sisters. She now lives in Africa, where she works as a missionary, but that hasn't affected our bond.

Tobore and I took one more trip to Saint Elizabeth, and this time I was to meet his parents. For me, it was an uncomfortable introduction. My eyes grew wide when we drove up to their house. It was what I considered to be a mansion! I immediately felt inadequate and out of place. Of course, his parents inquired about my family and background, but I had no idea what to say. In my head, I played out the honest conversation: "Well, my mum is unemployed, has kids with two different fathers, and lives in a one-room shack where we all used to wake up wet with pee, because someone was always wetting the single bed we shared. My stepdad is also unemployed, and has been ever since his job was made redundant at the rice factory, which happened about ten years ago. I really don't even know who my real father is, but the man who has claimed me as his daughter molested me when I was twelve."

Just imagining the looks on their faces was enough to make me shiver! Here I was, trying to make a good first impression, and all I could do was try my best to sidestep their questions about my family. The entire visit was awkward. On our journey back to Kingston, Tobore assured me that they would warm up to me in time, but I was skeptical. To me, it seemed as if his parents and sister did not think I was good enough for him. They quizzed me about my background, family, and their faces indicated that they disapproved when I would tell them the truth. I just knew it. They had a better house, wore nicer clothes, spoke better English. It was all there in what they said and didn't say. They were upper class, and I was the scum of the earth in their eyes.

I was torn and confused, wondering if I should just break it off immediately to spare us both the disaster that was sure to come in the future. I began to question the realistic chances of our relationship lasting long term.

When my year teaching at the high school came to an end, I found out the post would not be renewed, and that it was time for me to start looking for another job. Finding another teaching job in Kingston proved to be a difficult task, and soon I was applying for jobs outside of the region. I was finally offered a job teaching Home Economics in Manchester, about two hours from Kingston. The thought of a move was not appealing to

Chapter 4: Comfort Zone

me, and even less so to Tobore, who said that he might not be able to follow me because of his steady job in Kingston. But we both realised the reality of our situation. He could not afford to have me at home as a kept girlfriend, and it wasn't my ambition either. I also felt the break would do us good. Parts of me wanted out. I felt that we wouldn't work, I wasn't suited to him, and he was not standing up enough for us.

Accepting that new job bolstered my sense of independence, and it was a permanent job finally. I would be moving to a new place and starting my life anew. As soon as I got settled, I purchased my first set of furniture on hire purchase. I chose a rather luxurious sofa, dining table, and bed, along with a few other pieces. In my heart, I intended to make my flat comfortable for my man and myself. My hope that Tobore would soon visit me was ever present in my mind. I strived to make my apartment look like the home I had always dreamed of.

In time, I realised that I liked being on my own, but some parts of me desperately missed Tobore's company. I looked forward to every one of his visits, as we were now working out better as a couple. Maybe the move was what we needed. He always arrived bearing tons of presents, but most importantly, he would bring his love to me. Our lovemaking in these times was passionate, and every minute I spent tightly pressed up against his naked body was no less than amazing. We were carefree but committed to each other.

My new job was challenging but exciting. I was learning a lot and enjoying it immensely. When October came around, though, I was starting to feel very tired, and I was having a hard time making it through the days. It was only a little over two months into the school year. Then I started feeling frequently nauseous. One day I entered my food and nutrition practical room not feeling well. I couldn't figure out what was wrong with me. My students started to tease me about being pregnant. I laughed with them, thinking how ridiculous the idea of me being a mum was. It was unimaginable!

I was still at an age when young people think they are invincible, the age when something as adult as pregnancy doesn't seem like it can happen. I wanted to take a different path. Especially having seen what early pregnancy did to my mum. Tobore and I had never really discussed having children, and frankly, it was the furthest thing from my mind at that time. I was having fun, we just loved our time together, and I didn't want anything to change that. However, one day when I fainted in the middle of teaching one of my classes, my friend Gloria took matters into her own hands and insisted that I go on a doctor's visit. I relented and made an appointment for that evening after work, just to shut her up.

In all honesty, I was avoiding the situation because I was scared of what the doctor might say. What if he discovered I had a mysterious illness or a brain tumour? How would I afford all of the medical care and time off work? What would Tobore do if he had to take care of me every day while I wasted away until I died? Would he even stay with me? Such silly thoughts from a silly girl!

When the doctor asked my symptoms, he immediately ordered a pregnancy test, which I thought was preposterous. I kindly declined, not wanting to waste my money on something that I didn't need, but when he insisted, I complied. The doctor returned with the results in a few minutes. I was all ready to roll my eyes at him, but when he delivered the news that I was pregnant, I felt the earth move beneath me. I was confused and disorientated. The silliest questions spilled from my mouth. "How could that be?" "When did that happen?" It was the doctor's turn to roll his eyes. After a few calming words, he dismissed me to go home. Yet, he had not answered my most important question: Why now?

What makes us ultimately happy is sometimes disguised in shadows of turmoil.

CHAPTER 5: NEW LIFE APPEARS

***Hidden happiness awaits us if we stop to see beyond the now.
Only that is most times almost impossible.***

The doctor's office was far from my home, and I was so distraught that I couldn't think straight, so I hailed a taxi. That trip home seemed much longer than it was in reality. I sat in the back of the car, not speaking to the driver and simply overwhelmed with panicked thoughts. Being pregnant and unwed meant that I was going to lose my job, which in turn meant that I would have no way to pay for all the furniture I had just bought, or the rent on my apartment, which meant that I was going to be homeless! Not only would my grand attempt at independence be an absolute failure, I would also be an utter embarrassment to my family, and everyone who had faith enough in me to help me along the way. I couldn't stop the tears when a thought struck me: *There is no way to break the cycle you were born into, girl.*

As soon as I reached my home, I phoned Tobore and told him that he needed to come see me. While I waited for his arrival, I paced the floor of my apartment. The doctor estimated that I was about two or three months along already, which meant that I had already been pregnant when I moved into that place. My thoughts quickly turned into a petulant conversation with God. *God, are you for real? Why did you wait until I was getting my life pieces together? Why, why, why? Why now, why me?* I had so many questions for Him, if only He would answer.

I asked why He couldn't have let me know earlier, so I wouldn't have wasted my time on the move, wasted my money on the furniture. I asked why He didn't care enough to help save me the hassle, why He had allowed me to finally feel a bit of comfort in the false knowledge that my life was finally coming together. A mocking little voice crept into my head, reminding me of where I was from and that I needed to just accept the sad life laid out for me. A life of being considered a community's property and serving without question. The voice grew stronger and more challenging, asking, who do you think you are? Just how stupid are you to believe that you can change the history and lineage of so many women that came before you?

Tobore arrived very quickly, although to me it felt like hours had passed. I blurted out the news, my thoughts having worked me into a complete frenzy. My beaten spirit was just waiting for the next awful thing to happen . . . for him to leave me.

To my great surprise, he took the news much better than I had. A giant smile spread across his face. He was excited, but I was baffled about what he could possibly find exciting about my predicament. As he said soothing words to calm me down, my mind continued to work. I reflected on the opposite roles that a man and a woman played in that situation of life. Really, a man had nothing to lose when a girlfriend told him she was pregnant with his child. He would still have his job and he wouldn't lose his figure. Oh, I hadn't even thought about that aspect yet. I was about to lose the perfect, taut young body and wicked curves that I suddenly realised I had and never truly appreciated. I instinctively put my hand on my belly and thought about how men didn't have to face the massive changes that come with carrying a baby. I wondered if he would love me after I became all pudgy and round, after giving birth to his child.

As Tobore continued to hold me close and reassure me, I began to calm down. That night, he made such tender love to me that I felt my heart might burst. His arms made me feel secure and I began to believe that things would work out after all. We lay in bed deep into the night, tangled in each other's arms, discussing what would happen next. As the morning hours came upon us, we came to the decision that I would move back to Kingston and figure it out from there—that is how it was left, and it felt familiar versus staying where I hardly knew anyone. I also couldn't afford to pay for the apartment. There really was no other option, but a part of me resented it because I still desperately wanted to be independent and live on my own. I was also confused and a bit ashamed by my childish desire to simply run home to a mum who could give me the nurturing that I needed at that moment. But since my mother wasn't a loving, empathetic, or encouraging type of mum, that wasn't an option.

Tobore was the person I would have to rely on through the situation, and I recognised the truth in his words when he said I would eventually have to move from Manchester back to Kingston. I was resigned to that decision the next morning when I went to my school and delivered the news to my head of department that I was pregnant. They needed to know, as I was not being effective as a teacher due to my early illness. I felt I couldn't cope; my mind and body were in shock. She listened quietly and then informed me that I would have to give up the job, as my time there hadn't even exceeded a single term of classes yet. She reminded me that I had signed the contract acceding to the moral fabric and principles of the school policy, which forbade employment in that exact type of situation—being pregnant, unmarried, and in my first term. Nope, unacceptable. Inwardly, I was screaming about the gross unfairness of it all, but outwardly, I kept my mouth shut because I knew there was nothing to be done.

Tobore and I immediately made plans for my move, and before I knew it, I was out of my little apartment and back in Kingston. On arrival, Tobore brought me to the large house he was still sharing with his sister. His plan was for me to spend at least a few nights there while we got an independent living arrangement established. However, that was short lived as his sister wasn't very happy with the idea of me even staying there, and my heart sank when Tobore made no attempt to sway the decision.

Chapter 5: New Life Appears

I sat in tears, again overwhelmed by my situation. I was jobless, pregnant, and now homeless, without the protection of the man whose child I was carrying. I was so disappointed with Tobore, even though he continued to try to find a place for me to live on my own. Tobore approached a friend who lived with his girlfriend and their child, and they agreed to take me in. Lucky for me, they turned out to be lovely people, plus they treated me well and welcomed me warmly into their small home. Believe me, their kindness made me sad, as I felt as if I was invading their privacy and adding an unnecessary burden to their lives.

When my friends found out about my situation, many of them couldn't understand why I was living in these strangers' home, when my man was living in a large house that could have easily accommodated me, as well as our imminent child. I was filled with shame when I had to explain the circumstance of his sister's disapproval. Her impression was clear: I had impregnated myself to lure her brother.

A few weeks after I began staying with his friends, I was surprised and delighted when Tobore suggested that we find somewhere for the two of us to live together. I felt he was ashamed of how I was living while carrying his child, and his moral compass must have chipped in.

As soon as we settled into our new place, he sent word back to his family in Saint Elizabeth that we were living together, and I was pregnant with his child. They received the news tentatively, it seemed. I am sure his sister must have told them; however, their approach must have been to pretend they didn't know until he told them.

I understood the reasoning behind their hesitation. I was certain they were harbouring an unexpressed belief that I had become pregnant on purpose to trap him. Nothing was further from the truth.

I was still worried that by starting a family so young, I would be wasting my teacher qualification and impeding my chances of getting anywhere in life. But time moves on. Tobore and I settled into our life together and started preparing for the birth of our child. However, his family did not warm up to the situation.

I remember on New Year's Eve that year, Tobore phoned his parents to send season's greetings, but after the discussion he seemed sad. I knew that something negative had been said about our situation, though I never asked him about it. I didn't want to make it any more difficult than it already was for him. I felt like running away so that he could be rid of that burden and find peace again with his family. I knew that they were really disappointed with how everything was turning out between us, and with the baby on the way. Tobore would often try to hide their disappointment and disapproval from me, but I could always tell what was being said on the other end of the phone just by the look on his face. Even though he had finally started standing up for us as a couple, it pained me to realise why he hadn't in the first place. The emotional beating he was taking for me was almost unbearable. He was torn between the woman who bore him in her womb, who he adored and who meant the world to him, a family he had known all his life—and a woman who just walked in and stole his heart. It must have been a very difficult period for him. I saw it in his face after his calls home and when he came to bed. It was hard to watch. He was in constant agony, and I had so much guilt that I wanted to leave him.

I was still working on finding ways to improve my standing in the world, and another step towards independence was learning to drive a car. Tobore had one, but never taught me how to operate it, so I took it upon myself to learn because he felt I needed to be taught by an instructor and I was far too eager to wait. I remembered what little my uncle had taught me years prior. I began to sneak the car out at night while Tobore slept. Even with my growing belly in the way, I was soon able to expertly manoeuvre the vehicle. Although I was pretty certain that Tobore wouldn't get mad at me if I crashed the car, I was constantly worried that the police would be on my back if I got into an accident. Luckily, that never happened.

Chapter 5: New Life Appears

After living in our first rented place for only three months, Tobore and I had to move out of it because the landlord absolutely refused to fix anything, and the place rapidly became unlivable. We started thinking about the need to have more space once our little one arrived.

We were blessed to find a two-bedroom house in a much cleaner and safer neighbourhood. Our lives continued to move along, and we found more comfort in one another with each passing day. Soon, we began to talk about marriage, and that turned into a formal engagement, even though we had no idea when a wedding would be feasible. Whether it would be before or after the baby. We never discussed it with anyone else; it was kept for the most part between us.

At that time, Tobore was working as a shipping agent, which meant that he had to travel frequently, and I was at home by myself most of the time. To stave off the feelings of isolation and loneliness, I began writing. Putting my life's story down on paper proved to be therapeutic. I finally got the nerve to tell my mum about my pregnancy and engagement, but her response was rather unemotional, and I wasn't sure how she really felt. Her lack of response made me feel so anxious I lost my appetite. Looking back, I can see that I was in a deep depression during this time. Not having the support of my family, nor of my future in-laws or their extended family, some of whom lived a mere ten minutes' drive away from our place, weighed heavily on me. I wondered if that situation was hinting at how they would treat my child when it finally arrived.

I tried reaching out to the few friends that I had in Kingston, but they were busy with work. I had no one to talk to about my concerns and anxieties about becoming a mother, and successfully caring for that new life that would be entrusted to me. There was no one to help me strategize how I was to restart my career after the pregnancy was over. I needed a female who understood the challenges facing the fairer sex.

During that time, however, Tobore was my whole world, and I couldn't have asked for a better partner. He had grown very courageous, standing up to anyone who insulted or challenged our unborn child and me. He made sure that I didn't miss a single doctor's visit, paying for all of them and even attending them with me whenever his work schedule allowed. I had become confident in his love for me. All of his efforts made me feel happy and secure. Despite the challenges we faced on a daily basis, we still had fun. The days and nights inside our little home were filled with laughter, playfulness, and utter joy. Oh, how I loved him!

I would sometimes get to travel with him when he went out of town for work. I loved these trips. For me, they were a vacation. On one such trip to Ocho Rios, I got the chance to meet a famous female songstress who was my favourite Jamaican artiste at the time. I had been wandering around the hallway outside our hotel room moaning about wanting to go with Tobore to the concert she would be performing that night, when she happened to walk past us! I had no idea she was staying at the same hotel as us. Tobore was bold enough to strike up a conversation with her. He asked her to talk some sense into me about the fact that I was too far into my pregnancy to go to a concert full of jostling people. She was so kind and offered me an autographed card as consolation for not being in any condition to go see her perform. That placated me enough that I didn't hassle Tobore when he left with his work colleagues to see the show.

We decided that it was best to get married before the baby arrived, and began planning the ceremony in earnest. When we set the date and made the announcement, time went by with no word from his family to say that they were coming. I didn't know if they contacted Tobore separately to deny or accept the request. He was too kind to tell me. I resigned myself to the possibility that he and I might be the only ones there.

We were wed in March of 1998 in a simple ceremony, surrounded by about twenty friends and family, including Tobore's parents! I wore a white wedding dress that had been made by one of my friends who worked in a nearby US embassy, whose daughter I had taught in high school. We had to use a ton of fabric to accommodate my ever-expanding belly, as my due date was only two months away. The wedding was nice, but it was nothing like I had dreamt of as a child. Like so many other women, I had always pictured myself surrounded by a grand court of bridesmaids, my groom supported by his court of groomsmen, the maid of honour next to my side, the best man next to his, and a ring bearer and flower girls. My wedding was far from the fairy tale. We did get to have the ceremony in a church, though, which I had worried about since most churches frowned on marrying a woman so obviously pregnant. Luckily for us we knew someone who knew the pastor for the church we got married in. We even had a small reception at a well-respected heritage site in Kingston that Tobore had been able to secure because of his family name.

I remember being so relieved when I saw Tobore's parents sitting in the church. The dread that had been gripping my heart in the weeks before finally relaxed. His sister didn't attend though, and her failure to come, even though her residence was in the same town, was a show of her disapproval. As for my family, only a distant cousin made it to the wedding. I remember looking around at the small crowd that had gathered for the ceremony, and feeling utter happiness at marrying someone as wonderful as Tobore while feeling our baby kicking in my belly. However, that joy was tempered by the realisation that so few members of our families were present to share in the celebration. I began to grow anxious again about the reality of our situation. We were setting out in life on our own, without a strong support system behind us to help if we faltered.

We never planned to take a formal honeymoon. In some ways, the wedding itself was mainly carried out to help ease some of the shame our families—more so his—must have been feeling because of my pregnancy.

I remember someone asking me if I would have married Tobore if I hadn't been pregnant. My answer was a solid yes; I was madly in love with him. The pregnancy rushed our timing, but I would like to think that we were such a good fit that our relationship would have survived, and we would have eventually made it to the altar regardless.

The close and easy relationship that I craved to have with his parents did not come about even after we were married. I had hoped that once I became Tobore's wife and a legal member of his family, they would finally let their guard down and accept me, but that was just a dream.

> ***They say nothing worth having comes easily, yet we could benefit from balls thrown at us that weren't always curved.***

CHAPTER 6: BROKEN

Sometimes we go through life feeling broken, and something magical happens to change that, like the birth of an innocent life.

I was in my third trimester and still very ill on a regular basis. I had to carry a paper bag full of medicine wherever I went to help keep the nausea from turning into violent vomiting. When we were in the car, I would have to ask Tobore to pull over so I could throw up on the side of the road. Certain smells, like Irish Spring soap or the Styrofoam cups from Wendy's and Burger King, would trigger severe nausea. The doctor even prescribed Gravol injections, but they were painful and the trip to the office to get the injection made it almost not worth the relief that they brought.

I was so tired of all the medication and the continued feeling of illness. I tried on several occasions to reach out to my in-laws, hoping that I would hear some excitement in their voices about the upcoming birth, or comfort about the state of my condition. But there was little advice or support offered through kind words. My doctor often told me that my illness wasn't entirely physical, but a result of the extreme emotional and psychological torment I was feeling at the time. I tried to force myself to overcome the feeling of rejection and my desperate need to feel accepted. But my efforts were to no avail. I believed that if I were nicer or more solicitous, they would grow to love me. But each visit to their house ended with me feeling even more like an uninvited and unwanted guest. In reflection, some of these feelings were my own insecurities. Tobore worked hard to make me feel included, and eventually he got his parents and sister to ease up on their cold attitude towards me. My illness got milder when the tension from his family eased. I was filled with hope that our relationship would only continue to progress, especially for the sake of our child, who would certainly need the love and acceptance of both sides of the family.

A few weeks after our wedding, Tobore's sister announced that she was expecting a baby also. I was thrilled to hear the news because I was sure that our shared condition would help to improve our relationship. After all, she and I were now in the same boat, at least somewhat. My hope was never realised; she had no such intentions.

One day, when I was home alone, I felt a strange calmness in my belly. The baby wasn't moving. In a panic, I checked myself into one of our discussed private Christian hospitals. Before I could settle in at the traid, the emergency staff went into overdrive. The number of injections I got was shocking! I had no idea what was wrong, but it seemed serious by their treatment of me. When I became stabilized, I was discharged with the advice that I needed absolute rest and strict instructions for no solid foods. I was only allowed broth. Phew how would I survive this being a food, my mind thought!

Tobore was in the middle of a big project at work and felt that I was not fit to be on my own, so he took me to his sister's Collete's home. He outlined to her that I needed to just be on broth and no solid food, and I was left to rest in my husband's old room. However, when dinner was prepared, there was no broth in sight. I was shocked to find that dinner was fried chicken from a local fast food chain restaurant. The chicken broth and olive branch of peace I was expecting wasn't offered, so I retreated back to my room and cried silently. Did she disapprove of me so badly that she would risk my life, as well as that of her future niece or nephew? I went back to my own home as soon as Tobore was back home, as I knew that sort of rejection would only make me feel worse since I continued to be so severely ill. Tobore was an introvert and though he said nothing, I know he was aching inside.

Nearly eight months into my pregnancy, we decided to change my doctor. We became increasingly concerned about his lack of care and professionalism, and thought it best to make a change. That added a new stress to the end of my pregnancy, but I did start to feel a bit better under the new doctor's care.

We were busy planning for the baby's impending arrival. Tobore and I started writing down baby names we both liked. We had a good set of options for either sex: if it were a boy, we thought of Matthew or Michael, and if it were a girl, we liked Jasmine, Tempest, Tonya (after a student of mine, who was the daughter of the lady who'd made my wedding dress), April, or Ginell. I particularly loved the names Tonya and Jasmine. Our excitement was contagious, and my friends Jenna, Arlete, Janiz, and Violet organised a baby shower for me. When I arrived to a room full of my friends, I felt such a strong sense of love. I realised that I had finally cultivated a family of friends who cared for me and also loved me as much as a blood family should.

A few days after the shower, I began to feel unwell. I had a suspicion that something was wrong, and I soon convinced myself that I hadn't felt the baby move in three days. Tobore was working in town and I didn't want to alarm him, so I went to see my doctor on my own, and she advised that I get checked into the hospital right away. Tobore and I had already decided that we would have the baby in a private hospital, and we had chosen one that was not far from our home and the doctor's office. On arrival, I was admitted for observation. The initial examination revealed that my blood pressure was far too high; I had preeclampsia. Within minutes, the consultant informed me that they needed to perform an emergency caesarean section. At that point, I knew I had to phone Tobore and tell him what was about to happen. When I reached him, he assured me that he was on his way and would arrive at the hospital as soon as possible. I was very scared at the prospect of having to undergo surgery. The situation was extremely daunting, and I wished I has a sister there to hold my hand.

The hospital staff changed me into an open dressing gown that provided no privacy. But my embarrassment was soon overshadowed by the discomfort of having to lay spread-eagle, and the extreme pain of having a urinary catheter inserted without any anesthetic. I cried and prayed for it all to be over soon. Just as they finished prepping me for surgery, Tobore arrived. He was allowed to walk alongside my gurney, holding my hand, up to the entrance of the surgical theatre. I will never forget the feel of his kiss or the smell of his sweet sweaty brow as he leaned over to kiss me. He whispered that he loved me and assured me that he would see me in a bit. I was sure I was going to die and that was my goodbye kiss.

The anesthesiologist told me she would give me something that would make me feel sleepy, and that I would soon fall into a deep sleep.

As she started her work on me, I anxiously looked around the room and was horrified to see all the various apparatuses waiting for unknown uses. I broke out in a cold sweat. I had never been given an anesthetic before, and I kept thinking of the stories of people who were given a general anesthetic and never woke up. I tried desperately to calm myself down by thinking about the moment I was going to see the beautiful face of my child for the first time. Everyone had speculated that I was going to have a son, based on their assessment of the shape of my belly and other body signs that I didn't understand. I conjured up the image of my beautiful baby boy, of welcoming him into the world, and that was the last thought I had before everything went dark.

I awoke in a haze. My thoughts were so muddled, but there was a definite recognition of pain in my belly. It felt like I had been chopped with a machete right through my lower abdomen wall. I could tell that someone was talking to me, but the words being spoken made no sense. I could make out a jolly voice saying, "You have a lovely girl!"

I told myself I must be dreaming and that I should go back to sleep to await the announcement of a boy. I fell back into the solid darkness of unconsciousness. I was aware of the jostling of the bed as a porter transported me to a room for post-surgery recovery. I awoke just long enough to ask that person to please slow down and be gentle, only to hear a soothing voice tell me that we were going very slowly and smoothly, but I would feel the discomfort because I had a fresh wound.

Discomfort was not the word to describe the feeling I awoke to. Never before had I experienced such immense pain! I gritted my teeth and held back from sobbing as my loving husband leaned over me and began telling me all about the beautiful baby girl we had. He was so excited; his whole outlook on the world seemed changed. He gushed unashamedly at what a proud father he was. I was overcome with happiness and my reason for weeping was now because of our shared experience. I was finally happy, he was finally happy, and we were finally happy together, without the restraints that held us back from one another and our blessed life together.

Tobore and I just melted at the sight of our baby as we both cradled her. To me, something felt whole for the first time since we'd met, and we couldn't stop looking at our bundle of joy.

I told Tobore that I wanted to name our little miracle Winter, but when my father-in-law phoned the hospital to check in, he expressed his strong displeasure with the name. He asked to speak directly to me, and inquired why I wanted to name his granddaughter after the coldest season of the year? I didn't have any satisfactory answer to give him. In the end, we named our daughter Jasmine, but acquiesced to his family's instructions that her middle name be Elizabeth, one that had already been established in their family for several generations. I felt as if naming our child should be our decision alone. I seemingly had little say in giving my daughter her name, but to keep the peace, I agreed. The last thing I needed was to upset the in-laws who took so long in coming around to liking me. Again, I was made to feel like an outsider in my own life story.

In the hours following the birth, my hospital room was flooded with gifts for the baby and well wishes from visiting friends of both Tobore and myself. When the room finally quieted down, Tobore took the opportunity to go home and freshen up while I took a nap. He was one proud and happy dad, and I was just relieved that our little girl was healthy and breathing. When I woke up, I found that I was afraid to look at her, as I feared that all the medicine I had been given while pregnant might have caused some abnormalities. I mustered up my courage and said a pleading prayer to God. I was so grateful when I peeked into the bassinette and saw a perfectly formed baby girl. She was a pink bundle of joy!

My heart melted when I held her. I had never felt such a rush of unconditional love for anything before in my life. The nurse instructed me on how to breastfeed her. I was a little scared at first and felt anxious about how it would feel, but I watched in amazement as she latched onto my breast. Unlike me, she had not needed any instructions and knew exactly how to do it. The feeling was strange, but so full of emotion that my life bond to her was strengthened beyond anything I could have imagined. I looked up to the heavens and thought, *God, you have made my life so amazing with this one miracle.*

About two days after our daughter was born, we were told that the doctors had detected a heart murmur and she needed to have an echocardiogram to confirm the health of her heart. I was still terribly sore from the C-section and could hardly move, but when they told me that my little girl might not be well, I was determined to stay by her side for any testing she was to undergo. They told me that she needed to travel to a different hospital for the tests. The best place for her was the public hospital attached to the university, which we would need to travel to by car. Even though I had dreaded the pain associated with walking, talking, and even coughing in the days prior, when I heard that my child need-

Chapter 6: Broken

ed me, I got up and started doing all of the necessary activities. I didn't know where the strength and courage came from, but it was there, and there was no keeping me down. Tobore also became infused with a sense of protectiveness, nothing like I had seen before. He helped get us ready for the trip to the hospital, making sure we were quickly discharged and safely in his hands for the travel. Thankfully, the test showed that nothing was to be feared and that the heart murmur would disappear in time without intervention.

We settled into our home with our new little bundle of joy. I basked in the love of our small family and wanted to shut out the world and all of its hassles. Just one of our daughter's smiles made all of my insecurities and negative feelings disappear. I started to view my worries over how my in-laws felt about me as silliness. I realised that I didn't need to be accepted by anyone else's family. I had my own family now, and my life was complete.

Our little girl developed a bit of jaundice in the first week at home, so I sunned her, as it was recommended as the best remedy. I was still learning to walk standing straight up, and to cough without wincing in pain, but the duties of motherhood provided the strength to overcome my physical ailments without complaint. I was very distraught when I developed an infection that made breastfeeding difficult. I missed the bonding time with my daughter. Tobore had been able to employ a daytime helper, but he remained extremely attentive and helpful. He even washed the dirty cloth nappies, bathed, and changed our little girl without being asked. His enthusiasm for fatherhood was like nothing I had ever seen. Then again, who did I have to compare him to?

Tobore's parents and sister visited periodically, and they all seemed excited about the baby. I was so taken aback by their interest and tried to hide my confusion so I wouldn't come off as offensive. When I had been pregnant, they'd barely paid any attention to me, so all the sudden time together and easy conversation was very new. I remembered how people had said that a baby changes everything, and for the moment, it seemed like that was exactly what was happening.

My sweet little girl, Jasmine, was growing into a fine specimen of a perfect life. When she was a few months old, I decided it was time to start looking for a job, as our money was dwindling. I initially tried for teaching jobs, but they were scarce, and nothing came of my efforts. Then I heard of a job with the daughter of a famous singer from Jamaica, who still had strong ties with the local community. I found out as much as I could about the available position, which turned out to be for the guidance of disaffected young people. I took it upon myself to write a sample curriculum for what I could carry out as the teacher and student supervisor, and became involved unofficially on the periphery of the project. I was doing everything, from enrolling to coaching women who were lost on their path towards a better life, and I would often visit the office where some of the initial work was being done. I expected to be a teacher in the classroom and supervise the staff, which was why I was brought on. Eventually, I was offered a formal position to work on the project, and I immediately found that I loved being back at work, although my duties weren't exactly what I expected.

After about two months in the role, I started to feel anxious and disgruntled about the work I was expected to do. For the most part, my dissatisfaction was stemming from the fact that another person was home taking care of my baby and I was not by her side. I felt guilty that I was somehow abandoning my child. I had to remind myself that I was doing that job to feed and clothe her, and help Tobore, who had done a stalwart job of looking after both of us so far. Every day, I would have to take a fresh blouse to change into because my breasts would constantly leak. No amount of breast pads worked for me! My body seemed to know that my daughter was at home waiting to be fed.

I would pump enough milk for her each morning and leave it in the fridge. I was very concerned about her health and would not allow any type of formula to be used, since it was mixed with the local water. Before I left for work each morning, I would lie in bed and Tobore would fetch Jasmine for me so that I could feed her a good first meal for the day. She would stay on the breast for two hours sometimes, but the routine would get tiresome when she was on a marathon-feeding streak. The intimacy of bonding with my child through breastfeeding clashed with the intimacy that my husband and I used to enjoy.

I began to hate my husband being on my breast. Something inside told me that for now they belonged to my child. I shunned his requests to be together sexually, as I felt it was inappropriate somehow with an innocent new child in our house. I had no idea if that feeling was normal for new mothers because I had no close friends with children to ask such a personal question. I am certain now that I had some postpartum depression, but I had always tried to disguise my feelings of sadness, especially because everyone around me was so happy about the baby.

There was such a tumult of emotions coursing through me at the time. I wanted to recapture the carefree love I shared with my husband, but I was also aware of my time with my child. I would often come home more anxious to see her than to see him. I would be at work and become overwhelmed with the sense that my baby girl was crying out in hunger and that she needed me. At those times, it was such a relief to drive the car up into the driveway, run inside, wash my hands, throw a blanket across my lap, and let my daughter feed until her heart was contented. I just wanted her to know that her mum loved her and would never abandon her.

Sometimes our lives have to be turned upside down and rebuilt in an effort to take us to the God-given place we were meant to be.

CHAPTER 7: PUSHING FORWARD

I have realised that we can directly measure life by our will to endure, persevere, and survive.

Jasmine grew fast in her first year of life, and we soon realised that she needed more space than our current house provided. We found a slightly larger home where she could have more freedom to move around, and she could continue to express herself in her boisterous baby language. I was still working with the project associated with a popular musician, but I was starting to yearn for a different challenge. I saw an ad in our local paper for a sales representative role with a telecom provider. I took the plunge and applied, thinking it would be exciting to work in a field that was so different from anything I had done before. Something about all the challenges I had faced and overcome during my first year of motherhood had given me a lot of courage and self-confidence.

Still, I was a bit shocked when I got called for the interview. When I arrived, I met with a man who held a long career in the telephone industry. Even though he readily agreed that I was a long shot for the job, he treated me with respect and conducted the interview as if he was talking to a respected potential employee. He drilled me with questions about how to conduct sales in the field, as well as about general customer service issues. I had never done sales before (in an official capacity, but boy, did I sell those mangoes on the train!), but I knew that being friendly and easy to converse with was my strong suit. People used to tell me that I was a chatterbox, and in this interview, I chatted myself into a job! There was only one problem—it required me to have a car at my disposal all day long, and Tobore and I were still sharing one.

Chapter 7: Pushing Forward

I admitted my dilemma to the interviewer, but he could not see a way of us getting around that requirement. This new job would be a step up from the last one; it had new challenges, great job prospects, and came with a really attractive salary package. I sat up straight and looked that man square in the eyes, saying that if I had passed the interview and it was only the lack of a car that was holding me back from getting the job offer, then he needed only to give me three days to get a car. I recalled sitting in another office, begging the Minister of Education for his belief in me. I was confident that I could find a way in three days' time to overcome that obstacle, and I was thrilled when the interviewer agreed to my request.

I phoned Tobore at work with the good news of the job offer, and then the requirement of a personal car in order for me to accept it. As always, my husband delivered. He immediately went out and found an affordable car that would help me secure my new job. I felt as if my life was back on track. I had a new job and my own car.

In between doing the interview and getting prepped for this new job, I had taken the test and paid the fee for my driver's license. It was the easiest way to ensure I had a license for the new role. At that time in Jamaica, there were a lot of under-the-counter schemes run by the civil servants. There was little oversight and many times you would pay the fee only to be failed and told to return to take the test the next day, no matter how well you had driven. With this knowledge, I headed for the bulls-eye and paid so I could get it at once. This was how the instructor made his salary.

Shortly after acquiring the car, Tobore was in Saint Elizabeth, visiting his parents, and I was at home in Kingston with the baby. I decided on a whim to make the drive down during the night so we could be with him when he woke in the morning. Now that I had the option, I wasn't about to settle for staying home alone to care for the baby on my own. I wanted to talk to him about the anxiety I felt about starting my new job, and how it would affect my being a wife and a mother. On reflection, I think I was missing him, but also wanted his parents to see me differently.

I think I wanted to prove to him that I was capable of driving and taking care of myself outside of our house. It never occurred to me how stupid, how very stupid, I was being by heading out into the darkness all alone with little experience behind the wheel. If I'd had a lick of sense, I would have never endangered my child and my life for such a petty reason. Needless to say, when I arrived at his parents' home in the wee hours, they were incredibly angry and Tobore gave me a proper telling off. I did not rise to their anger, as I quickly saw why they were so upset with me. I deserved Tobore's tirade, and his words of anger that were solely borne from his love and concern for me and our child. They, too, were really happy that I had found a new job, and it felt like all of us were getting along much better. To be honest, Jasmine helped. They loved our little bundle of joy and were so distracted with her, they forgot about my background and me.

I started my new job, and although the money coming in was good, I again started feeling that same sense of guilt over being away from home for such long hours. I had thought I was gone from my baby too much with the previous job, but it was nothing compared to now. I was constantly on the road, travelling from customer to customer to sell advertising space in the telephone directory. The company itself had a monopoly in Jamaica, so the locals didn't always look on it favourably, but they took the space if they needed it because there was no other alternative.

One of the clients they sent me out to deal with was a large international paint company, and when I arrived at their local headquarters, they wanted nothing to do with the company I was representing. They pointed out all of the non-working telephone equipment that they had already paid for, and all of their issues with trying to get the company to resolve even the simplest of problems. And here I was, trying to sell them an expensive glossy ad! They were having none of it.

I decided to take a different approach and transformed my sales pitch into a customer service offering. In the end, I helped them to fix their existing problems and they showed their gratitude by giving me one of the biggest sales I ever secured. That experience taught me the skills in customer service that I would use to excel later on in my career.

That year, I made money like I had never seen before. Our little family wanted for nothing. I began to not mind the expectations of the job so much because I was now able to collaborate with Tobore to provide for our daughter. Tobore and I would always pool our earnings by sitting together to plan our budget whenever I got my paycheque. Even after paying all of our bills, we were able to afford all the gadgets we wanted. We were only in our early twenties but we were doing better than anyone I knew of in my family or our age group.

Things were going so well that I suggested a family holiday somewhere exotic. I felt guilty that I was away from Jasmine so much. I realised that Tobore was starting to think I was away from home more than our society saw fit for any woman with a husband and child. I had also started formulating an idea for a new business, thinking that we could start something in the clothing trade, either in exporting or importing. I chose Panama for our vacation that year and it was a wonderful experience. One that I had never dreamed would be a part of my life when I was a young girl living in the ramshackle homes of my family and friends back in Saint Elizabeth.

Things continued to go well at work. I was at the top of my game, and that year I won the company contest for the largest sale; having secured the contract for the Caribbean and South Florida telephone directory, that netted the company over eight million Jamaican dollars in profit. The prize was an all-expense paid holiday to a large theme park in Florida. I was to attend a company-wide conference with winners from all the other international offices. Since it was technically a working holiday, families could not attend. I stayed at the resort itself and was driven everywhere by a private golf cart. I hate to admit it, but I found the time away from the hectic life of daily work and family to be wonderful. Even though I had to attend all-day meetings, I could go back to the quiet of my private room that had been serviced by the cleaning staff and wait for room service to deliver a hot meal.

Like any accomplishment in life however, my success only served to set the bar higher for the next year. The pressure at work was intense. The upper management expected me to exceed my prize-winning record, which put further pressure on my home life, in particular my marriage. I came home one day during regular work hours to find my husband busy doing the daily chores. He had given notice and left his job, feeling that one of us needed to be at home. I didn't see this coming. To date, the reasons as to why Tobore and I differed on him being a stay-at-home dad are still blurry. I felt terrible; I had never intended him to become the stay-at-home spouse, but he felt I had left him no option.

I suppose in many ways we were comfortable financially, as my salary was good, but he also wanted to spend every moment he had with Jasmine, and the demands of his job meant he wasn't seeing her enough. I suspect those were motivators to walk if one opened the door to such a thing.

At that point, our communication had broken down completely. Neither of us understood what the other wanted, and we were making decisions based on our misunderstandings of each other. There was nothing to do about his job. He could not go asking for it back, and I had to work even harder since I was now the sole breadwinner. So, we drifted even further apart. He began to feel the same isolation and dissatisfaction with life that I had felt in that first year after our daughter was born. I endured the stress he must have felt to come home to a lonely spouse and growing child. We both recognised that our roles weren't balanced, but we couldn't figure out how to resolve it, and we had no one to help point us in the right direction.

Tobore was a wonderful father to Jasmine, as well as a wonderful husband. He had dinner on the table often; every time I would see the plates set out, heaped with nourishing and delicious food, my heart would ache because I knew he needed me at home. It was killing me because even though our marriage was young, it was also frail and brittle from the tribulations of our lives. To make matters worse, clients would often present urgent and complicated issues at the end of the workday that required me to work late, often missing dinnertime at our house completely. I would try to make up for it by cutting some of my days short, but it interfered with my work to the point that my performance was suffering, and my bosses were starting to take notice.

I felt trapped in a no-win situation. Leaving my job was not an option because one of us needed to work. But my extended hours away with clients, coupled with the growing discord between Tobore and myself at home, led to jealousy and distrust. Tobore started accusing me of cheating because he could not imagine how someone could be busy with clients for so many hours of the day. We were constantly quarrelling and I had a short temper that was then being set off by the smallest of things.

I had not given up on my marriage, though. I made a concerted effort to be encouraging towards Tobore to restart his career. He admitted that he had been looking for jobs, but his old firm was not hiring, and no other industry showed interest in his application. I suggested that he go back to school to bulk up his qualifications. These conversations didn't yield much. We never seemed to finish them with a productive plan that we both agreed on and could work towards. I think we both expected the other to do their part, and we didn't see that teamwork required sacrifices on both ends.

I thought our problems might be solved when my company offered me a promotion. The new position had the same duties but was based in a different location and offered a bit more money. I interpreted that opportunity to mean less work time and more time with my family.

We moved to Mobay and used the compensation I had received the previous year from my large prize-winning contract, along with some help from Tobore's father, to purchase a piece of land. We saw that empty piece of bush land as the tool to restore our marriage; working together to build our dream home would heal our wounds and bind us together again.

We rented a two-bedroom flat near the regional hospital and started making the architectural drawings and interviewing the necessary contractors. We were both relieved to realize that the project was indeed strengthening our bond and we started feeling closer than we had in months. Tobore seemed happier at least, and overall, we were at a good place. He didn't seem to mind what the outside world thought. In that moment we had each other, and the baby made us complete.

I was doing well at my new job and my successes soon got the attention of another large company in the wireless communication industry. I received an offer from a competitor, and it was too good to turn down. Sadly, it meant I needed to move to another part of the country. Luckily for us, Tobore had secured a new job with a supplier of aircraft food and was now working at the nearby airport. Jasmine was old enough to attend a nursery and we no longer required a full-time caretaker in the house. While Tobore and I struggled to make our daily life an easy and happy existence, Jasmine existed in a carefree world.

When I was offered the position with the new company, I consulted with not only my husband, but also his family, to discuss all aspects of the job to help us make the decision. I told them I had carefully considered it and recognised it as a great opportunity. I was careful to verify that I wasn't blinded to some key issues that could be detrimental to our family's situation. I was interested in the job, as it also offered me the opportunity to further my studies with a scholarship, and I was eager to do something like that. Tobore's parents had always believed a woman should have the more traditional role within the family, so I was thrilled when they agreed with my assessment, and I quickly accepted the offer.

At that time, my sister Kem, who was about fifteen years old, had sent word from Saint Elizabeth asking to come to live with us. She was the third child born to my mum after me. She was also mum's favourite child, as she had a heart condition that made her fragile. I had loving memories of playing with her when she was a toddler. I knew that we could offer her a stable home life and opportunities that were not available to her back in the one-room home that they were all still living in. I felt like the salary at my new job afforded us the luxury of taking on that responsibility, and because Tobore and I were bonding again, I felt no anxiety about the presence of another person in our house.

Upon Kem's arrival, Jasmine was thrilled to have another person to play with and pamper her. It was good to be living with a blood relative, though we hardly knew each other in such a space. I was overly cautious with her around Tobore, purely from my old scars and experiences, as some of my old memories of Dave started resurfacing. I would insist that she always dress appropriately, and would try to avoid her and Tobore spending too much time alone if it could be helped.

I had to be a bit different around her too, as it related to my husband and how I dressed. It took some getting used to, but gradually it all slotted in and we made an okay family.

The company I now worked for was relatively new in the industry but very successful and growing at a rapid rate. The output and demand for its services was much greater than anyone expected, which was wonderful for income, but also a substantial burden on its employees' time. I began travelling a lot again. There was no formal office space in our region, so I worked out of my home and sometimes out of the car. On paper, my job responsibilities were clear-cut. In the initial stages, one of my responsibilities was to work alongside a colleague to negotiate with local landowners, so the company could acquire their land for our operational equipment to be erected. Basically, I saw my job as wining and dining people while I sold them the company's concept, maintaining compliance, and being the face of the company in that region. I was good at it, and was soon internally promoted to the position of Dealer Account Executive.

But the same problem arose as with my last job. My time at home was limited, and I carried out my job responsibilities under a cloud of private shame over my family suffering from my absence. Tobore and I talked about it from time to time, and I was aware that his family wasn't happy with the outcome. I felt like I was being torn in two directions. My heart wanted to be a full-time wife and mother, but my mind craved the challenges that only my career could provide. Perhaps I was a bit overzealous at the time because of my roots in a community where very few people went to work or had a career. Especially the women.

Jasmine was growing so fast; it was a treat to pull up the drive and see her face giggling away at the sight of either me or her dad. My job satisfied something deep within me that was almost pathological. My talent at what I did only further fed the fire that was consuming me. Yet, that wonderful aspect of my life was causing my family to fall apart. I was fully aware of the whispers around me, telling me that I was selfishly sacrificing family for my career. Unfortunately, I didn't know how to confront them and tell them that I wasn't doing it purposefully. I just didn't know how to balance both. My family wasn't going hungry, we were financially secure, and I used these facts to justify my being away from them far too often.

Before I knew it, the relationship between Tobore and I had again deteriorated into fighting and dislike. He reinitiated the blatant accusations of my cheating, and I responded by losing respect for him for believing that I had such low character. We both recognised, yet tried to ignore, the fact that the fracture in our relationship was rapidly reaching an irreparable point. Tobore was convinced that I had a lover tucked away somewhere, and I began to suspect him of the same. We grew so far apart that even though we lived in the same house, we communicated as if we were separated by continents.

Our rented home was a good distance from the land on which our dream house was being constructed. Tobore had lost interest in the project and it was I who kept it going. I would travel alone to spend hours at the site and oversee the workmen to catch the common mistakes that would have otherwise cost us so much money. Soon, I took over the whole project in earnest, travelling to the hardware store for items and taking on the payments for the construction crew and materials. Even though I didn't want to admit it, I was building a house for a family with no husband or father.

Jasmine would often accompany me on these trips to the construction site and it was our time to bond. I would tell her about all the dreams her dad and I had for our family house, how we would all live there in a bubble of love and happiness. The workers recognised Tobore's absence as an opportunity to slack off. One day, I arrived to find that the workers had erected a column on the veranda that leaned and was clearly unstable. I immediately pointed that out, citing that it would not support the weight it needed to, and told them that they needed to remove it and start again. They challenged me in an obvious way that related to me being a woman. I was used to these arguments by now, and I had grown clever at making up some story to cover my husband's absence and assuring them that he was still overseeing all of their work.

Finally, our house was completed enough for us to move in. I was still hoping that this residence would magically heal our family, but when we moved in, it was even more painfully clear that Tobore and I were over as a couple. Kem and Jasmine evidently hated our arguing so much, they would cover their ears, and sometimes Kem would take Jasmine for walks to escape. I started dreading going home to the arguments and tense silences. If it weren't for my daughter, I would have never returned to that house. The silence gradually took over and there was no longer any communication. We were married in name only. I felt utterly abandoned and was sure he did too. We were at a fork in our relationship, even though my husband and I slept under the same roof (but in separate rooms sometimes). Our relationship became so broken that soon after, we both found comfort in someone else. I am still unsure if it was the strain we endured from the onset, or something more specific. Was I upset he left his job?

Did I outgrow him? Were we too young? I don't know. All I know is at that point we were falling apart and had no support system to help us find our way back.

We quarreled and fought, but knew we had to discuss our indiscretions and figure out how we could move past them in the healthiest way possible for both of us and for our child. Even though I was guilty of the same offence, his admission nearly killed me. We both knew there was nothing to be done but for one of us to move out. Tobore's brother arrived one Sunday afternoon and helped him pack his belongings, removing them, and him, from our lives, while I sat in silence on the veranda, combing our daughter's hair. Before they left, Tobore came and said goodbye to our daughter. I felt as if my world had crashed down around me, but I couldn't fall apart in front of our child.

That night, after I put Jasmine to bed, I cried until my eyes were swollen. I had no idea how much I would miss Tobore's presence in our house and in our lives. I realised that despite the undercurrent of anger and dissatisfaction, I loved him deeply and relied on him for our family's stability. We had just lost our way as a couple. I realised that Tobore had been a part of my life since I was a teenager. I started to feel ashamed that I hadn't properly appreciated him. The fact was, neither of us had appreciated each other in the end. I thought about how I had lost sight of what was truly important over the past couple of years. We really were still too young to be able to handle all of the events that life had presented us with. I thought of how we might have benefited from more emotional support from our extended families, but that time had passed and there was no going back and no blaming anyone except ourselves. My primary concern then had to be our child. I had to protect her from the pain that Tobore and I were feeling during our uncoupling. We were both amazing parents to her in that period of our fallout, and thankfully she had Kem, who was a good distraction for her.

Even though my sister was still living with us, it was challenging to keep the house together without Tobore around. I had to hire workers to do many of the routine chores that were too cumbersome for my sister and me, such as maintaining the yard. Hiring men for certain jobs served another purpose, bringing a male presence to our house that gave us a sense of protection. We gradually adjusted to life without Tobore. He would arrive every weekend to pick Jasmine up for her overnight visits with him, and there was never a problem during these hand-offs. He maintained a fabulous relationship with our daughter.

Jasmine was a very clever little girl. She took notice of everything and would catch the importance of even the subtlest experiences. One day when she and I were out running errands, she pointed out a house and told me it was a girl's house that her dad would take her to. I was confused by that designation and asked her, "What girl?"

She answered with a sense of impatience, "Mummy, that's where Aunty Femi lives." I eyed the place suspiciously, but when I asked who Aunty Femi was, Jasmine simply replied, "Daddy's friend." I did some investigating and found out that "Aunty Femi" was a topless bartender who worked at the local joints, and indeed, she had lived in the very house that Jasmine had pointed out. And so, I began to get some insight into what Tobore's post-marital life consisted of.

Shortly after that encounter, the company I worked for organised a grand function in Montego Bay, at which two internationally acclaimed songstresses would be entertaining. The invited clientele came from my territory, so I also got an invite, but I knew it would be a working evening.

I dressed in one of my finest gowns and waited for Tobore to come and pick up our daughter to watch her for the evening. He arrived with a young woman in the car who he introduced as his friend. I didn't pay much attention to her, as in my mind we were over, and I didn't think he would be brazen enough to bring a lover to meet me with our daughter present. She seemed insignificant at that moment in time, but now I wished I had paid more attention. Jasmine seemed well acquainted with her, so I decided not to worry. Besides, I was so excited about the night's concert that I simply accepted his explanation and left knowing Jasmine was safe with her father, and he was just offering his friend a lift somewhere, or something as simple as that.

The isolated life that Jasmine, my sister, and I led in our house passed by without much incident, but I continued to miss Tobore and the relationship we once had. I started attending counseling and decided to ask Tobore to come back home for Christmas that year with the intent of initiating a reconciliation. I had the entire plan laid out, and at first everything went as expected. We attended Jasmine's kindergarten Christmas play, and I leaned in close to tell him in an intimate whisper that I had something to talk to him about afterwards. He walked me to the car and stood by my side as I strapped our sleepy daughter into her car seat. I became suddenly shy and my awkward movements showed it.

In my head, I was dying to ask him to come home, to spend Christmas with us, to lie next to me until dawn, to talk and rekindle our love for one another. I knew we could work this out. He then filled the silence by saying that he wanted to tell me something. My heart leapt. I was flooded with relief, thinking that he wanted the same thing and that we were really going to be a family again.

My relief turned to shock, though, when he said, "I have gotten someone pregnant. The girl you met the other day, in fact. I wanted to tell you myself. I didn't want you to hear it first from someone else."

I don't think I even responded. I was so shocked, I couldn't even speak. I started the drive home and that was when the tears and anger came. I didn't know what to do, but like a child tattling on a friend who had offended me, I phoned my mother-in-law and told her that her son had gotten someone else pregnant. Her response made me fume even more, but I had no argument to counter her when she said, "Until I hear it from my son, I won't believe it."

I hung up the phone. Suddenly, certain things from our past became clearer to me. It was obvious they did not believe my words. In fact, they seemed relieved that we were crumbling. I guessed that they were saying, "I told him so," in their minds. Our separation was no surprise to many of our friends and family, and neither would be the news of his impending fatherhood. The relationship between my in-laws and myself had deteriorated badly and the original strain that existed was now a deeper well at this stage. I was not able to approach them to discuss a reconciliation, as the belief among many was that I was the one cheating, or who had cheated and lead us to our breakdown. With this view in mind, I dared not approach them again, and so I left it at that. Thankfully, time has healed the wounds and we now have an amazing relationship where I can pick up the phone and call them these days and we all talk lovingly.

When we arrived back at the house, I handed Jasmine over to the care of our house-helper and my sister. I then made my way to the kitchen and began drinking every bit of alcohol I could find. Within hours, I was an incoherent mess, on the edge of eternal unconsciousness. My sister got me to the hospital, where the doctors pumped my stomach to remove what alcohol hadn't yet been absorbed, and in doing so they probably saved my life. They kept me in the hospital under observation for a few days. I found out they were going to discharge me on a day that my sister was working, and our helper had off. A friend of mine brought my car and Jasmine to the hospital to pick me up. I was ready to go home but I needed to drop my friend back home first.

The next day, another female friend of mine called me in great distress. She wanted to talk, so I invited her over. Not only did I have something to tell her too, but I also needed a distraction. We spent the entire day cooking, laughing, crying, talking about men, and burying our sorrows in each other's friendship. It was getting late, so Jasmine and I dropped her home and rushed back to start preparation for work the next day.

It was around seven p.m. when Jasmine and I pulled into the driveway of our house. I had been talking on the mobile phone with another friend. I told him that I would call back as soon as I got inside and got Jasmine settled down. I had the phone still cradled between my shoulder and my ear and was holding a sleeping Jasmine in one arm, while trying to open the front door with the other. Suddenly I felt something cold and metal press hard against the side of my neck. My eyes swung to the side and I saw the muzzle of a gun and four men with their eyes trained on my frightened face. In a quick second, one of them swiped the phone from my ear while another took Jasmine from my grasp. It was a miracle she didn't wake. The one with the gun pointed at me, grabbed my arm harshly, and pushed me forward, instructing me in a quiet, sadistic voice to open the grill by our front door. The two other men, who had been silent so far, stepped forward and told me to give them the cash card for my bank account. As soon as they had the card they left and the other two hustled me into the house.

I was escorted at gunpoint to the bedroom and I saw one man put Jasmine down on the sofa, where she just curled up and continued sleeping.

The two men were hurling all sorts of insults at me and started recklessly wandering throughout the rest of the house. They stopped occasionally and poured out little packets of cocaine, which they snorted in front of me unashamedly. I was absolutely certain that I was going to die, and my thoughts turned to how I could save the lives of my daughter and my sister, who would be coming home from work at any moment. When the men were out of the room on one of their rampages through the house, I snuck a call through to her and left a message to not come home and to call the police. I hung up just before the men returned to ask me for the keys to unlock all of the stores that my company owned. I think they believed we had monies in there overnight, but they also hoped to get their hands-on mobile phones, accessories, and phone cards that they could pedal easily on the black market. I began then to realise that this was a robbery based on my job.

I told the men that I didn't have any of the store keys, explaining that I wasn't responsible for that part of the operations. I told them that I only supervised the stores. I went into a babbling explanation of how the company was structured, but the taller one cut me off with a sharp laugh. "We're not interested in your work!" he yelled.

I was shocked into silence, my mouth hanging open mid-sentence. He became very serious, looked me straight in the eye, and told me in a hissing voice that they had been sent to kill me. They said two names of people I knew but none of it made sense to me. I could not understand why these people would send them to kill me or even disrupt my life so terribly. I have my assumptions but have since kept them to myself. It is still so blurry; I would hate to be wrong.

I made a panicked plea for my life. I told the man that I would pay him more than the person who sent them, if only he would spare my life. He said that he had already accepted the payment to kill me and he was a man of his word and would not renege on his contract.

The man with the gun then started asking me about a man he had been told I was seeing. I told him I wasn't seeing anyone, but he said that he didn't believe me. He stalked around the bedroom, saying that I must have pictures of that man and me together, but there weren't any pictures of that imagined relationship to be found. Then he said I seemed like a nice girl, nothing like the cold bitch he was told that I was. The other man pushed me back onto the bed and pointed his gun directly at my chest. I was certain my life was about to end. Back in the living room, however, my daughter had finally awakened. She was so innocent. Curious as any two-year-old would be, she came running into the room to see what her mummy was doing. The guy with the gun aimed at me spun around and trained his gun on her. My heart skipped a beat. I thought he was going to shoot her.

I fell off the bed onto my knees and screamed out for him to hold his fire and not to kill my child. The scene was tense, but everyone managed to remain calm in the seconds that followed. The man allowed Jasmine to come to me. She came into my open arms; tears were streaming down my cheeks. She was such a sweet babe, and as I held her tightly to me, she told me not to cry. I knew that the situation was growing dimmer as each moment passed. The men were obviously agitated and their whispered conversations with one another were becoming more aggressive. I heard some of the words creep through and I knew what was being planned.

One of the men left the room to go rummaging again and the other turned his attention back to me. Fearing I knew what was about to happen, I told him that there were condoms in the drawer next to where he stood. I was thinking if I somehow survived this night, I didn't want to come out of it with HIV. A smile crept across his face and he said he didn't need one. He had come prepared with his own stash of condoms. I panicked and blurted out a feeble lie that I had a sexual disease hoping it would deter him. His jolly mood continued, though, and he laughed and told me that he knew clean women like me were always careful; he was confident I didn't have anything transmissible.

There was no hiding the danger of the situation from my daughter then, and she had begun screaming and crying in a hysterical manner.

I was still holding her and trying to comfort her when that man came close, leaned in and stroked Jasmine's face in a blatantly sexual way. He nearly cooed when he asked her to tell him how old she was. I answered for her, telling him sternly that she was only two years old. He kept his eyes trained on her only and told her in a soft voice that it was too bad; if she were three, he would have had to fuck her too. My body convulsed and I nearly threw up. My subconscious was crying out to me that she had been spared; it was only me who was to be subjected to his violation.

Everything happened rather quickly, or maybe I just thought it did. The mind protects you from the horrors you experience by erasing them from your memory sometimes. What I do remember was during the course of that violation there was a phone being answered. I remember the two men waiting at the cash point were angrily demanding my security code to get access to my accounts. Some days I remember much more.

Let me be very clear. The bastard held me down at gunpoint and raped and molested me inches from where my daughter sat cowering on the floor. My baby, Jasmine, was crying hysterically and I could not reach out to comfort her. That horrid man teased and taunted me in some kind of sadistic dance he played in his mind. He grabbed my breast hard and licked my face, boasting how lucky I was going to be. I was so disgusted I could feel the vomit rising in my throat. I called out to Jasmine to turn her head and close her eyes. I told her to put her hands over her ears. I promised her everything would be okay. But I knew better. Nothing would ever be okay again.

All at once, that vile man was on top of me. He kissed me, trying to shove his tongue into my mouth. I spat at him. He hit me hard, telling me if I did that again I would pay. I was so terrified. I took that to mean he would do something to my child, my baby, my light in the darkness. I looked to see Jasmine sobbing in the corner between the bed and the wall. My heart was breaking. I then decided the best I could do was to endure whatever was to happen in silence. He pulled the clothes from my body. He bit down hard on my nipple, exclaiming how aroused I was. Aroused In terror, perhaps.

I wanted to scream and cry out from the pain but dared not. He shoved his fist inside of me. That pain was almost unbearable. I thought I might lose consciousness. The entire time I heard his heinous laughter as he waved his gun in my face.

My mind and body had gone numb. Like I was in some horror film, I could only watch myself. He waved a condom in my face telling me I was not worthy of a child of his. I thank God for that. He entered me, and that time I could not stop the vomit. But I made no sound as the tears streamed down my face. My only thoughts were that I had to do everything to protect my daughter. He enjoyed himself immensely at my expense. I just lay there cold; feeling a part of me was dying.

The other man came back into the room with a bunch of keys that he had found somewhere in the house. He assumed they were keys to the stores. He told his accomplice that we all needed to go to the shops so I could let them in. I felt broken. I felt as if they had torn my soul right out of my body. Then they told me how angry they were at me for making them wait so many nights. They said that they had been waiting for me since I had been in the hospital. They mocked me for taking so long to recover before I was discharged. I got a sick feeling in my stomach as I realised this really couldn't be merely a robbery gone badly. The Mayor and his family lived next door and had far more money and exploitable power than I did. I was only twenty-four years old. How much did they really expect to get from me? I wondered if it could be true that they were hired to simply kill me?

The two men then told me to get dressed. They forced my daughter and me into my car outside at gunpoint. As we drove, the two who had gone to the bank called again and I could overhear them talking casually about how they would get rid of me shortly. They made me take the driver's seat and ordered me to start driving. I felt a glimmer of hope when they instructed me to drive down a road where I knew the police station was. I nearly got caught by the speed trap set up there. I was so grateful to have the chance to be rescued by putting my foot down a bit harder on the gas pedal. But there was no such luck tonight. There were no policemen sitting and waiting to catch a speeder.

One of the men sat next to me in the front passenger seat and kept his gun aimed at my knees the whole time. He told me not to do anything stupid. If I had been alone, I might have crashed the car or driven it right into the police station, but the other man sat in the back seat with his gun aimed at my baby. I didn't give up, though, and tried appealing to their consciences. During the earlier part of the night, I had given them nearly sixty-five thousand in cash that had been kept in a safe at the house.

I offered them more money if they would just let me and my baby go. They merely instructed me to keep driving. We drove through the mountainous and gully regions of Montego Bay, Jamaica, and we finally ended up in the city centre. They directed me to one of my company's stores, but I had been telling the truth when I told them that I had no keys to open the shops. They were livid when they realised that. One of them slapped me hard across the face as he grunted in frustration. The one who I had begun to think of as their leader was upset too, but he remained calmer than the other and told him there was nothing to be done. That I had told them the truth.

We were hustled back into the car and they instructed me to drive them to a well-known place by the seaside. By then all their cell phone credits had run out and they started using my mobile phone to make contact with their two accomplices at the bank. They set up a rendezvous point and made me drive to a shadowed area. I sat in stunned silence and listened as the men told me that I was to leave Jamaica.

"Go abroad," they said. One of them stifled a little chuckle and told me that when my daughter was grown, I should tell her, "Life is fucked up." It was at this point they decided not to kill us, but then they pointed their guns again and told us to get out of the car. My mind went crazy. I started to remember all of the recent news reports from the Middle East, where women were being executed in open areas to send a message to the public.

I stood trembling in the darkness, holding my child to my breast and prayed to God for his mercy. The first shot was so loud it nearly burst my eardrums, but the volley of shots that followed made me realise the men were firing into the air above us. They jumped into the car of their accomplices, who had finally arrived, shouted a final warning that I was to leave Jamaica immediately, and drove off. They just left us standing there.

A part of me thought that Jasmine and I must be dead, and that if I looked down, I would see our bloodied bodies lying beneath us and realise we were just ghosts, doomed to haunt that beach for eternity. I frantically searched Jasmine's tiny body for gunshot wounds and could hardly breathe when I found none. My entire body . . . my entire spirit. . . was numb. I couldn't believe we were rid of the men and still alive after that dreadful ordeal. By some miracle, the men had left my phone behind, and I called the police and the friend I had dropped off at home before that nightmare had started. The police had told me to stay put, but I was afraid that the men were going to come back and finish the job. I put Jasmine back in the car and drove myself to the closest police station I could think of. I was trembling the entire way and could hardly keep straight on the road. I don't even recall arriving at the station. The police later told me that they found me outside in the parking lot, collapsed over the steering wheel. For years, I didn't share much of what happened in terms of my sexual violation with most of the people I was close to. Yes, I shared the robbery, but just brushed over it like that was all it was. Part of it was shame, and the feeling of being dirty, soiled. And it just was a bit tabooed, I suppose. I was able to keep the dirty abuse secret just as my father had taught me as a teenager. One of the lessons you learn is to go mute. After all, in my community, I was someone with status and this would drag me to the ground. I wouldn't take that risk.

Watered baptism is said to be the only thing to cleanse original sin, thus sins are stained and embedded in us. However, forgiveness is saved for the contrite, making it hard to erase the embedded evil.

CHAPTER 8: YOUR GUT

I've learnt to let my instincts and gut guide me in all I do, regardless of how things seem.

The days that followed our ordeal were miserable and confusing. We were staying in a hotel in Montego Bay about twenty minutes' drive from our home, where the ordeal happened. I was in a zombie state. Not eating, tense at every sound or car that passed me, and I was fearful of everyone around. I was not interested in going on the road unless it was absolutely necessary. Jasmine had no clue, but perhaps she did, as she was suddenly extremely clingy. I was not present emotionally to deal with her, so I was glad friends were around to help her. That comforted me. The police sent a team out to my house to dust for fingerprints among the ransacked rooms and in my car. They said that they would only be able to match a person to any evidence once they found a suspect that they could use for comparisons. I was shocked to hear that the chances for swift justice were so slim! This told me that I was now even less safe than I was the night of the attack. The police were meant to help me feel safe, but they were not doing that, days after my attack. That signaled to me that I now needed to disappear. The officer explained that our assailants must have worn gloves or cleaned up the evidence. He also explained that since the men didn't steal any physical objects from the home besides the cash I gave them to ransom our lives, it wasn't really considered a straight-forward robbery or assault case according to the legal definition at the time. Nothing was removed from the house. I was alive, but far too scared to even admit all of what had happened to me. My standing in the community left me riddled with fear, and inside, I wanted the police to drop it all, so I kept some of the details to myself. My pride and dignity were trashed and all

I wanted to do was disappear and have the ground swallow me up. I had walked from room to room with an officer to make an inventory of what had been stolen from my house, but found everything was still present. They had not taken a thing. Not the fancy electronics, the TV or stereo, none of my jewelry, and even the stash of cash I had hidden secretly were all still in the house.

The realisation that the robbers had truly had no interest in our belongings shook me to my very core. I was trembling like a leaf and could hardly breathe when I remembered the man sneering at me that they were simply sent there to kill me. Earlier, the police had sent me to a hospital in Montego Bay for treatment of my physical wounds. There, too, the doctors had given the grim news that there was little to no physical evidence from my attackers they could retrieve from my damaged body. Even though the house was released from its status as an active crime scene, I could not return to living in it. I got assistance from an organisation I was close to that put the three of us—my sister, my daughter, and me up in a hotel. Thankfully, I had money in the bank, as there was a limit on how much you could take from the ATM, so we had money to survive on. Tobore was very distant during this time of our greatest need. His version is that he did not want to be implicated, and that, too, was a hard tablet to swallow. If he could have at least been there for Jasmine, if not for me, it would have been a lovely gesture.

I worked with the police to trace the calls made by the assailants from my cell phone that night. Unfortunately, that was a time when tracing technology was still new in Jamaica, so the only information they managed to get was that one of the calls had been made to a well-known ghetto area. August Town, Saint Andrew.

We stayed at the hotel for a few days, just long enough to finish dealing with the police. Thankfully my job gave me time off until I was fit and ready to return to work. They were amazing to say the least. At a moment like this in your life, you need a breather to just collect your thoughts, as everything you know becomes distorted. I gave the police my assumptions about why I was targeted, but I did not feel they were taking me seriously. After all, I had no evidence, so they had very little to go on.

As soon as the investigation was completed, I felt compelled to flee so that I could gather my wits. The only place I could think of that would provide a calming and safe environment was Florida, probably because of my recent experience there with my previous company. Jasmine and I flew out a few days later, as soon as we secured our visas. Kem stayed with friends while we went on this trip that we needed. I wasn't sure where my sister went the night of the attack as I warned her not to come home and saved her that horror, but she re-joined us the next day at the hotel. However, the distance did not calm my nerves the way I had expected. I was an emotional wreck. I couldn't eat, and my nights were spent either sleeplessly pacing the room or jolting up from a nightmare that would force me to relive the trauma once again.

A friend called and told me that Tobore had moved from Montego Bay back to his parents' place in Saint Elizabeth. There was very little communication between us at this time. I was told he quit his job without giving a reason for his sudden departure. I wondered if he'd left out of fear for his own safety after hearing what had happened to me, or if he simply feared being questioned about our separation and his impending fatherhood. With that in mind, the fact that my attacker had said they had been sent to kill me by someone I knew kept playing over and over again in my head.

The time in Florida was doing no good, and I knew Jasmine and I couldn't hide out there forever. I needed to figure out how I was going to move on with my life. I wondered if I could simply force my mind to shut out the trauma, and return to my home and my daily work schedule. But my assailants' final warning to me was to leave Jamaica. Would I dare go against it? I could not help but fear they would come back to finish the job if I returned. Regardless of what my ultimate decision would be, I knew I couldn't make it and carry it out from my cousin's home in Florida where we had been staying. I steeled my nerves, packed up Jasmine, and headed back home to Jamaica to face the situation head-on. It was hard, as parts of me wanted to run off and become an illegal immigrant, but I knew that was a stupid idea, so I quickly dismissed it.

Jasmine seemed happier in Florida, and a lot of that could be linked to my physical and emotional behavior of being at ease. We played kiddies gold, hung out with friends and family, and were immersed in a more relaxed new world where Mum was not looking over her shoulder constantly. Upon my arrival back in Jamaica I checked in with the police to see if they had any news, and of course they did not. They told me to just be vigilant, lay low, and be safe.

I found that the love for the family home that I had built with my ex-husband was now dead. I stood at the front door and realized our home was really just an object made of brick and wood, nothing more. My life within its walls had been ended by those four men, and I walked its hallways like a ghost. I employed a security guard for the house, as we now had nowhere else to go. The hotel was not permanent. But still I could not find solace. Kem moved back in and the three of us stayed in a single bedroom. However, I was still too terrified to sleep the whole night through. One night when I couldn't calm down, I called the friend whom I had spent the day with prior to the attack. The one whom I had been on the phone with when the attackers had arrived. The one I was said to be having a relationship with. My sister and Jasmine were beside me in the bed fast asleep. While talking to him, my heart nearly seized when my ears picked up an unusual sound, almost like footsteps on the roof of the house. The security guard was in the front room at this time. I told my friend I would call him right back.

At first, I thought I must have been hallucinating because of my hypersensitive state. I ensured the two girls beside me were still sound asleep. I didn't want to alarm them. I was sweating and really beginning to panic.

As I gently opened the curtain to see if I could get a peek at what was happening, I saw the mouth of a gun. The person holding it could not see me, but I saw him and I froze so as not to alert him of my presence. Panicked, I shook my sister awake. I quickly stifled her gasp of surprise by cupping my hand over her mouth.

I whispered that someone was outside. I was certain it was the men coming back to kill me. I feared there was no escape for me that time and my imagination went into overdrive. I imagined these coke-fuelled fiends with spy-level skills that allowed them to disable the guard and my sister and make their way inside to shoot me in front of my baby girl. I gently got off the bed and tried to get everyone on the floor without any sound; my hand was still over my sister's mouth to keep her from panicking.

I grabbed for my cell phone and frantically dialed a friend of mine on the police force who had been at the house earlier that evening. I gave him the pre-arranged signal we had come up with to alert him that there was an immediate danger to my life. He understood and rang off. I then used my shaking fingers to dial the local police station, which was only a seven-minute walk from my house. Within moments, I heard the scream of a siren and my police friend calling to say that he was the one pulling up outside. He instructed us to stay in the house while he surveyed the perimeter of the building along with the security guard, whom he found unharmed, too afraid himself of the gunmen to move, and frozen on the sofa in the front room. Several minutes later, I heard the noises of several cars alerting us that the local police were finally arriving.

The sirens had chased the men off and we were safe for another few hours, but I knew they were not going to let up. I knew that was the last night I would spend in that home.

The next day, I went to Santa Cruz to stay with a friend and started looking for somewhere to live. Not long after, I found a house to rent in Santa Cruz with enough bedrooms for Jasmine, my sister, and myself. This was near to my siblings and Mum, which was one good thing to come from all this mess. But it uprooted my office and Jasmine's school. It was impossible to send her to the same school, as our new life was now over two and a half hours away. Thankfully, my employer was flexible, and they agreed I could move since my new location fell under the areas I managed. So, the transition was only our new living arrangements, as the area already had existing clients that I could get up and running in no time.

The financial hardship of the loss of the money the men took was having an impact on my bank balance and my ability to afford life as whole. Disappointingly, Tobore stayed away and didn't offer any emotional or financial support to me or Jasmine during this harsh ordeal.

However, as we finished packing up the old house and started loading the car with our personal belongings, my sister Kem told me that she was not going to join us. In my mind this owed to the fact that Santa Cruz was a village-type area and slower than Montego Bay, plus she had a good job at the airport and did not want to leave it. I could not blame her. I was disheartened that I was going to take on that new phase of my life completely alone, without any help to take care of Jasmine. I was frustrated at her timing too, since I had already committed to the massive rent for a larger place that she was supposed to contribute to while living with us. Thankfully, one of my younger sisters, Anna, came to live with us instead. That was such a relief and comfort for Jasmine and me.

I completed the move in a daze. Everything was happening so quickly, and I still hadn't had time to process the trauma of the events or what they really meant to my life and my sanity. When we arrived in Santa Cruz, I contacted the lady who had been employed as my helper right before the attack. I thought she might have had something to do with the incident. In my view, she was used as an internal source to know my whereabouts. I was so stressed afterward that I hadn't had time to consider the frightening implications of the suspicious circumstances under which she had requested the day off before the men showed up to begin their reign of terror. My suspicions were confirmed or strengthened after this chat?

My new life in Santa Cruz was the same as it had been in Florida. Every night after the sun set, I would be besieged by the normal noises of the boisterous city around me. I would pick out individual sounds and convince myself they were whispers of the men coming to kill me. The entire trauma of that night in Montego Bay replayed constantly in my mind. I was becoming a shell of the woman I used to be. The only things that kept me going were the fact that I needed to pay my bills, so I had to work. And my precious Jasmine. I knew I couldn't continue that way and be an effective mother to her. I had to do something.

I had an aunt living in London who invited me to come visit her. I jumped at that idea, especially because I was set to take an exam for my bachelor's degree, and I had been struggling to complete it as part of the job I was currently in. I was offered a scholarship to finish a bachelor's via distance learning, and I was determined to complete this regardless of my disheveled life.

I could not concentrate. A total change of scenery sounded good. London was far away, but my aunt was family. She had left Jamaica many years ago to immigrate there. She and I weren't close at all. In fact, my only interactions with her had occurred when I was a young child. But when I wrote to tell her that I wanted to accept her invitation, her response was positive and warm. She and Mum were close, and after she learned of my mishap, she was ready to support us as much as she could. I had barely shared what had happened to us with anyone outside of our *close* family and that was a small number, so telling my aunt was hard but necessary. In fact, I had decided not to share much of my sad story after the reaction of pity and utter shock I received from the few I did open up to. I could see how difficult it was for some of my friends to decide on how to support me. Some would cry, shocked, unsure of how to react, and that made me introversive about the issue.

I couldn't afford to take Jasmine out of school at that time, but I needed time and space to myself to think and unfreeze my zombie-like state. My in-laws volunteered to keep Jasmine while I was out of the country, and she was excited about the prospect of staying there because her daddy was also living in their house. I felt certain that despite the threats that were being aimed towards my life, no one would seek to harm an innocent child, so I entrusted my daughter to them.

Tobore was busy with his new baby that was on the way, and I was trying to pick up my pieces. The exam was a good distraction, and going to a new country was exhilarating. There was no talk of a divorce, as I suppose it was such a new territory for us both, and perhaps unconsciously we may not really have wanted to do it.

I got my ticket for London and boarded the plane with two things in mind—completing the final exams for my bachelor's and emptying my mind of the horror of the attack. When I got to London, my aunt was such a blessing. In the downtimes, she lifted my spirits and took me all over the city. We even attended the wedding of some very distant relatives. Before then, I hadn't realized I knew other Jamaicans who had relocated to the UK. The whirlwind social schedule helped me forget about the stresses that awaited me back home. I began to see that as long as I had my daughter with me, I could build a fulfilling life anywhere, even there in that new country. Though the people, and certainly the weather, in that country were vastly different from my home, I felt a sense of safety. The news reports on the TV spoke of crimes that were nowhere near as heinous as those that had become routine in some parts of Jamaica at that time. Certainly, I didn't hear of anything as blatantly violent as the attack I had just experienced in my own home.

I began to dread going back to the life that Jasmine and I had been living back in Jamaica. Even on the nights that my mind had calmed enough to allow sleep, I had been awoken by the intermittent flashes of lights being shone in our windows by the police who still made routine

Chapter 8: Your Gut

patrols of our house to assure our continued safety. My auntie recognised my internal torment and suggested that I register with some local employment agencies just to see what opportunities there might be in London if I decided to stay.

I thought very carefully about the reality of our situation in Jamaica. I thought of how I could no longer stand to drive the car with anyone sitting in the back seat, as I would suddenly fear that person might pull a gun on me or Jasmine. I thought of how I would drive far out of my way, meandering to get to my destination, all to avoid any crowded areas where my attackers might see me and force their way into my car. I thought of how I could no longer make myself drive anywhere as the hour of sunset neared, since the dark was much too frightening a reminder of our plight. This was no way to live and I knew it. I acquiesced to my auntie's wisdom and registered with several agencies before making the trip back home.

I left London with a bittersweet feeling. That city was so completely different from any place I had ever visited before, yet I felt safer there than in the country I had spent my entire life. When I returned home to Santa Cruz, I could not wait to go and pick up my baby Jasmine. I had never been away from her for such a long time. Upon my arrival she, too, could not wait to see me, and we just cuddled for a good ten minutes as I collected her from her father. I did my best to settle into life again. My company rearranged my responsibilities so that my territory alignment was to include the parish I lived in and the adjoining ones. That meant that I was now responsible for the parishes of Saint Elizabeth, Hanover, Westmoreland, Manchester, Trelawny, and Saint James. That was June of 2002, and I was doing my best to return to my normal life of hard work and taking care of my growing daughter.

One day, as I was travelling from an appointment in Manchester back to our rented home in Santa Cruz, my cell phone began to ring incessantly. I had purposefully ignored the first barrage of ringing because the hill I was driving up was particularly steep and treacherous, the site of frequent accidents. Yet, when the phone started ringing a third time, I pulled to the side of the road, panicked with the thought that there may be an emergency at my daughter's school or the house.

When I answered, I found that the person on the other end of the line was indeed calling with life-changing news, but not in the way I had imagined at all. The caller was in fact a secondary school principal from the Mitcham borough in London. She stated that she had received my credentials from one of the job agencies and she was anxious to speak with me about current and upcoming employment opportunities with her school. I was slightly taken aback by her interest in me. After all, I had not taught in four years. *It must be divine intervention*, I thought. *God's favour must finally be turning towards me again!* I refocused my attention to the words being spoken into my ear from so far away. She was already starting to conduct the interview with me right there on the side of Spur Tree Hill.

I hadn't really expected anything to come of my registering with the agency and here we were with an interview! Oh, how one needs to expect more from simple touch points.

It was all happening so suddenly. My mind started to buzz with excuses to get out of the interview. What if, at the end of my interview, she was to offer me the position and expect me to commit to moving there? A pessimistic voice in my head reminded me that teaching was not something I had a flair for, like I did with sales. It was not something that I would even enjoy at that point in my life, as it couldn't afford me the lifestyle that I had grown accustomed to. Mentally, I wasn't in a good place to absorb the stress of working with children. That same little voice told me that even considering a move into the teaching field would be a step back. After all, teaching was something I had used to get a start in life, but it had never been my dream job.

In the background, I could hear the woman's continued questions. Somehow, I was managing to answer them coherently, and based on the tone of her voice, she appeared to be pleased with my responses. Then it seemed to me the conversation was ended abruptly, with her making a firm job offer and asking when I could start. I was dumbfounded and searched for how to answer that last important question. There was so much to consider! I mumbled some platitudes to give myself time to think. A part of me thought I must be crazy to not just hang up on her absurd offer and go about my daily business. That part of me was seized by the fear of leaving my country. After all, the job I held now gave me financial stability and the ability to afford much more than Jasmine and I could ever need. I had just imported a fancy new car from Japan, which was my weekend car. Very few people at my age could afford such a luxury, so who was I to throw it all away? I still owned the house in Montego Bay, but it was now rented, so it was not a financial burden and I could count it as a solid investment for my future. I was now living closer to my mother and she was providing a new type of emotional support I had not known before. Finally, I was still legally married, even though I only saw my husband occasionally and he had started a new family with another woman. My feelings for him were certainly tangled and complex.

But then another part of me began to intrude on my torrent of thoughts, and it was the voice of logic. Despite all of the successful contracts I was still managing to secure in my fragile post-trauma state, I lived every moment of my life with fear and paranoia. Jasmine and I still lived under constant police surveillance and our activities were restricted. That was really no sort of life, no matter how many amenities and gadgets I could afford to buy.

With that final realisation, I made an impulsive decision to accept the job. The voice on the other end of the line was filled with happy relief, as she rolled out the details of my employment and told me the agency would finalize the details. My start date was set for September twentieth I had less than two months to pack up all of my life and migrate to the UK. I hung up the phone and sat in awed silence for a moment. It appeared to me that God had just opened the door leading to the next chapter of my life. I called my mum and told her the news. She was shocked, but mostly unsure if I should move to another country or stay close by her, where she could essentially watch over me. I also called Tobore to tell him I had accepted a job in London. He expressed elation at my decision and told me that was the best way for me and Jasmine to move forward. The one thing Tobore and I knew at that stage was that Jasmine would stay with me. In Jamaica, in most cases, it is just a given that kids stay with mums.

The sincerity in his voice reminded me of what it had been like in those years during college when he was my staunchest supporter.

Alone, I sat silently in my car on the side of that steep hill for some time, trying to gather my emotions. A part of me felt afraid of the unknown. I wondered what life would be like once I moved to the UK. Granted, London had looked inviting while I was on my short visit, but what could I really tell about a place after just a two-week visit? In reality, though, it didn't matter what my fears were. I had accepted the job and now needed to get Jasmine and myself ready for the big move.

Changes can creep upon you forcing you to sink or swim.

CHAPTER 9: YOUR GUT

The world is your oyster explore babe explore!

Within days, the job agency forwarded the various documents that I would need to send to the British Embassy to obtain my work visa. They informed me of the vaccinations that I would be required to get in order to teach in the UK. Before I knew it, I had an appointment with a nearby doctor in Santa Cruz and left his office completely up to date on my immunisations. Everything was happening so fast I couldn't keep up.

A few weeks later, Tobore accompanied Jasmine and me to the visa interview session, which was conducted in Kingston. That day, it was raining in sheets, and I phoned the Embassy ahead of our travel to ask if it was necessary to make the trip due to the rain. The woman who answered my call laughed good-naturedly at my question and told me that if I intended to live in the UK, I needed to understand that rain stops nothing. We hastily jumped into my car and made the trip to collect our visas.

Jasmine and I got our visas, and I was scurrying around trying to get all the family's affairs in order before we left. The family here did not just mean my daughter and Tobore, it meant all my siblings as well. All my mother's and stepfather's children combined. Before I left for the city of gold and honey, how we referred to England, one of my obligations (or what I felt like was my obligation because I was the eldest) was to ensure all my siblings were, as we say in Jamaica, "set up." That meant I would ensure that each one had something to help ensure his or her future while I was gone. After all, taking care of everyone seems to have always been my job, even today.

Part of me felt guilty to be leaving them knowing they didn't seem to possess my resilience to survive, or so I felt. I didn't know what was waiting for me in the UK, but I felt I needed to ensure all my siblings had a start for their lives. So that was what I did. For my eldest brother I had a shop stocked with inventory. It was what he said he wanted—to be an entrepreneur. The sister that followed him was given money to pay for hairdressing courses; she said she wanted to be a hairdresser. Anna, the sister who had moved in with me soon after I moved to Santa Cruz, still lived with me. Her school fees were paid off. I had to cut off all of Sarah's family, as they reminded me of the pain and the dirty secret I carried around, and I didn't need that reminder. The sister after Anna was also given money to go back to a full-time education. I gave Kem the option to come with me to England and remain a part of my house. If she said no so be it, I would hold my head straight and forge my new life. In my mind, I had done the best I could for each of them. I gave them all a start in the lives they wanted, something someone had done once for me and that I had used to the best of my ability.

I had to leave the house in Montego untenanted while we were gone, as I just needed to get away from its ghost. It held far too many bad memories, and getting it rented was not happening quickly. I didn't want to make a rush decision and sell it, as it was the first sense of security I had somewhat created for myself. That meant the mortgage still had to be paid, and, obviously, that too was my responsibility. There was also the car I had just recently purchased, my Honda Accord with the three-litre engine. It was no baby car, as it was all glammed up. That was a massive loss of money. I hadn't envisaged having to leave Jamaica anytime soon or I wouldn't have bought a new weekend car. During the week I drove the company car, a Honda CRV.

As my migration was so sudden, I ended up selling all that I could of my belongings for little or no money. I sold everything at a bottom dollar price. Some items were given to people who promised to pay me later. Little did I know that even before I had ascended into the sky, these

Chapter 9: Your Gut

people had no plans of repaying me. That is how most of my money was diminished, with my naïve desire to escape and leave everything behind me. Even with all that, I still felt I had more than enough to start a new life across the pond. I had a job waiting for me and newfound family and friends there for support

With everything in place for our emigration, I resigned from my job with the company that had been so much a part of my life over the past few years. My heart was heavy, and I began doubting my decision as I delivered the news to my supervisors. I constantly reminded myself of the promise of the new life awaiting me in London, one that would bring me out of the fear I lived in currently.

The plan was for me to move to London first, where I would set up a home for my daughter and sister to join me later in October, as Kem had decided she would join us on our grand new adventure. In the meantime, Jasmine would stay with her paternal grandparents. Although I knew Tobore's parents would look after my daughter well, it was difficult for me to leave her behind. I kept my focus on the knowledge that it was the best decision for us as a family, and eventually, we would all be together again because Tobore had told me that he would like to come with us as well. I was so excited, and we actually went to dinner to celebrate our new move away from all the pain and hurt we found ourselves in. Jasmine was happy to see Mum and Dad together. You could just tell from her wanting to sit between us at dinner.

His plan was to join us there in December of that year. Things had not played out well with the new woman he'd been with. I was excited to finally have the opportunity for Tobore and me to work on our marriage again, away from all the stresses of our families and the demands that we were surrounded by at the time, including the baby on the way. I thought a fresh new environment might do us some good.

In August, only a few weeks before my scheduled departure, Tobore's girlfriend gave birth to their daughter. The news of her birth ripped my soul in two. It felt as if someone had defiled the one sacred event that he and I shared. It was a difficult period for everyone involved because Tobore and I had begun seeing each other on a regular basis. The tension was thick between everyone. Tobore and me, and Tobore and the mother of his new child. I could only imagine the torment he felt, or how it compared to my own, because we never spoke directly of it. As a woman, I also felt sad for the mother, though it was difficult to see it as I was in the middle of this threesome. But there were moments that I would place myself in her shoes and think about how hurt she would be feeling during that period in all our lives. That thought did not last for too long, because if I lingered there, I would not want to go back to Tobore and try to fix our marriage, our lives. So, I quickly snapped out of it and focused solely on our future and our life together.

Here we were, Tobore and me, with a child who, in essence, was the core of our relationship, and she needed her father. But at the same time, he had just brought a new child into the world, and that child needed a father just as much as mine did. I was torn with shame that I would be taking the father away from his child like someone had taken mine away from me at one point. I was beginning to feel like I should start a blog about my life and make the domain name Confused.com, with a capital C.

I stayed with Tobore in Montego Bay the night before my flight to London, at the flat where he was now living. I awoke in his arms feeling extremely nervous. I pulled myself from the bed, jumped into the shower, and started getting ready to leave. All of a sudden, there was a great commotion at the door of his flat. His baby's mother had arrived at the doorstep and was demanding entrance. The scene was heart wrenching, and I felt an unexpected wave of guilt and shame even though Tobore was still my husband. She was crying and shouting at the two of us, clutching at her heart and screaming out in pain as if it was breaking. I felt guilt grip my heart that the cost of my husband and I restarting our married life would be the destruction of this other woman and the future of her newborn baby.

Finally, things calmed down when she realised that her pleas to Tobore were falling on deaf ears. He had not even let her in the door. Eventually she just left. I stood in the silence that followed and collapsed in his arms, sobbing. I felt like our marriage had been broken in so many ways. Not just by that situation, but also by everything the two us had been through in the past year, together and separately. Our ride to the airport left me feeling that we were facing so many uncertainties as a couple, and I wondered how we could possibly survive. I could not bring myself to voice all of the questions that were swirling in my head. Could I bear the guilt of separating a man from his newborn child? Was I making a mistake by trying to reconcile with him? Would moving our family to an unknown country be our downfall? How would Jasmine survive being away from me while I left her to set up our new home in the UK?

As I dropped her off at her grandparents' house and said goodbye, my heart was palpitating. I kept asking myself if I were doing the right thing. She was crying, as she knew I was leaving, but for how long her tiny brain could not quite work out. I was torn up, snot everywhere, and as Tobore gently removed her from my arms and gave her to her nan, my heart broke.

What if they didn't send her to join me? There were so many what ifs, but nothing I could do now, other than deciding to stay in Jamaica, could fix any of them. And would staying even fix them? I remained silent as we drove to the airport, lost in my thoughts, questioning my decisions.

As I boarded the plane, I looked back at the landscape I was leaving. I bid farewell to the country that I had known my entire life. The nine-hour flight seemed to last for an eternity. I watched movies, walked around the plane, and even slept. It was frustrating to wake up and still be thousands of miles up in the sky, with hours left until I was to reach my destination. I fought the urge to stand up screaming for the pilots to turn around and take me home! I was reminded of the feeling I'd had as a child living at the will of everyone else in control. I reminded myself that I had made the choice to get on that plane, and I was taking the chance of restarting our lives away from everyone we knew and loved.

The airline served lovely Jamaican food, and I greedily wolfed down my meal, not realising that these authentic flavours tantalizing my tongue would only be tasted again when I someday returned home to Jamaica. Finally, the announcement was made that we would be landing in thirty minutes. Even though it was the same airport I had flown in and out of for my first visit to London, I was utterly disoriented and overwhelmed when I disembarked from the plane. In my anxious state, the airport seemed to have grown by miles since my visit a few months ago. My ears were blocked. I couldn't hear the announcements directing people to customs, and the entire ground I stood on felt unsteady. I thought maybe there was an earthquake starting, but realised that everyone else around me was moving with calm purpose.

I was surprised by the cold chill in the air, even though we were inside. It was most certainly the wet, chilly weather that London was famous for in the autumn that was sneaking into the building. I snapped out of my daze and tried to catch up with the other passengers from my flight. I assumed the direction they were all going was the correct one. I knew it wasn't snowing outside that early in the season, but all of the other passengers were retrieving heavy coats from their luggage; I was not prepared for that at all.

I joined the queue to clear customs and followed the instructions for those without UK citizenship. The line was much longer than the one for the British citizens. It was obvious that our flight was not the only one that had landed at that time. There was a great assortment of people in my queue. I took in the various shades of skin colours, the assortment of traditional clothing I had never seen before, and the cacophony of strange languages. I was relieved to finally recognise some of my native people, a family who had travelled on the same flight I had been on. But I breathed a sharp intake of breath as they were gathered up by the stern authorities and taken away. I wondered what they had done because they didn't look suspicious to me and seemed much more relaxed than I was. I was struck with panic. Would they come and detain me as well?

Another lady from the flight must have sensed my anxiety and confusion because she leaned over and whispered, "Drug mules." I was surprised at my ignorance, but breathed a sigh of relief, realising that my hypersensitive state was more the norm for people legally immigrating to a new country.

I reached the customs window without incident. The officer hardly looked at me, simply stamping my passport and telling me in a bored voice, "Have a good day." I settled myself in the arrivals section of the airport. I was so anxious to call home and tell Tobore I had arrived safely and hear my daughter's sweet voice, but my Jamaica-based service was unable to pick up a signal and I realised I really was on my own.

Sometimes it's best to be unsure of what lies ahead of us because if we knew, there wouldn't be any great adventure or ability to build resilience.

CHAPTER 10: THE UNKNOWN

The unknown is sometimes started with excitement and anticipation that isn't realised at first. It's then that we have to accept we weren't prepared for the unknown.

I had been told that a representative from the employment agency would meet me in the arrivals area of the airport and take me to the home they had arranged for me to stay in while I settled into my new life and job. But as I looked around, I couldn't make out any particular person among the hundreds of people who were crowded around, waving frantically to loved ones and rushing to hug long-missed parents and lovers. To me, the room was cavernous and filled with laughing, chatting people whose lives had just been completed by the dear ones now in their arms.

On the edge of that melee were a few men standing somberly and holding up placards with arriving passengers' names printed on them. I was so relieved to realise that maybe one of these men might be from the agency and waiting patiently to collect me. I walked past each man in turn, carefully reading each card to find the one bearing my name. When I reached the end of the line, I doubled back to look again, thinking I must have somehow missed the one with my name on it. But my second search was as fruitless as the first. I began to think I might have landed at a different airport than the one where they were expecting to pick me up. I rechecked all of my notes from my previous conversation with the agency. I even rechecked my boarding tickets, which clearly read Heathrow Airport, and when I asked an employee walking past, he confirmed that I had landed at the right place.

Chapter 10: The Unknown

I began to think that the agency representative might simply be running late. I settled myself in a chair close to the area where the pick-up gathered for each arriving flight, so as not to miss my person when they arrived. After thirty minutes ticked by, I found another airport employee and explained my situation of just having arrived and finding no one to pick me up and having no service on my mobile. The employee directed me to a bank of public phones, but when I went to use one, I remembered that I had yet to exchange my Jamaican dollars for British pounds. Luckily, someone nearby noticed my plight and graciously handed me some coins, and I immediately dialed the agency.

The woman who answered the phone was surprised to hear that I was waiting at the airport and admitted they had overlooked the fact that I was landing that day. I breathed a sigh of relief when she said to sit tight because they would send someone to come get me right away. In that case, however, "right away" really meant another hour and a half, and the representative I was expecting turned out to be a cab driver who barely spoke English. I felt a rush of camaraderie for a fellow immigrant, but soon understood that our conversation would be limited to monosyllabic words.

The driver took me to a hotel and gestured for me to go inside and check in while he waited with my luggage outside. When I went to the reception desk, though, I was told that there was no Ava Brown on their guest list. At first, I assumed that the agency may have used a variation on the spelling of my full name that was causing confusion, but after the receptionist checked the guest list again, with every possible variation of my name, she still came up with nothing. A sense of panic flooded over me. Here I was in the middle of London, homeless, with nothing that the agency promised, when I could have been easing into my king-sized bed back in Jamaica with the knowledge that my house-helper had taken care of all my family's needs.

When I expressed my predicament to the cab driver, he understood and made some calls back to the agency. As he chattered away in a mix of English and some foreign language I didn't understand, I began to feel like I was a product being bartered in the human slave trade. I realised I was at the mercy of the employment agency. I had trusted them to bring me to another country, and I knew I already owed them something for getting me my work permit. Little did I know how the process really worked. The school I would be working for had paid thousands of pounds to the agency as a "finder's fee" for me. The cab driver finally finished the call and told me that we were at the wrong hotel, and he would take me to the right one.

We drove in pensive silence to the north of London and stopped in front of a tall building with the term *hostel* in big white letters above the door. I had no idea what a hostel was, but I learned exactly how it was different from a hotel as soon as I entered it. The communal living atmosphere reminded me of the dorms I had lived in while at college. But here I was, a woman with a husband, a child, and a successful career behind me. I was no longer a teenager who was comfortable sharing a single bathroom down the hall and noisy, tightly packed bedrooms.

That time, the cab driver brought my luggage inside and drove off after gesturing me towards the reception desk. There my name was on the guest list. I was given the key to my room and informed that I would be sharing a room with eight other people. I could hardly believe what I was hearing . . . Eight other people? How could that be? Even when I lived in the cramped, single-room house as a child, we didn't have nine people in it. My quick assessment of the lobby did not bode well, and as expected, when I reached the living quarters, I found filth and chaos. The bathrooms looked like they hadn't been cleaned in years, and there was a buzz of activity, with people of many different colours, races, and languages jostling about the narrow hallways, in and out of our room.

In Jamaica, the language was either Patois or English, but here there was Russian, French, Italian, and Polish. I soon realised that the many people of different origins were interacting as one group, and that made me feel like even more of an outsider. In addition, I was keenly aware that I was the only black person and that made me feel even more isolated.

"What have I gotten myself into?" I asked myself out loud, but either the people around me hadn't understood me, or they were just far too busy getting on with their own lives to care about a new addition to their already crowded home.

The room we all shared was about 14x15 metres with three-tiered bunk beds along the two side walls and two flat beds in the centre. There was absolutely no privacy. I had been assigned one of the bunk beds, which was covered in the filth of an unknown amount of people who had slept on it before me. I envisioned myself in prison and couldn't believe that I had condemned myself to that sentence of suffering. I tucked my belongings in the small space that had been spared for me and went to bed that night in a state of complete disillusionment. I cried myself to sleep lying on the disgusting pillow. I missed my home, my daughter, and my husband. I felt so cheated and misled. I was ready to go back; I even looked at my ticket to see if I could go back. The crazy thing is I knew I was on a one-way ticket, so this was not even an option. With no money to spare either, it was even dumb, but I was lost here. I needed to feel the sun, familiarity, and there was absolutely none here.

Settling into my new life in London quickly proved to be more emotionally difficult than I could have ever imagined. I ended up spending more than four nights at this hostel; it seemed like four months if I am honest. Every night as I lay down to sleep, I lamented the life I had left behind in Jamaica, blinding myself to all of the difficulties I had endured. I only remembered the good times and all my successes. I berated myself for having left an excellent paying job, my friends, and family. I would constantly cry myself to sleep thinking about how I had abandoned the simplest pleasures of life in my home country. I missed being able to knock on a neighbour's door just to say good morning, or the ability to ask friends and family for a favour and being confident of the laid-back response being a kind, "No problem, irie mon," in our friendly, sing-song accent. I consoled myself by remembering a piece of advice that my dear friend Dee had given me during a particularly difficult period of my life: *God doesn't take us through dirty water to drown us, but to cleanse us.*

I had arrived in London with nothing more than what had fit into my single piece of luggage, bringing minimal clothing and only what I thought would protect me against the intense wet and cold weather I imagined existed year-round. Establishing my new life with these relatively few possessions was a daily reminder that I had consciously chosen to leave behind a lifestyle of luxury and certainty to start all over again. I felt as if I were back in the first week of college, the poor girl without the appropriate items to do my work and without any friends. However, the fear that still lurked in my heart about the men who had attacked me on that fateful night compelled me to reflect on the justifications I had given myself for moving to London in the first place. I reminded myself that Jamaica had once been a colony of England and of its significant influences on our culture that were still evident even today. I told myself I was just being a silly girl. How different could the two countries really be?

My roommates seemed to be settled into the hostel lifestyle. But I found it very difficult to adjust, especially with the lack of privacy and the requirement to share a toilet and a shower with so many strangers. The shower was on the third floor, and I had to take six flights of stairs to get there, carrying with me all of the toiletries I would need. I would wearily climb the stairs every morning, my arms loaded with my towel, toothbrush, soap, toothpaste, lotion, underwear, and most importantly, bath slippers to protect myself from contracting the fungal skin diseases that were rampant among the community. I would also take my clothes to get dressed for the day, since the shower room provided the only privacy, and

Chapter 10: The Unknown

I was incredibly uncomfortable with the sexually liberal attitude that I was seeing all around me.

The hostel provided meals for all of its residents, but I had an extremely hard time eating the daily dinner rations of bland mashed potatoes, runny brown gravy, and fatty English sausages. Sleep was never easy and an undisturbed eight hours was impossible. I soon found out that my roommates all worked different jobs and kept different hours. Some worked in the food service and others at the twenty-four-hour cab dispatch offices. As such, we all kept different schedules, and the lights in the room were going on and off at all hours of the night. It seemed as if we were all in a constant overlap of going-to-work and coming-home schedules, with someone coming in at dawn, exhausted from the late-night shift, just as somebody else was crawling out of bed, exhausted from lack of sleep, to get dressed and join the morning commute. It felt like I was simultaneously living out a multitude of scenes in a movie that was set in fast-forward.

Another difficulty in that living situation was the potpourri of smells that assaulted the nose throughout the day and night. I was sure that I smelled as strange to the others in the hostel as they did to me. We were such a mismatch of body odours that revealed our cultural beliefs of how much bathing was appropriate and what kind of foods were eaten in our varying nations. Almost everyone sought out their native foods when they were outside of the hostel. The breakfast menu was not much better than the dinner menu and just as unchanging.

The smell of eggs frying in stale oil permeated the entire building every morning as the sun rose. I would drag myself down to the breakfast area, because if you missed breakfast, you were on your own until dinner.

The cleanliness of the dishes we ate from was equal to that of the rest of the hostel, and the food was of very low quality. My first morning there, I looked down at my plate and imagined it shouting, "Don't eat from me! I am not clean!" The bread looked as if it had been obtained on sale after being rejected from the production line, the eggs were runny and barely warm, and the sausage was undercooked to the point of being nearly raw. My stomach knotted, and I nearly gagged at the thought of eating that meal, but I knew I needed sustenance for the day ahead of me. I had not yet begun my teaching role, and I was no longer even grateful for it, the way I was feeling then. Whatever wealth I had acquired remained back in Jamaica for the time, and with money being tight, the food at the hostel was my only option.

My most important duty was to find a place where I could get my phone activated so I could hear the voice of my sweet daughter and remember the reasons I needed to endure that situation. To create a safer life for her and me, and to create a more stable home life for our family.

Being in the wilderness without a familiar object is like being left to die, but faith will allow you to survive until rescue can come.

CHAPTER 11: DEEP END

The mundane things in modern life, like technology, can be one's best friend in the desert.

I found a mobile phone shop about twenty metres from the hostel that sold SIM cards, which I hoped would allow me to access international calling on my phone. The price was steep, especially considering the very few pounds I had to survive on, until I started to receive my salary from the teaching job in a few days' time. It was a long wait at least two weeks in fact. I was incredibly hopeful as I handed over money and watched the salesperson insert the card into my phone. I was practically breathing down his neck as he held up the phone in the air, and together we watched the screen as it searched for a signal. I laughed out loud with glee when the signal bars filled up to the highest range, showing strong connectivity. Finally, I was returning back to civilization and I was able to make calls to the people that mattered. The school, Tobore and Jasmine, and my mum!

It was my second day in London and the agency had not left any messages at the hostel. I checked to see if they may have been trying to contact me through my mobile phone, but there were no messages on it either. It was strange; prior to my arrival, they had been in routine contact, constantly reassuring me that they would take care of me when I arrived in that new country. After the debacle at the airport, I couldn't imagine them forgetting me again so soon. I called the agency's main office, but only got a receptionist who told me I could not call the school, as it was the agency's role to introduce me. I did not want to break protocols, so I obliged. She had no power, but could only promise to pass on my message to an upper-level staff member. I left my mobile number and asked for a return call. My anxiety was again beginning to heighten. I thought in a panic of how much I was at the mercy of these people whom I had no reason to trust. I only had their word. Again, I thought of all the stories I had heard of unsuspecting immigrants landing in a country only to be placed in indentured servitude or outright slavery.

A tense two hours later, my mobile rang, and I was greeted by the branch manager of the agency. He apologized profusely for all the messy planning up to that point, but I couldn't get a word in edgewise. I had no way of proving if he was serious and would do as he said, so I had to wait and see. When he finished his jovial rant promising that everything would be well from then on, I was finally able to express myself. And express myself I did! I let out a barrage of complaints starting with the disgust I felt about being treated as nothing more than an after-thought and finishing with the horrible living conditions at the hostel. He waited on the other end of the line in patient silence. He then told me I needed to collect my belongings and find my way over to the office in south London to discuss the details of starting my job right away, and to get settled into a better living environment. I was still fuming, though, and yelled into the phone, "I am in the north right now! Don't you have an office nearby that could find me a more tolerable place to live?

His reply was curt. He told me again that I needed to find my way to their office, which was located on the south side of the city. He capped it off with a biting comment, "You said in your interview that you were a dedicated employee who wasn't lazy."

I was so offended. I wanted to end the conversation right then by telling him to just fuck off. Instead, I bit my tongue and kicked the wall. We both knew that I needed his help due to the predicament I was in. I took a deep breath and thought to approach the situation like I would have with any cantankerous client in my old sales job. I kindly asked if the agency would send another cab to come and get me, but felt like I hit a wall when he snapped, "I would imagine you can read and in doing so get yourself from point A to point B. You mentioned in our chat that you travelled to the US frequently. Well, it is the same here, just a different country. That is what working adults do, and I trust you are not a child. We don't employ children either." He cleverly placed a chuckle here to break the tension.

I stood in stunned silence and then thought about how I was to accomplish that feat. I mumbled something about getting a cab, and he replied by telling me to have the cab drop me off in Mitcham Town Centre, then to give him a call and he would provide me with the necessary walking directions from that point. He then hung up and all of the frustration at the indignities he had thrown at me came boiling to the surface. I let out a giant scream and stomped like a two-year-old. The passersby must have thought I was a mad woman!

I steeled myself for the travel to the Mitcham Town Centre, wherever that was. I consoled myself with the thought that at least I would be leaving that disgusting hostel. However, when I went back up to my room to gather my things, I found my bag lying open and broken on the floor. My things were strewn about and all the money I had brought was gone, along with the more expensive items of clothing and desirable personal care items. Thank God I had tucked some money away in my purse and taken it with me when I left on my errands. There was no way to know who had done it, as everyone had access to where the tenants' luggage was kept. My only recourse was to pack up what was left, improvise a quick fix to the latch so that it would be semi-functional, and check out.

I didn't know where I would be sleeping that night, but I didn't even care at that point. As I dragged my broken bag through the hostel's front doors, I felt as if I were wearing all of its grime on my skin. A white man, whom I recognised as one of the young immigrants from Kosovo that was living at the hostel, noticed my struggle and offered to help me.

I almost wept at his simple gesture of kindness. I realised then that the cold personalities I had encountered so far in London were almost

Chapter 11: Deep End

more than I could bear. In that moment, my heart ached so much for my home country that I thought it might break. Never in your wildest dreams would a Jamaican man stand by and ignore a female in need of physical help. The young man could see my turmoil, and without a word, he took the bag from me and carried it down to the curb.

I didn't have to wait long for the cab that had been called by the front desk to arrive. I loaded my things into the back and directed the driver to Mitcham Town Centre. Before we set off, I asked him how much it would cost, but he said he couldn't say for certain as the cab fares were based on the mileage covered. All I knew was that London was large. I had no clue how far my destination was from that point, and I prayed that the money I still had in my purse was enough to cover the fare. My body and mind were so drained from the emotional turmoil of my first few days in London that the movement of the car lulled me into a deep sleep. I remember clearly how I dreamt about Jamaica, imagining that I was seated on a plane and on my way back home. I felt a gentle tap on my shoulder and smiled, thinking it was my baby Jasmine waking me up as she normally would do. But when I opened my eyes to see only the Rastafarian immigrant face of the cabbie, tears streamed from my eyes.

"Madam," he said, "we are in Mitcham." I was still very groggy and looked around, searching desperately for scenes that would tell me I was really alighting in Jamaica. But there was only the drizzly London weather and people tightly wrapped against the chill with their heads down and hands tucked firmly in their pockets as they stalked through the town square. The shock of that scene was too much, and I started bawling outright. The driver was at a loss about what to do with me. He stepped away and instead busied himself with removing my luggage from the car and setting it carefully on the sidewalk. I finally gathered myself enough to ask him what the fare was: forty pounds. It would take nearly half of all the money I had in my wallet.

Chapter 11: Deep End

When I handed the money over, the cab driver asked me what was wrong. I shrugged off his question and told him that I was fine, but in a hurry to make an appointment. I did not want to air all of my complaints in the middle of a public street to a perfect stranger. Still, he placed an empathetic hand on my shoulder and told me to be strong. As he handed me a card with his number on it, he said, "It all comes together at some stage. I meet new immigrants from the Caribbean all the time and they are always overwhelmed by this massive city. With time, it will get better." I felt like God had sent an angel to deliver just the right message to strengthen my resolve to go forward.

I tucked his card in a safe place in my purse. I felt like I was no longer a complete stranger in that country. I now had met one person who was willing to offer the hand of friendship. As he got back into his cab, he gave me one last piece of advice. He told me the quicker I picked myself up the better it would be for me, because the path to my future in that new country was going to be rocky. And soon, I discovered that he was right on both of these points.

I finally snapped back to reality and made the call to the agency to tell my handler, whom I had begun to think of as my owner, that I had arrived in the town centre. He asked me to tell him a landmark near my location and then told me that I was a short twenty-minute walk from where he was currently doing some business, which was closer than the office.

When I arrived at the destination, I found the man was a tall, white Briton. He formally introduced himself for the first time, and I learned his name was James Tuckader, and I could call him Mr. Tuckader. In an unexpected gesture of kindness, he said that he had driven near to the town centre to do some business and pick me up. The drive to the office in Clapham was completed in absolute silence, and that time, I was much too anxious to fall asleep.

When we arrived, he directed me to a small room with a desk and quickly got down to the business of explaining the details of my employ-

Chapter 11: Deep End

ment. Where I would be working, what hours I was expected to be there, and to whom I would be reporting. Without any unnecessary pleasantries, he then took me back to his car and drove me to the school that I would be working in—a large public high school. We sat in the main reception area, on hard plastic chairs, for a good forty-five minutes.

All that time, there was a din of boisterous teenaged shouting and jostling in the surrounding corridors. I was utterly confused because the schools in Jamaica were so strict, and the children were expected to be well-behaved in all grades.

Finally, the door to one of the inner offices burst open and a thin, sallow-skinned white woman rushed in and made a beeline straight for us with a stern look on her face. She introduced herself as the deputy head teacher. Even though she was brisk and unfriendly, I was impressed with her efficiency. She spoke with us briefly and handed us over to the school's financial officer, who then surreptitiously handed an envelope to Mr. Tuckader. I assumed it was the agency's finder's fee that was paid for me. It made me really feel like I was being sold like a slave. I realised from my eavesdropping on their jovial yet argumentative conversation that the school was paying quite a tidy sum for me. The financier was an obese white woman, who wore a tent-like, bright yellow, floppy housecoat with frills. She flapped her arms about when she spoke so that she looked like the giant talking bird character from a popular children's show back home. I did not realise then that was her regular daily attire and that the students and staff alike secretly referred to her by the name of that very same character.

When what I imagined to be the financial transaction was completed, she stood and shook hands with me, commenting on how smartly dressed I was for their humble school. I thanked her, but soon realised that it wasn't really the compliment I had assumed it to be. I was wearing one of my power suits, which I was so accustomed to wearing in my executive job in Jamaica to convey a sense of professionalism. I had thought it was

Chapter 11: Deep End

appropriate because the teachers in Jamaica always dressed professionally and modestly, with all unnecessary skin covered up and tattoos hidden. The concept back home was that teachers were supposed to be models for the students to emulate.

I had dressed in my suit out of respect for the teaching profession and for the children I would be mentoring. But as I started paying attention to the students and teachers who were going back and forth in the corridor, I realised that I was terribly overdressed. I lamented the fact that even the dress that made me feel successful and capable in Jamaica only made me feel awkward and uncomfortable in a first world country. I buried these feelings and held my head high as I was given the grand tour of the school. At the end, I felt totally lost in that new world and thought I was intruding where I so clearly didn't belong. We passed classroom after classroom filled with screaming teenagers who were left on their own and were jumping around the room. At first, I thought we must be in the drama department, where pupils were practicing for an upcoming play, but as the tour continued, I realised that these were just regular classes, and that the teachers simply had no control over their pupils. The tour guide must have noticed my surprise because she told me not to worry. The wild behaviour was only expected at the beginning and end of the school year, when the children were still hyperactive from summer break.

The guide told us that the next stop would be the technology department of the school, where I would be working. She gave an embarrassed titter and admitted that the school was so large that even though she had been there for two years and was a senior manager, she didn't know where that block of classrooms was. I was set to start teaching the very next day. There was a lump in my throat. I knew right then that the rocky path in England the cab driver had foreseen would include both my personal life and my professional one as well.

Sometimes we end up in situations where running is our best option, but when we find that there is nowhere to run, we just stand.

CHAPTER 12: TRANSITION

Life can sometimes toss, shove, and send you into the wilderness before it brings you back to civilization, the place you ideally want to be.

The transition from being an employee in the private corporate sector to the state-run school system was a shock, to say the least. In addition, the school's curriculum and teaching role was completely different from what I had been trained for in my home country. I was confused as to how two countries that spoke a similar language and had a shared history could be so different. My fellow teachers and the school staff turned out to be very polite and eager to help me get settled in my new teaching post, but I could not shake my homesickness and the feeling of culture shock. I struggled to overcome my subdued mood and match the enthusiasm of my colleagues, but my smiles never reached my eyes and belied my belief in the Jamaican proverb to be wary of overly friendly people.

My general disorientation in that new setting only strengthened my paranoia that had been born on the night I was attacked. I remained on high alert in any situation involving strangers, including all of my colleagues and pupils. My inability to form any bonds within that social group pushed me deeper into a depression. For the first week, I would start each day by arriving in the classroom before the students, so that I could gather myself to be an effective instructor. Inevitably, as I would look around the empty room filled with desks, my resolve would crumble, and I would sink into a ten-minute sob fest. My crying was so intense in those days that I would hear myself gasping for breath and moaning out loud. I remember the horror that would strike my heart when I heard myself, and it would make me cry harder. I also worried about what my colleagues would think if they heard me, so I would bury my head in my handbag to suffocate the noises of deep emotional pain that were coming from within me.

I could not escape my misery. I wanted to be gone from that strange place where I did not fit in. I wanted to be back at home with my daughter and my husband by my side. I wanted the past year to have been only a bad dream. I began to convince myself that the threats to my life were not real after all, that I had somehow misunderstood my attackers' parting words, or dreamed their second visit to my home. I was desperate to return to the familiar world that I now felt foolish for having fled. There were so few black people in that new town, and my uniquely dark skin colour made me feel even more isolated. I yearned for the days when I could have simply walked around my local community and found any number of extended family members to complain to or commiserate with. Here, I didn't even get a simple good morning from passers-by on the street. I even began to miss the distant and sometimes tenuous relationships that I had with my mum and siblings.

On that first day at the school, the man from the agency had excused himself shortly after my tour of the building had begun. As he tried to sneak off, I grabbed him by the jacket so that he wouldn't get away without telling me where I was to be staying that night. After all, I had checked out of the hostel, and my luggage was still in his car. He told me that he would drop my bag off in the school's main office and I could find it there at the end of the day. For the second time that day, I found out that it would be up to me to take care of myself.

When the tour ended, the ladies in the school's main office were kind enough to make some calls to various B&Bs in the area. After several calls, they found one with a vacancy in the south of London. When the secretary asked me to approve the price of twenty pounds per night so that she could make my reservation, I agreed with trepidation in my heart. Twenty pounds was almost the exact amount of money I had left in my wallet. The secretary also provided me with the bus schedule so that I could catch a ride directly from the front of the school to my new lodgings. The bus was crowded with people traveling home from the end of the workday across the city, and in the hubbub, I missed my stop. I was relieved to find that the next stop was only a five-minute walk from the one where I should have gotten off.

I found the B&B rather easily and felt like my luck was finally changing. The building was a paradise compared to the hostel. As I approached the shining oak reception desk, I wondered just what would have happened if I had had no money left to pay for it? I shuddered to think that the agency would have just abandoned me to sleep on the street at that point, with their commission in hand. There was no need for them to concern themselves with me anymore. The receptionist took my money as prepayment for the night and informed me that there was no access to a phone line. I smiled, because for once today, a challenge was not insurmountable. My phone was still showing a strong signal, and I would be able to call home as soon as I got settled.

The collective cost of my taxi fare, the bus fare, and the lodging fee left me nearly broke after the rest of my money had been stolen that morning. I had no money for a proper meal before bed that night, so I focused my energies on taking a much-needed shower in the B&B's clean bathroom. Then I found a small shop where I could purchase a loaf of sliced bread and a two-litre cream soda. Those items would serve as my dinner until I managed to get some money wired from my account in Jamaica or my first paycheque arrived. I retired to the privacy of my well-kept room at the B&B and picked at the inadequate meal. In Jamaica, I was accustomed to a hearty dinner each night, which would include everything from oxtail, rice and peas, coleslaw, and potato salad, to fried chicken, bacon, and eggs. My help had been a lavish cook! My new life in England was so different to that in Jamaica that I felt as if I had been transported to another world and not just another country.

Chapter 12: Transition

Having that little bit of bread and soda in my stomach fortified my spirit more than it did my physical state. Despite my situation being nothing as I had imagined it to be, I recalled my natural strength of perseverance. I resolved to make the move work, no matter what, by reminding myself of the fact that my daughter and sister were coming to join me in October. There was no way I was going to allow them to arrive to the same frightening uncertainty that I had.

When I drifted off to sleep that night, I had serene dreams, filled with my daughter's sweet laughter and the sensation of her little arms hugging me. Before I knew it, the alarm was jolting me awake, alerting me to the impending workday ahead of me. I had slept so deeply that I was disoriented by my surroundings for a few moments. Finally, the realisation that I was in London, about to start teaching at the high school and needing to check out of the B&B to go to a new place a friend had helped me find down the road, crept into my mind. I took another long shower, luxuriating in the extreme cleanliness of that bathroom compared to that of the hostel. As the hot water cascaded over my head, covering my body like a blanket, my brain and soul woke up, and I steeled myself to handle all of the new challenges that lay ahead of me that day. The B&B served a hot and hearty breakfast, and I ate as much as my stomach could hold, knowing that my next meals would only consist of the leftover bread and soda that were now tucked among my other belongings in my luggage.

Even though my heart was aching to hear the voices of my daughter, my sister, and Tobore, I hesitated to call them with only complaints about my first few days in the place that was soon to be their new home. Instead, I placed a call to Jos, a childhood friend who was now living in the UK. Jos offered to provide me with a quick loan of British pounds so that I could rent a place before my financial matters were settled. Since I was expected to be at work all day, I would have to use the evening to look for a place to live permanently. I hoped I would find something immediately and not have to return to the B&B, as night-by-night lodging was always more expensive than a monthly rental.

I borrowed a local newspaper from the reception desk and scanned the advertisements as I finished my breakfast. Without thinking, I immediately started to seek out houses that matched what we had in Jamaica, but the exorbitant rates that were published next to each listing quickly jolted me back to reality. There was no way I would be able to afford a dwelling large enough for each of us to have a separate room and extra space for socialising. I scanned the adverts until I reached the section at the end that was more "poor man's housing," and I took a sharp intake of breath when I realised that even these prices were incredibly high by Jamaican standards. In all my considerations about accepting the teaching job in London, it had never occurred to me to consider the drastic difference in cost of living, which reduced my already low pay to nearly nothing. I cursed myself for having made such a rash decision to immigrate. Clearly, I had not thought it through adequately.

I caught the bus to work and was again overwhelmed by the newness of my surroundings. The buildings were tall and crowded together. Everything looked the same to me, including the people on the streets, who all wore dour expressions and kept to themselves. When I arrived in my classroom that morning, I met the first of my students. The informal interactions between pupils and teachers struck me as it had the day before. I planned to overcome this and establish a sense of decorum in my classroom by instructing my students to take their seats and give me their attention while I gave a very formal introduction about myself.

I stood straight up in front of the class and gave a proper oration about who I was, where I was from, and what my hopes were in regards to helping guide their lives and enriching their education. I asked the pupils to introduce themselves one by one.

When we got to one boy who was of Caribbean descent, he concluded his introduction by saying to me, "Hey, I have seen you somewhere before."

I immediately labeled that boy as the class clown, and I was more than ready to put a stop to his attention-seeking behaviour. I brushed his comment off with ease but was thrown off balance when the boy stood up, pointed at me and exclaimed, "Oh yes! I have seen you before, in the paper! My mum and dad just came back from the big reggae show in Jamaica, and you were in the paper they brought back."

I laughed his words off, but that just riled him up more.

He looked me straight in the eye and said, "I will bring that paper tomorrow and prove you wrong." He was so emphatic that I agreed that he should bring the paper in so that I could see myself in print.

Turns out, he was right. When he came in the next day with the paper, there I was staring out from the front page, dressed to the nines at one of the last big galas I had attended for the telecom company. The fact that I was standing next to a singer who was very popular worldwide at the time impressed my students and gave me a bit of respect in their eyes. I silently thanked God that was the story in which I was headlining, and not a report of the brutal crime that I had just survived.

The resources at the new school were nothing like I had ever seen before. I felt like the students were being educated in the lap of luxury. Back at my high school in Jamaica, we had learned about photosynthesis by picking leaves off of trees outside and holding them up to the sun to squint at the structures that the bright light made semi-translucent. This school was full of the latest technology and clever exaggerated representations of even the smallest of molecules and elements. Even though these resources were advanced, I lamented that, as a teacher here, I wouldn't have the opportunity to teach the children the important life lesson of improvising and using their creativity to overcome a challenge. There was a limit as to how much autonomy I had as a teacher. Very different from back home, and I dare say another lesson in my new life.

My strict demeanor allowed me to gain some semblance of control over the pupils in my classroom. However, my impression from the first day in the school was correct—most of the other classrooms seemed completely out of control. I found out that the lower grade feeder schools for that high school were all same-sex schools, so for many students, it was their first experience attending school with the opposite sex. The titillation that these students felt at being in a co-ed structure meant that many teachers were merely policing the hormone-driven students rather than teaching them. I noticed the sexual tension in my classroom, which was visible in the way that the children sat themselves on opposite sides of the room according to gender. I laughed inwardly because the room looked like a community ruled by two rival gangs who had no trust in each other.

I made a concerted effort to help the girls and boys begin to interact with one another more naturally by formally assigning seating that mixed up the two. The seating arrangement was met with much loud grumbling, but I overruled it all and the students benefited from it in the end. Sooner than I had dared to hope, I hadn't taught Food Technology in over eight years, and yet here I was again. I guess when you know a subject matter, it is like riding a bicycle. I found my footing in the classroom and the lessons started to interest the students. I did try to instill the importance of smart dressing, despite the fact that there was a uniform as part of the dress code, but that was largely a failure. The style for boys at the time was to wear their trousers down past their hips, so that their ass was literally hanging out, covered by thin cotton boxer shorts with wild prints on them. It was also the style to look a bit grungy, but boys of that age need to bathe, and they often smelled rather "ripe" from their boisterous activities.

I was continually surprised when the students would show up completely unprepared for lessons, carrying no pens, pencils, or books. There was a particular group of boys and girls who were already quite hardened to life and who accepted no amount of guidance. The boys would almost always skip class and instead wander the corridors in search of their own entertainment. Unfortunately, that entertainment consisted of accosting anyone they found alone. That even included the staff and teachers,

Chapter 12: Transition

whom they harassed relentlessly, because they knew that the law would favour them if they made any false accusation of abuse. I soon found that I was not immune to their torments. On one particular occasion, one of the rougher girls in this gang shoved me up against a window and threatened to thrust me straight through the glass in retaliation for my having reprimanded her during class. When I made a complaint to the administration, I was told there was no recourse since it had happened without any witnesses besides her group of friends, who, they assured me, would lie for her.

My personal living situation got settled pretty quickly. I found a small flat to rent in a multi-story building in an ideal location. It was near the train station and bus depot, as well as several grocers and banks. The floor plan consisted of a front social room (which also served as a second bedroom), a proper bedroom, kitchen, and bathroom. My flat was on the ground floor, and the flat below ground level was occupied by a number of African men living together in a place of similar design and size. The men, though packed in together and sometimes rowdy, were courteous whenever we met. But I was still very fearful of strange men, especially when they were in groups, so I always kept my distance.

While the place was cramped and dingy, it served my purposes. I dismissed my disappointment by reminding myself that the flat was simply a stopgap along the journey to my great life in London. Still, I greatly missed all the luxuries of the home I had abandoned back in Jamaica, and I began to worry about what conditions my family would be expecting to live in when they finally arrived. On our weekly phone calls, I tried to paint a picture of life in the UK and how it differed from the life we lived back home. To be frank, I am not sure that you can grasp the difference unless you actually live in it. All I could do was try and brace them for what was to come. Would they condemn me as a failure when they found no king size bed with Egyptian cotton sheets, en-suite bathroom, or walk in closet?

When I moved in, I got a better appreciation for just how dirty the last tenants had left the place. The carpets were thoroughly soiled and there was a prevalent underlying odour of mould that began to cling to everything I owned. I had no money to clean it, but I was also working so many extended hours at the school, doing after school clubs and extra *free* sessions with my students, that this didn't allow me any time to care about it. I had managed to make a friend among my colleagues at the school. Another young teacher named Soha, who immediately proved herself a trustworthy confidante. It was she who recognised that the struggle with my finances could be resolved by getting a flat mate to share the cost of rent. Even though Jasmine and Kem would be joining me, I was seriously struggling to pay the bills, and my circumstances would be even more burdened with their arrival. My first reaction to her recommendation was horror. Without thinking, I argued that it was impossible. I was a woman, I was a mother and a wife, and I owned my own luxurious home back in Jamaica. "Communal living was for youngsters who were just starting out," I stated flatly. She simply looked me straight in the eye and asked me if I had really just described myself. She also explained that she knew that the agency wouldn't be paying up front, so I would need to wait some time for my first paycheque, and that it often took longer than expected to get international banking matters resolved.

I was utterly frustrated to realise that she was right. I had very little money left from the loan I had taken from my friend Jos. I really had no choice but to get a flat mate if I were going to be able to stay in the dirty little hovel I had managed to acquire. I put out an advert in the free local paper but had little time to devote to vetting interested parties. Ultimately, I accepted the first woman who turned up in person and agreed to pay the amount I asked for. If I had been thinking straight, I would have realised right away that person was not someone I would have chosen to live with under any other circumstances. But given my situation, I didn't have much of a choice.

My flat mate had grown up in the local ghetto, much like I had, but the similarities ended there. Where I spent my days and nights tirelessly working to improve my situation, she sat around primping for social outings. Her mass of bleaching creams, coloured wigs, and scanty outfits took up a large portion of the front room. She was up at all hours of the night and would frequently return loudly from a boisterous night out in the wee hours of the morning, which affected my sleep and made settling into my new work routine a challenge. I made a mental note that professionals must flat share with like-minded professionals.

Much like a marriage, a successful union of flat mates relied on compatibility in the majority of things. The situation with my flat mate could not last, and I realised that the flat itself was absolutely unsuitable for my arriving family. I had settled into my role at the school and started to feel confident with the town itself, so I started looking for a new place where my daughter and sister could move with me. It was the end of September and they were expected to arrive in less than a month.

In the meantime, I began readying the dingy flat for the possibility of our needing to live there—minus the flat mate, of course, as she was now behaving in ways that I found harmful for my sister and daughter to be around. She was also an illegal immigrant, I came to learn later, and that could be detrimental to my own immigration standing in the country. I certainly could not risk that. I missed my daughter immensely, so getting the house prepared for her made me happy in a way that nothing else had since my arrival. There wasn't a great deal I could do with the flat, but I began to clean as much as possible. I was like a new mother who was nesting before the birth of her baby. I freshened up the foul carpet, obtained a nice, but cheap, duvet cover and some soft, plush toys. I even sought out ethnic food shops to gather some familiar foods, to help ease their introduction to that new life. I also learnt where the libraries, parks, schools, and churches were located.

As my excitement mounted, October seemed to approach at the pace of a snail. My flat mate was given notice of the arrival of my family, so we would be sharing tighter than we already were doing now. I began calling home frequently and spending all of my extra money on phone cards. Finally, the day arrived when they would land at Heathrow. There was no way I was going to let them experience the isolation and uncertainty I had when my flight had landed. I jumped in a taxi headed for the airport. It felt like I was driving across the country instead of just across town. In my anxiousness, I managed to arrive at the airport several hours early, but I didn't care. I was just thrilled to finally be reunited with my baby girl.

After their flight had landed, the arrivals area became thick with people awaiting the arrival of their loved ones from the interior. I couldn't see past the crowds and was afraid I would miss Jasmine and my sister. As I craned my neck to look above the mass of people ahead of me, I heard an all too familiar voice saying, "Excuse me, has anyone seen my mum? Where is my mum?" I flew through the crowd towards the little angelic voice of my daughter who was now four years old. There she was—such a big girl, confidently walking into the arrivals area, decked out in her denim jacket and matching jeans and a dainty pink bow laced through her hair. I flung my arms open wide, and she landed in them like a little angel settling onto a cloud. We hugged in a deep, long embrace, and I felt complete. Suddenly, it didn't matter how much I disliked that massive city and its strange culture; my life was filled with sunshine because my daughter was back with me.

I next grabbed my sister in a strong embrace, and we headed out together to face the challenges that London had to offer. On the ride to our flat, I could see the looks of amazement and trepidation on their faces as they scanned the city outside of the cab's windows. I was reminded of my first day here, and I became even more determined to ensure that their experience would be easier than mine had been. They told me all about the flight and the newness of all they'd experienced while crossing the Atlantic. I told them about my job and the town in which we would be living. The chattering continued when we got to the flat. My sister updated me on all the community news I had missed since September. We stayed up so late into the night that the cold began to creep in from the outside. Even though I had the front room cleared and set up for my sister to live in—thankfully my flat mate had moved—we all snuggled in my bed together that night and fell asleep.

Neither Jasmine nor my sister cared about—or maybe didn't even realise—the poor state of the flat or the neighbourhood in which we were staying. Even though it met none of the high standards I had made them accustomed to back in Jamaica, they showed me that the only thing that mattered was that we were together again. As I drifted off to sleep that night, happier and more fulfilled than I thought possible, I began to think about the next big thing we needed to prepare for. Tobore was coming in December.

The presence, support, and comfort of family are the best remedy for the soul.

CHAPTER 13: READJUSTMENTS

Readjustments can sometimes feel like a crisis on self-esteem.

The adjustment of us all living together in the small flat took some time. I managed to get Jasmine registered at the neighbourhood school and helped Kem find a job nearby, which was literally a two-minute walk from our home. I was pleased to see how quickly these two girls acclimatized, and it served to inspire me in the same vein. Certainly, just having had my two beloved family members by my side made London feel less like an island of banishment and more like our home. Even though I was still working long hours at the school, I took odd jobs like newspaper rounds and some cash-in-hand roles to get the extra income we would need to be able to afford an adequately sized place that would accommodate the three of us, as well as my husband when he arrived in December.

I was excited about Tobore's arrival, but also somewhat apprehensive. I felt we were strong enough individuals to overcome all the hurt that had passed between us and mend the frayed connection. My prayers were that our relationship would work out, since we would have left our major problems back in Jamaica. In fact, I believed we had already forgiven each other for all of our past transgressions and were ready to move on. Accepting the reality of his other child and suppressing my sense of utter betrayal had been hard, but knowing that he was sitting at home equally excited about coming to join me eased my pain.

As December rushed towards us, I became more comfortable making the types of phone calls to just simply say, "I miss you." One morning, when I had quickly finished getting ready for work and had a few extra minutes, I ducked into one of those iconic red telephone boxes and made such a call, even though it was two a.m. in Montego Bay. I still remember the smile that was on my face as I held the phone to my ear, waiting to hear the sleepy voice of the man who had recaptured my heart. But to my surprise, a friend of his answered the phone, telling me that Tobore had gone out for a walk and had left his phone behind. Something in his tone piqued my feminine intuition, and I knew I was being lied to. After all, I knew my husband well enough to know that he did not have the dreamy spirit of a poet who went for contemplative walks on the beach in the middle of the night.

As I hung up, my mind immediately went to the memory of the day before I'd left for London, when his "baby mama" had been beating at his front door and screaming in heartbroken anguish. My fingers moved over the phone's number pad without me consciously moving them. I dialed her number. She answered on the third ring and my number must have shown on her screen because she simply said, "Babe, it's for you," as she handed Tobore the phone.

To be perfectly honest, I don't recall exactly what else transpired on the phone call after that moment. I do, however, remember how I physically felt. All of the hope I had for our relationship wafted up and out of my body, like steam rising from a boiling pot. All the dreams I'd carried inside my heart, that had buoyed me through the past months, disappeared into nothingness. Blackness started to close in around me and I nearly passed out; the phone slipped from my grasp and clanged sharply on the glass pane of the telephone box enclosure. I managed to keep myself upright as I staggered out of the phone booth and made my way to my school for the workday. I cried the entire walk.

My mind was spinning. How could Tobore have done that to me—to us—right after we had agreed to start over? How could he so blatantly disrespect all the hard work I was doing to set up our new life? All I had done to ensure that his own transition would be easier than mine had been? The night we'd spent together before I left, we had made a solemn promise to one another. Recommitting ourselves to the marriage vows we had taken so many years before. He broke that promise. I was so distraught that when I arrived at work, I didn't care what the kids did that day. I allowed most of my classes to simply do their own thing. I sat at my desk in a near comatose state. I just stared at the floor and tried not to dissolve into tears. I couldn't have been more relieved when the day finally ended.

Back at home that night, I didn't speak to anyone, and I couldn't eat. I just wanted to shut the world out. In my mind I reviewed all the conversations Tobore and I had shared since my arrival in London. I searched desperately for any clues as to his true intentions, anything that I might have blinded myself to. Eventually, I called a friend back home in Jamaica. I needed to unload my misery and find some support, but the conversation only led to my learning that Tobore had gone back to his lover's bed the day after my flight left. I think he was having his cake and eating it too. I also recalled in our early days of dating he always said he wanted to live in the UK or Switzerland, and in that moment it all made sense. I felt betrayed by them both and was left wondering what the fuck I had done with my life again.

Even though I was disgusted at the thought of Tobore coming to join us, I continued to look for a house that would fit our family. In November, I located a two-bedroom maisonette that was tiny, but a vast improvement over our dingy little flat. There was a garden in the back and a charming corner bathroom right off the kitchen. I never could get used to the English design of putting the toilet beside the kitchen, but until I could afford to design my own home, I would have to live with the style that was normal in that country. In fact, many things that were normal fixtures in a middle-class home in Jamaica were considered amenities accompanied by a premium price in London, including the en-suite bathroom, a power shower (which sometimes simply meant a shower head), a garden, dedicated or merely convenient parking, double glazed paneling, and central heating.

Chapter 13: Readjustments

The perception of England back in its previous colony, a largely poor one, was that the motherland had streets paved with gold. While my expectations on arrival were not quite so luxuriant, they were certainly higher than what I had been exposed to so far. I came to realise the importance in the distinction between how things appeared when one was on holiday and how they actually were for the full-time working citizens. Despite all my petty complaints, the maisonette was the best that my budget could afford.

My sister Kem, Jasmine, and I moved in, and we instantly fell in love with our new, clean place. We were cramped, but cozy. In addition, despite what had transpired between Tobore and his lover, he had told me that he was still planning to join us. I began to dread what was in store. Were we soon to be back enduring each other's company in a broken relationship with no hope of survival? I was not going to be the one to stop his visa and deny his entry. That was just not in my DNA. So, I allowed it. I guess I was just too soft, and at the time, broken in some respects. My pride was bruised, as I took him back after all that, and this was my repayment. It wasn't a nice place to be.

December arrived before I knew it, and I found myself in a cab on the way to the airport to pick him up. I was surprised to find that a part of me was still happy to know that he was finally arriving after all that time. Maybe Jasmine's excitement for her daddy's arrival had rubbed off on me. Jasmine and my sister joined me on the trip to the airport, and to a stranger's eyes, we made a very joyous welcoming party. The journey home was more subdued and reflected the true feeling, or lack thereof, between my husband and me.

Over the next six months we made a somewhat valiant effort to rekindle our unconditional love for one another, but all our interactions were tainted with the mistrust of the past. I did try to identify exactly what our fundamental problems were so that we could attack them head on. But looking back, I realise I was too close to the situation to be able to carry out that kind of self-assessment in a productive manner. The clarity of hindsight, supported by the years in between then and now, in which I have matured, has allowed me to see what my faults were in the crumbling of our marriage.

I suffered greatly from low self-esteem, which had been further weakened by my experience with the attackers that had caused me to flee Jamaica in the first place. I had always felt inadequate next to Tobore, with him being from such a strong and wealthy family compared to my own. But then I also felt somewhat unworthy of him. I was plagued by the feeling that I had failed as a wife. I blamed myself for him straying into the arms of another woman and creating another child. With the move to London, I felt that I was failing him even then. I felt that I was the one who moved him from our luxurious life to a struggle for survival in a strange country without our families or lifelong friends.

We endured a tense life under the same roof for about six months, with no progress being made towards each other. Then one night, during the last weeks of the spring term at my school, our frustrations with one another came pouring out in a massive argument. At the end we were both physically and emotionally exhausted, and I knew we could not go on like that without utterly destroying ourselves. In the silence that followed, I was the first to speak: "I will move out of the flat." I was not prepared to live this unhappily anymore. It wasn't what I came here for. If I had moved from Jamaica to the UK and survived, I could get through this too by moving towns or boroughs. Tobore was independent. He had a job and could look after himself, so he was not my responsibility anymore.

Within a few short days, I had secured another two-bedroom flat and moved my sister, Jasmine and myself into it. I had settled with Jasmine into one of the two bedrooms so that Kem could have a room to herself. However, as our move-in day progressed, Kem never showed up after she removed her things from the flat we were vacating. As the afternoon wore on and I'd had no contact with her, I began to get nervous. "Oh, God, please don't let this be Jamaica all over again, where Kem left me to foot the whole bill, but was also an emotional letdown," I pleaded in silent prayer. I certainly did not have the income to afford that flat by myself. I calmed myself by rerunning all the conversations we'd had in the previous days, when she had constantly assured me that she would stay with us and had helped pick out something we could afford on a two-person income.

As evening began to fall, Kem finally called. My heart sank as I listened to her tell me that she had decided at the last minute to move in with her friend instead of Jasmine and me. Her words were a slap to my face. I reasoned with her about the rental contract that I had signed with the agreement that she was to live with us. Her answer was only to suggest that I abandon the new flat and find a smaller one that I could afford without her. When I explained again how that was impossible because I would lose all of the money I had deposited, she remained unmoved.

If I broke the rental agreement, I would have no money for a deposit on another place, so I went ahead and stayed in the flat with the knowledge that I had to find a flat mate, and quick! Luckily, the advert I put out in the next day's paper was answered promptly by a lovely white girl from Yorkshire named Jenna. Before we knew it, she moved in, and I finally felt some relief from my financial worries. Jenna wasn't the cleanest person, but she tried. She was kind-hearted and helped out as much as she was able to. For example, she would wash her dishes, but she never remembered to rinse the soap off them. I would have to go back and rinse anything in the cabinets so that Jasmine and I wouldn't get sick from eating the soap residue. She never thought to clean the bathroom, and I often felt like I was cleaning up after two children in my spare time. I began to picture myself as a child, doing endless chores every waking hour when not in the classroom, and I became convinced that my lot in life was to clean up after others. Still, I couldn't complain because she was always on time with her rent.

When spring rolled around that year, it blew Kem onto our doorstep, asking to move in with us because she no longer had any place to stay. Of course, I could not leave her out in the cold. Jenna was still occupying the second bedroom and paying her part of the rent, so there was no room, even if I had wanted to forgive my sister so quickly. I told her that I could not make my flat mate vacate the house, and explained that there was no room. It would also be terribly inappropriate of me to cram another person in the single bedroom that Jasmine and I shared.

Not surprisingly, Kem was quite upset with me. She cried and said that she was in need, that I was her blood, that she had come to rely on me as her fortress of protection when the world was not treating her kindly. It pained me to see that, but I had no option. I had to harden my heart and realise the truth in what everyone had always tried to tell me. That I was a softie in general, even more so when it came to my sister, and she knew it and often abused it.

Still, I could not absolutely turn her away. I told her that I would find someone else who could help her out and provide a temporary, or even permanent, place for her to stay.

Tobore had recently moved out of the flat we had rented together, and I had helped him find a flat to rent through the woman who owned the house. Even though their situation was cramped, I thought that they might be able to accommodate one more person. I made the call, and within thirty minutes, the whole situation was resolved, and Kem had somewhere she could live temporarily.

That stressful situation made me reflect on the freedom that came with owning one's own home. I missed having my own place terribly. The move to London had proved regressive in so many ways. I had stepped backwards in my career and was living more like a college student than a woman who was a mother and provider. I decided that I needed to get my life together and focus on buying my own place. But this was hard, as the monies owed to me in Jamaica were not forthcoming, and the house was now tenanted but just enough to pay the mortgage back in Jamaica. So, my focus had to be on making money here to buy a place regardless of how tiny it would be. I knew I would have to rely on my traits of perseverance and determination to make my dream come true. I mentioned my new plan in passing conversations to some of my friends and was told to calm down because I was being too ambitious for my own good.

"After all," they said, "you have only just come to Britain in the past year, and so many others have been here for years and years and they still cannot buy a house." I didn't know anything about these other people, so I began planning how to make that idea work out.

Perseverance can be the platform on which goodness is staged.

CHAPTER 14: WEAPON

The most significant weapon people can use against us is our own mind.

I was shocked to find out at the end of the school year that my salary had not been divided on a twelve-month schedule, and that staff provided through an agency were not considered for work during the summer holiday. It meant no pay over the summer holidays. Damn, my heart froze wondering where the hell I would find the resources to survive over the summer.

I also found out that I was still considered a temporary worker, known as a "supply teacher," provided by an employment agency; Someone the administration could choose not to extend on contract for the next school year. I understood why the agency had decided to hide that fact. Who in their right mind would have given up their whole life and journeyed more than forty-five hundred miles to take an unstable job that could be revoked after only a few months? I began to panic when I thought about how I was going to be able to afford our monthly rent, and I lamented that I would never be able to save up to make my dream of purchasing a home a reality.

I was anxious to prove myself to the school in any way possible so that they would see what a good worker I was. I needed them to consider me an indispensable part of their teaching staff who should be hired on a permanent basis with a salary increase. I took on all sorts of extra duties and never said no to any requests that were made of me. That was difficult since I also needed to take on other jobs, such as cleaning homes in my spare time, for additional income (cash-in-hand was always a savior, as I tried not to jeopardize my visa conditions). I was still trying to save up for the months in the summer when I would be unemployed or add to the savings for a down payment on a house.

Because of all the extra duties I was doing at the school, I had made a request of the deputy head teacher to please consider an increase in my salary, which was lower than that of the staff teachers. Instead of getting a response to my request, I was told by the head of the faculty that I had been assigned to run an after-school club, in addition to all the other things I was doing on a voluntary basis. I didn't argue, and instead called the agency to see if they had heard anything about my status at the school or whether an increase in my salary was at a negotiation stage. The answer was a resolute, "No, we haven't heard from the school at all in the past five months."

Since it appeared that nothing was going to get done without me pushing it forward, I scheduled a meeting with the head of the faculty to discuss the disproportionate level of my workload and compensation. When we met, I was ready to use the extra club assignment as a bargaining chip in my negotiations, but she quickly shot that idea down. I was told that although clubs were technically voluntary, I wasn't employed in a position that allowed me to turn it down, and that it was being assigned to me. She ended by firmly stating, "That is the role of the Food Technology teacher."

I was absolutely frustrated! Even though I didn't mind running a club for the students, it was unfair that I was expected to take it on without any consideration for my desire or time.

Unfortunately, the head of faculty was right. I wasn't in any position to deny that assignment or bargain for something better. They had me over a barrel. I had to accept whatever situation they put me in, regardless of the blatant unfairness of my doing equal or more work than the permanent staff, while getting paid much less as a supply teacher. My work permit was tied to that school. My conversation with the head of staff had left me far too timid to fight back and potentially lose everything I had worked so hard for.

During my short time at the school, I had already seen numerous other supply teachers come and go. Since I was so busy and their tenures so short, I was never able to become friends with any of them and ask how they planned to survive the summer break with no pay. I started thinking about what other type of job I might be able to find for the six-week period but remembered that my visa had a stipulation that forbade both work for any other entity besides the agency that brought me in or recourse to public funds.

With that realisation, I gathered up my courage and went to the head teacher to ask if there was any way that the school could pay me a retainer fee for the summer holidays, to make up for the absolute lack of income I was to have during that time. I was disappointed, but not surprised, when she told me no. I called the agency again to find out if there was anything I could do to avoid the situation of financial stress that was impending, but was told that these terms had been explained to me before I'd arrived. I was in no position to argue, as I had been in such a fragile mental state when I had accepted the job. For all I knew, they had detailed every last bit of their policy, and I had simply not understood it. I didn't blame myself too much. After all, I would have never imagined that anyone would have set up a system in which they expect people to stay tied to an employer who does not provide any work for a part of the year, and then restrict the employee's ability to do anything else gainful during that off period. Thankfully, Tobore gave me some small allowance to cater to Jasmine's food needs, but I will never understand men—they don't seem to realize that a child needs more than food; they need a roof and so much more.

The one good thing about my job at the school was that the official workday ended at half past two. This meant that I could dash off to pick up my daughter at the end of her school day and sometimes take her to some of my after-school clubs, even if I had other after-school duties to attend to later in the day. I focused on that fact and decided not to let myself get depressed about the other things that were out of my control. Before I knew it, summer was upon us. I knew the next six weeks were going to be tough, and I prayed that God would bring us a miracle by stretching the little bit of money I had managed to save so that we could eat and keep a roof over our heads. It was hard, and I mean strenuously hard. It meant watching what we ate, shopping around for bargains, and staying in as much as we could to save money. If we ventured out, it had to be somewhere free like the park, which we could walk to, or just a stroll. It was living on a shoestring. Switching off the sockets when not in use to save on the electrics, and cooking once or twice a week to save fuel, something that was so foreign to me. I hated stale food but desperate times call for desperate measures and we were, in fact, in desperate times. I did not like school much but prayed that the summer would end for one reason and one reason only: to be paid.

The time off passed relatively quickly, and I returned to work on the first day of the autumn term. Things progressed without incident, and I was saving every penny that came into my hands. Before I knew it, I had saved up enough to start looking for a small house in the area that I could afford to buy. I found one and was thrilled to start the process of securing a mortgage.

As that part of my life began to come together, my life at work started to unravel. A tension had grown between the head teacher and me. It stemmed from the disagreements we'd had at the end of the spring term. I wouldn't have minded if the tension had remained unspoken, but I started to notice that the head teacher was acting on her displeasure with me. Several other employees who were much newer to the department were suddenly offered promotions, and I was completely unaware of the process by which they were selected for that honour. That baffled me, especially because I had been designated as a form teacher—one who performed with excellence and was given newly qualified teachers (known as NQTs) to shadow them to learn the job. I loved being a form teacher, and I was quickly assigned many NQTs because I was able to form such great relationships with my students and I was a great example for them to learn from.

However, before I could use that as an argument to support my request for a similar promotion, there was an unfortunate and unfair incident that occurred, involving a boy in my class who had HIV and me falling on my sword. The boy's infection status was strictly confidential, and as far as I knew, the NQTs were not privy to that information. Because of that policy, I neither spoke to my newest NQT about the sensitivity of that information, nor provided her guidance in how to handle it. By the end of her first week, I found out that she had told the entire NQT group of the boy's illness, and I was furious! I spoke to her in private about the issue, but I could not calm down over her immaturity and the injustice that had been done by it.

My disappointment and anger did not subside, and it showed itself in my interactions with her. In the end, I was called up by my supervisor and reprimanded for my behaviour towards the NQT. I didn't want to make the situation worse than it was, so I didn't explain why I was so angry. Her behaviour would have cost her job and ruined her entrance into a teaching career. I took full responsibility for my behaviour towards the NQT and remained quiet on everything else. The meeting was attended by the assistant deputy head teacher, a fellow Jamaican who had immigrated many years before and who had abandoned all traces of her heritage. As the meeting ended, and I sat contrite in my chair with my head held low, she gave a single comment. Her biting advice to me was to get rid of the Jamaican attitude I carried, thinking that I was better than others.

That situation threw me over the edge. I no longer wanted to work under these conditions. I went home that evening and called the immigration department just to enquire how I could apply for my own visa so that I could be freed from the enslavement that I was in. I wanted to get

Chapter 14: Weapon

out of the constraints of being tied to the school or agency. I didn't want to be a caged bird anymore; I wanted to fly and be free to do so. But I knew doing so was risky, as I would certainly be flagged as a visitor with questionable intent. The immigration representative told me the steps involved, but also warned me that there were no guarantees and that my application may in fact damage my future plans related to my current status. She explained that by starting the process, I would lose the four years that had been granted in the original visa, and my stay would be valid for only one year. I didn't care at that point and just wanted out of the bind I was in with that job that felt like indentured servitude.

Starting the process required a reference from my current employer. That would be tricky as it would alert them to my wanting to leave their employment, and I was worried they wouldn't let me go, as I was basically cheap labour. I decided to tell them that I was requesting the reference to continue my studies to get a bachelor's in business administration. In the end, the deceit actually worked in my favour without my planning it, because I found out that my original degree wasn't accredited, and I had to get another degree that the British regulatory bodies would recognise.

My real plan, however, was to take the letter of recommendation to the home office to apply for my own visa. I filled out the application for the "highly skilled" visa, and my stay time was immediately reduced to one year. When I told my friends and family, their only response was that I must be mad. They asked why I had decided to limit myself to one year, when I was struggling enough with the ability to try to make a successful go of that move in four years. I, on the other hand, felt like a slave that had just been freed. I didn't even care about the mortgage application and the fact that I could be granted the mortgage any time from now and maybe couldn't even provide any further financial paper work needed. My freedom mattered more than any security or a house at that time. I was not going to stop the application, as the gods may shine down on me and grant me this home. At least, that was my background thinking.

The next day, I went to the head of faculty and told her I was thinking of resigning. I was arrogant, maybe, but wanted her to know she no longer had a hold over me. That her shackles were off, only she didn't know that, so I was here to educate her, I suppose. She sat back and looked at me with an emotionless expression on her face. She advised me in a cool voice to seriously consider my immigration status before I made any decisions. I told her that, as a matter of fact, I already had considered it, and I had found a way where it wouldn't be a problem. She made no reply, but merely raised her eyebrow in curiosity while her mouth turned down in a hint of displeasure. I could suddenly see my situation with clarity. I knew that the visa status was a way of holding workers like me as prisoners. I felt confident in my decision to get out of that place before it destroyed me.

I went home feeling rather pleased with myself, knowing I had gotten the best of my jailers. I knew it was ego, but I didn't care. I was so proud of myself for finding a way out of that restrictive mess I was in. I realised that I could use the head of my department to my benefit in that situation as well. That man had been a completely ineffective manager, who needed to justify his position by assigning pointless tasks and publicly berating the staff beneath him. He was intensely jealous of the relationships I had established with many of the pupils and teachers, where he, on the other hand, had not. The students recognised him for what he was and wouldn't warm to him.

A week before, I had handed in some students' end of term reports, but he refused to accept them because he wasn't happy with the way I had structured one of the sentences. Even though I knew there was nothing grammatically wrong with the passage, and I'd double-checked it with the head of the English department, he insisted that I change the sentence. If I didn't, he threatened that would cause my report to be delayed and that I would be written up for tardiness. I was certain he was acting out of his displeasure with the recent NQT issue, of which he had limited understanding. Because of that, I refused to change the sentence just for the sake of appeasing his unnecessary demand.

When he realised that I had not cowed to him, he came rushing down the corridor where I was talking with some of my year eleven pupils. He was yelling and flailing his arms at me, reprimanding me for being disobedient, as if I were a child. I was incensed at his audacity in such a public setting, and I sank to his level, shouting back until we were engaged in a full-force shouting haggle. I stood my ground, refusing to change the grammatically correct sentence just to meet his preference. I left school that day in a huff and listened to the advice of a colleague in my department to take the next day off as a sick day to let the situation calm down. Unfortunately, my absence just made the issue worse.

When I went back to work the following day, I was immediately called into the office of the assistant head of faculty and told that I had been labelled as disobedient. This was now going to be added to my employment file with the school, and it would be nearly impossible to live that down. I was so disheartened by the unfairness that I wanted to take the day off again, but several other teachers happened to be out so I was told that there was no way they could forgive me if I left that day. I gave in and attended to my classes. As the afternoon approached, however, I was called into a meeting with one of the school's deputy heads, who explained that my absence the day before proved I was a waste of the school's funds. I tried to stand up for myself, and we entered into a debate. She wasn't being fair, and I felt too hurt and mistreated. I resigned on the spot, without even considering that I had just signed the paperwork for a mortgage on my first home in the UK.

As soon as I calmed down, I realised what a tremendous mistake I had made while I was in a snit. I berated myself for once again not being able to handle conflict gracefully and mindfully. But that's who I was, a young woman who ran from conflict rather than facing it head-on and fighting the battle to the end. The day was just around the corner when Jasmine and I would complete our sale agreement and move into the house I had just gotten a mortgage for. Yet, at that point, I had no idea how I was going to pay for it. My head raced with the fear of our situation. I wondered if there were any way I could call the mortgage company and cancel the sale, but I knew everything was done. The papers were all signed, and I was holding the key to another burden in my life.

Ego can ignite a satisfaction deep within us, regardless of the consequences.

CHAPTER 15: PRISON

Money is a prison for those born without it.

The first month my mortgage was due came quickly, and there had been very little work where I could earn money. I was unaccustomed to the employment practices of the UK, and I didn't realise I could register with multiple agencies to increase my chances of finding employment. Gradually, I became savvier and the work began to trickle in. By the beginning of November, I had worked only a total of three weeks over the previous two months. December wasn't any better, and I only managed to find work on four days out of the entire month.

Our savings were rapidly dwindling down to nothing, and I asked myself continually how I could have been so stupid and egotistical to put us in that situation. The proud part of me would always retort, "How dare they treat you that way?" Certainly, I had grown up poor, but I had dignity, and I was sure that they were cheating me at that school. But, in my anger and haste, I had robbed myself. No one had forced me out; that was all my own doing.

The jobs I found through the other agencies were in the teaching profession. But instead of getting a classroom of pupils that I would teach on a daily basis, I found myself running from school to school. One day I would be assigned to a school in East London, the next day I would be in the north, and the next in the southwest. I felt dizzy and unsettled at the constant moving about, but I couldn't complain because the bills were being paid. For the second time in the UK, I lamented that I had given up stability for instability. I was immersed in the life of supply teaching and I just had to deal with it.

The high school I was assigned to next was set in an immigrant area of the city and was largely composed of students that were from African nations. I learned the lesson that day that sharing a skin colour does not equate sharing a culture. The children were louder than I had ever experienced. Every conversation was carried out at the top of one's voice. I kept trying to shush them in the hope of creating the Jamaican decorum. One of the permanent teachers watched my fruitless efforts for a while and then came over to explain to me that in many cultures in Africa, talking softly in the presence of other people was considered extremely rude because it indicated that you were trying to secretly talk about the others around you. Loudness was the African decorum.

There was one African boy in my classroom that was surprisingly louder than all the others. When I tried to engage him in the lesson, he instead focused on my obvious West Indian heritage and began making a slew of disparaging remarks about people from my region. I addressed him by explaining that I may be Jamaican by birth, but I was African by origin.

He was pleased with my remark, announcing to the class that it was a good thing to hear that I embraced my origin, but that some in the Caribbean didn't.

I used the opportunity to explain to the class that it might be due to the fact that our fellow Africans had sold us into slavery and that's how we wound up in the Caribbean in the first place. Many people have forgotten that to this day. I was shocked by his retort. He said that all the Africans who were sold into slavery were the lowest and the weakest of their people. They weren't good enough to be worthy of staying with the better part of their race. His prejudiced attitude made me want to vomit even more than being faced with a mentally impaired teenager the day before, who had pooped on himself and managed to smear the mess all over. My heart was sick too, because I knew that ignorant kid's views echoed what he heard at home. I wondered to myself if there was any hope for the future. That experience was not my only introduction to prejudice that day. During a science lesson that I was sent to cover for a teacher who had fallen ill, I was happy to find a Jamaican girl among the pupils. However, one of the boys in the classroom was very focused on bullying her. Right in front of me, he announced that all Jamaicans were born with a criminal record. I could not believe what was going on in that school! I felt like many of these children already had poisoned minds at a young age.

Since my career as a supply teacher provided no permanent job, I became very frugal, saving for the ever-present possibility of there being no work on any given day. I took any job I was offered, in fear of the same eventuality. One day in October 2006, I didn't receive the usual early morning call for a placement. Instead, I used the morning to attend a parent-teacher conference at my daughter's school. When I arrived, the teacher showed me a poem that Jasmine had written. The poem was entitled "ANGER." While the teacher focused on the exceptional cadence and advanced word usage, I focused on the message and realised that this hectic existence I was leading interfered with my time with my child. The poem spoke to how angry she was feeling that mum was constantly rushing around, that we were not a family. In essence, she was not enjoying life in the UK.

I was not a neglectful mother by any stretch of the imagination. I never considered the time I spent with her as a sacrifice of my time that could otherwise be spent making income. I loved every minute we would spend in the evenings doing her homework or simply talking about her day over dinner. I decided that I had to carve out more time to ensure she felt that I was *fully* present, and we needed to do stuff together that counted and mattered to her. I was not going to allow the rat race to dictate my life. One day I would get to decide on my location, time, and freedom, but until then I was going to be the best mama I could be.

> **When all around you seems to be a whirlwind, just stand still and allow the calm to take effect. It will sort out the chaos.**

CHAPTER 16: UNBROKEN

Societies differ and can make or break you, so you must be mindful to stay unbroken, as those same societies will eject you if you are weakened.

The home I had purchased was a flat located on the third floor above a street-level café. At first glance from the street, it looked like an eyesore, but once I stepped inside, it was as if I had stepped into a charming cottage straight out of some fairy tale set in a hushed forest. However, I soon found out that serene calm only existed when the owner of the flat below was away from home. Turns out, the previous owner of my new flat had neglected to mention that his reason for selling was because of the nightmare neighbours that lived below.

My first encounter with reality came the day after we moved in. When I met those neighbours in the building's entrance, they were blatantly cold towards me. I thought they might be upset at the noise created by our move-in, but my apology was met with nothing more than a hostile dismissal. I soon found out from the neighbourhood gossip that these people hated all blacks and were very vocal about their dismay that "niggers" were coming into their building.

I handled the situation by steering clear of them whenever I saw them and making sure that our house was very quiet so they would not have anything to complain about. However, my attempts were all for nothing. These people wanted Jasmine and me out as soon as possible. I started receiving threatening and derogatory messages on my front door. Reporting them to the police didn't make much difference. We tried on numerous occasions but got literally nowhere.

So, I ignored them. I had hoped that their interest in getting rid of us would fade if they got no response. Instead, they began a more aggressive campaign. Back then, whenever I was in the building's common areas, no matter what hour of the day or night, the neighbours would suddenly appear with their pet Rottweiler in tow. They would leave just enough slack on the leash for him to run at us viciously while he snapped his jaws at us with only a centimetre or two to spare. They would even leave the dog in the stairwell, the only exit for my flat on the upper floor, so that Jasmine and I would be trapped in our home.

The situation only escalated from there and turned into an outright campaign of harassment and threatened violence against my young daughter and myself. I started to feel stressed and harassed all over, like when I left Jamaica. I had run away from one prison, but we found ourselves in yet another.

When the situation got too dangerously close to physical violence, or when I would fear for our lives, I would call the police. If for no other reason than to document the threats in case we were found dead in our apartment the next day. Unfortunately, that whole situation fell under the definition of a civil matter, and until the people caused bodily injury to us, there was nothing concrete that could be done by the authorities.

The threat of the neighbour's hatred and their snarling dog was as bad as the threat of the four gunmen I had fled in Jamaica. I was also under massive stress at that time to continue to afford the mortgage payments. Since my work was not stable enough, I found a flat mate to move in with us and ease that financial stress. The lady who answered my advert was kinder than I could have ever hoped for. Abina quickly become my confidante and dearest friend. She filled a place in my heart like a sister. Together, we bore out the trials with the downstairs neighbours.

Despite the fact that the troublesome neighbours would raise hell if even the smallest of noises crept out of our flat, they would routinely host all-night parties, often going on full-force until the sun started to lighten the morning sky. We simply tried to sleep through it all, but some nights were just too much. Both Abina and I had work the next day. On those nights, one of us would steel our nerves and go down to politely ask to have the blaring music turned down, explaining the late hour and our need for sleep. All we ever got in return was verbal assaults or threats that they were going to get the dog on us. Invariably, we would find used needles and alcohol bottles in the stairwell the next morning. The stench of marijuana would permeate our walls and cling to everything in our upstairs flat.

I worried constantly about Jasmine being exposed to the drug smoke that clouded the stairwell and wafted in through our adjoining ventilation system. Thankfully, Tobore had her sometimes, so she didn't have to endure this torment constantly.

The couple that occupied the downstairs flat fought with everyone they encountered, including their party guests and each other. The fights between the couple were epic! She was always drunk, and he was always high. During their most violent blow-ups, which always happened outside of their apartment door, I would have to intervene to help protect the young woman from the beating her partner was giving her. Yet, her gratitude never extended beyond the few minutes after she had been saved from his pummeling fists.

I never saw either one of these people keeping a routine work schedule. We soon figured out that neither held a job but lived off government subsidies for the disaffected. However, most of the social help they received was immediately translated into alcohol or drugs. The rest of their money went towards the latest technology and luxurious items I could only dream about having. It was shocking to see the material items those two could acquire while never holding down a job.

Meanwhile, Abina and I were working our butts off and struggling to make ends meet. By summer, I was really in financial trouble. Not only was I in arrears for the TV and the telephone bill, but I also had a large amount of debt on a credit card, for which I couldn't afford anything beyond the minimum payment. But things soon got worse when the bank holding my mortgage sent a certified letter stating their intent to take me to court over a complicated matter involving paid bills that were misclassified in their system and were accruing massive late fees and penalties. I would have to hire a lawyer to help me rectify the issue, which was growing more serious every day. Anyone who has dealt with a lawyer knows that not only do they cost significant money, but they also require a significant amount of time to adequately understand the situation they are addressing. My free time and every extra cent I had started going towards the lawyer.

Things were getting so bad that one morning, I had to spend the majority of the single pound I had left in my purse just for postage to send some required documentation to my lawyer. When Tobore dropped Jasmine off shortly after, I panicked with the thought of how I would be able to afford food for her. She would be hungry. The refrigerator was empty, and I only had twenty pence in my wallet.

The phone rang and I was greeted with a less than lucrative offer from one of the employment agencies I was registered with. The consultant asked me if I was available for work. When I said yes, she became very chipper. But I became more despondent as she talked. The work paid little, and I would have to pay her two hundred pounds out of each week's wages. On the face of it, the amount was paltry, but when you are living pound to pound, it adds up. I kept thinking how a full five days' fee would be two hundred pounds, which equated to one "cost" too many, or a portion of the week's groceries for us. But I wound up taking the job. People in my situation had no choice but to accept terms that in the end benefited others.

These experiences with temporary employment served to remind me of the importance of higher education. I recognised that having a solid education and a firm set of degrees behind your name were critical steps towards steady employment and a more secure life. I stressed these ideas to Jasmine and supported her in every educational pursuit. She excelled at her studies naturally, but I was always there to push her further so that her life would be easier than mine was.

The next teaching placement I was offered was in Luton, which was about an hour away from our home by train. I struggled with the idea of the long commute and how much of my time it would take away from all of the other things that needed my attention, but an old Jamaican adage kept creeping into my head: "When a man is drowning, even a moving mosquito is an option." However, my apprehension melted away when I heard that the job was permanent.

Before the lady from the agency provided any of the details of what the work would be, I accepted. I knew that whatever the tasks were, I would work my hardest to master them. All that mattered at that moment was that I was finally gainfully employed. I let out a joyous shout of praise to God.

Struggles can be medicinal.

CHAPTER 17: TEMPORARY BREAKDOWNS

While trying to carve out your own destiny, you sometimes leave dents in someone else's.

The new job afforded stability that I had not had since I'd first arrived in London. I was catching up on my bills and adjusting to the long commute. Things were finally starting to come together, and I was so relieved. But that calm was only a temporary break in the storm of my life.

Shortly after I started my new job, I received a frantic call from my family back in Jamaica with the news that my sister Anna had been picked up by the police and was currently sitting in a jail cell. At first, I didn't understand what I was being told. How could my nineteen-year-old sister be in jail?

I learned that after I'd left for London, she had run away from home. I immediately felt a twinge of guilt. I was the one who had made her move back into my mother's home before I left Jamaica. She had come to live with me after the attack, but she had cultivated a clandestine and age-inappropriate relationship with a much older boy who was my helper's relative. My only way to curb the situation, and hopefully stop her from getting pregnant or being taken advantage of anymore, was to send her back home.

Apparently, she was terribly unhappy back under my mother's thumb, and she absconded in the night only a few days after I had left for London. I was shocked that no one had bothered to share that news with me until now. The excuse was that none of the family knew where she was. They had reported her disappearance to the police, but even the police didn't seem very concerned about it. The general consensus was that she was just being a rebellious teenager.

However, now that she was locked up in jail for aligning herself with the wrong crowd, everyone realised the seriousness of the matter. When my mum called, I could tell from the tone of her voice that the situation was much worse than I had imagined from that first phone call. She said that the situation my sister was involved in was so scandalous that it was even being covered on the nightly national newscast.

I didn't need to hear another word. My family back home needed me, and I felt partially responsible for putting Anna on whatever path led her to that sad state. I used every last bit of credit I had to purchase a plane ticket back to Jamaica so that I could meet with the local bank and try to secure funds for her bail. I was not even worried about my overall fear of going home, as in that moment all I could see was that my sister needed me. I called in to take some days off of my new job, dropped Jasmine off with my sister, since Tobore worked shifts, and went on a mission to save Anna from the treacherous situation she had gotten herself into.

When I arrived in Jamaica, my plan was to stay with a few different trusted friends. But I was given a rude awakening when I tried to actually help—an unforeseen consequence of my having left the country. I had taken the title for my house in Jamaica to the bank to use as collateral for a loan to make the bail. But when I started to fill out the required forms, I was informed that I was ineligible to post bail due to my resident status in another country. I could not believe what I was hearing. There was nothing I could do for her.

With the bad news in hand, I went to visit my sister in the juvenile centre where she was being held. The sight that greeted me broke my heart. There she was, separated from me by thick black metal bars. Her eyes were wide with fear. I ached with the desire to save her, to tell her that I was there to take her away. When I told her that the law forbade me from helping her, she began to weep uncontrollably. The pain in my chest was tangible, like someone had scooped out my heart and left only a raw, gaping hole. I wanted so badly to hold her and tell her everything would be okay. But it wouldn't be. This, I could not fix.

When I left, I went immediately to my mum's home. Little by little, the circumstance of what had put Anna in that predicament came to light. They had found out that my sister had been living with some unsavoury people who had very bad reputations around town. Apparently, she had become intimately involved with a man who was on Jamaica's national most-wanted list of criminals. The news only got worse from there. People said that she was known to carry a gun and flash wads of cash around. I couldn't stop picturing the little girl I knew, play-acting as a character living in the wild, wild, west. The person they spoke of was not the Anna I knew.

That situation was nothing like a child's game of cowboys and Indians. As I sat and listened to an almost unfathomable tale, my mind drifted. I didn't want to hear it. I needed to distract myself. I began to take stock of my surroundings. My mum's place, while still humble, seemed much nicer than it had been when I was last there.

However, the matter at hand involving Anna completely overshadowed my curiosity about that. The conversations shared with different family members all ended the same way. Everyone lamented how embarrassing it was for our family as a whole. She had brought a great shame upon us, which flowed throughout the entire community. I was stunned to hear them speak of Anna in such a fashion. I was told that people were now openly accusing all of us of supporting and benefitting from her unsavoury exploits.

By evening's end, I finally got the full story about what led to her arrest. She had accompanied a group of boys when they went to rob a supermarket. Things got out of hand when the owners resisted, and the boys ended up killing them. They had almost gotten away with it, but the group was living in a rented home, and when they stopped paying the rent, the landlord sought to eject them from the property by reporting to the police that they had a stockpile of guns on the premises. When the police searched the house, they indeed found a multitude of guns and ammunition, some of which matched the evidence from the supermarket killings.

I couldn't believe what I was hearing. I felt like I must have fallen into some Hollywood thriller movie plot. How could that have been real? How could my very own sister, who was still a child, be involved in that sordid affair? Robbery? Murder? I couldn't make the information align with reality. My memory of little Anna was shattered. My guilt overwhelmed me. If I hadn't left, maybe . . .

In the end, I had to catch my plane back to London. There was nothing I could do for Anna, and my job and child were waiting for me back at our UK home.

My life in London continued as if the horrible plight that played out in Jamaica did not exist. I finally received word that Anna had been released and was living once more with my mum. She was on probation and needed to report to the police every day. My mum told me that she was very calm and quiet. She stayed at home and didn't even try to go out. We both expressed our relief that she must have learned her lesson and had been scared straight out of her dangerous lifestyle.

It quickly became apparent, though, that Anna wasn't merely acting out a penance to her wild ways. She was simply staying at home and sleeping a lot because she had a general sense of feeling unwell. We all equated her malaise to depression and didn't give it much thought beyond that. As the day of her trial approached, however, the family began to notice an alarming deterioration in her physical appearance. Again, we all thought it was due to the stress of the trial. Everyone believed the entire ordeal was taking its toll on her overall health. She was found not guilty of any of the charges. We were then sure she would perk up and start to feel better.

We were completely mistaken, however. Over the next few days after her trial finished, her health deteriorated at an alarming rate. She was unable to walk, and her body was covered in unexplained lumps. In fact, there was talk of voodoo possession of my sister. One of my other sisters called me in a panic, asking me to come home right away because they didn't know what to do but knew that something was terribly wrong. They had gone to visit several doctors, but none could come up with a diagnosis.

I had just surrendered my passport to the home office for my visa to get extended. I therefore couldn't make any trips outside of the country. I felt trapped and helpless. The news that came from home was worse every day. She couldn't walk, doctors couldn't fully diagnose, there wasn't any money for medical bills. It was overwhelming. Finally, God performed a miracle, and my passport, along with Jasmine and Tobore's, arrived at my house by post. I immediately went to the travel agent and bought plane tickets for Jasmine and myself.

I spent the next days packing and getting our London lives in order for the time we would be gone. The day before we were to leave, I was exhausted and fell into a deep sleep mid-afternoon. My nap was interrupted by the jangling of the telephone and the weight of my housemate, Abina, coming to sit beside me on the bed. Her hand on my shoulder was so gentle as she leaned in to whisper for me to wake up. Before I put the telephone receiver to my ear, I knew something was dreadfully wrong. It was one of sister's voices on the other end. She told me that Anna had just died.

I couldn't believe what I was hearing. How could that be? She had just been to a new doctor and they had again found nothing wrong with her. She had been scheduled for an exploratory surgery that morning. We all believed she would have had a diagnosis soon and would start the treatments for whatever was causing her illness.

I crumpled to the floor as the truth of what I was hearing sunk in. Even after my sister had hung up, I sat frozen on the wooden floor in my flat, unable to move or even hang up the phone. The disconnected buzzer alerted Abina to come and take the phone from my hand, but I never heard it.

When I was able to move again, I knew I had to change our tickets to fly out that night. Unfortunately, I could not simply change the flights. Instead, I would have to relinquish the old ones, apply for a refund, and purchase new ones. Since the refund would take up to eight weeks to be processed, I was stuck without the necessary funds to afford two flights. The only way I could afford to go home then was if I went by myself, leaving Jasmine with my sister Kem.

I travelled to Jamaica on my own and met with my family to bury our little sister. The funeral was a low-budget affair, and most of the cost was left to me since I was still the most successful of our family. It was also left up to me to identify her body in the morgue and to claim it for burial. While I picked through her clothing to choose something for her to spend eternity dressed in, I thought the sadness would kill me. I was also to deliver the eulogy at the funeral service. I was at a loss for words that could adequately describe the absolute tragedy of her last year of life. It was so unjust that she would not be allowed to live out her life and redeem herself in the community's eyes.

My poor mother was in so much distress; I began to fear for her health as well. Although I had grown up seeing her suffer the life of the desperately poor, that was nothing compared to the suffering she was experiencing now. The grief radiated from her. It permeated the entire family. I was again plagued with guilt for leaving my family to pursue a new life so far away. I couldn't stop wondering if Anna would still be alive had I only chosen a different life path. After the funeral, we received word from one of the doctors she had seen in the days leading up to her death that they had finally come up with a diagnosis—lupus. I also found out that she had been baptised in the church right before she'd died. She was merely nineteen years old.

She was gone too soon.

Death is a thief. It robs us of our loved ones and keeps a hold of all the person is and was.

CHAPTER 18: FIERCE

Some events in life can rob you of your soul, but our bodies function, nonetheless.

The death of my little sister changed my life in more ways than I could have imagined. I had become fiercely protective of my own child. I felt like I could leave nothing to chance when it came to her future well-being. I swore to myself that she would never find herself feeling unloved or unwanted. I wanted a kind of guarantee against her feeling the need to seek out security and intimacy from friends or lovers who could turn around and take advantage of her.

After we laid Anna to rest, the journey back to London was a hard one for me. Not only was I drowning in my sadness over that lost life, but I was also weighed down by the knowledge that I had spent my very last pennies on travel and funeral expenses. For the first week after I returned, I could think of nothing but memories of Anna. My heart ached with the unfairness of the situation. I cried out to God, asking why the young had to be taken.

Anna and I had shared a birthday, and I kept playing back the memories of all the celebrations we had shared together on that day each year. The memories were sweet, but caused as much pain as they did comfort. Both Anna and I had been born on the twenty-eighth of February, but when my birth had been registered, the officials had made a mistake and wrote February twenty-second on my birth certificate. It had never caused any problem, so the family just ignored it. But since my sister's death, I could no longer find joy in celebrating in her absence. As the years went

Chapter 18: Fierce

by, I just accepted the twenty-second as the day that was for me alone, burying all the happiness of the past along with my sister.

The Luton teaching job had fallen through due to my travel back to Jamaica. I was back at square one, waiting for the phone to ring each morning with news of any temporary position. The positions were very few and far between, so I registered with as many employment agencies as possible, not caring what the industry was that they served. I was ready to take any work, as long as it brought in money.

The first job offer I received was as a contracted cleaning lady for a large firm. Since there was nothing else coming my way, I swallowed my pride and forced myself to go in with a bright spirit. The whole way in, I chided myself for thinking that job was beneath me. After all, I took our rubbish out to the bin and dusted our house every week, how different could it be? Well, the answer to that question came the minute I met my new supervisor. Apparently, the job wasn't so much general cleaning, but was specifically scrubbing public toilets for ten hours.

When the supervisor told me about the job's sole duty, she gave me a swift look up and down, and commented that I wasn't dressed for the job. I must say I was happy to hear that, thinking that she would find another duty for me to earn the day's pay, but it was not to be. She dismissed me, despite my assurances that I was willing to do whatever they needed of me regardless of my attire.

As I left the building, my eyes were already stinging from trying to hold back the flood of tears. I felt like I had reached my lowest point. I couldn't even get a job as a toilet cleaner! By the time I reached the bus stop, the tears were running freely down my face. I couldn't get on the bus while I was blubbering like that, so I ducked under the bus shelter to get out of the rain and called my friend Jade for moral support. She comforted me, and we prayed that God would see me through that rough time. We prayed that He would lead me down the right path that would provide work for me and an income for my family.

Over the next several weeks, work opportunities continued to be scanty, so I began looking for alternative means to afford the basics of life, such as food and utilities. When I looked into the possibility of getting help from social services, however, I found that my immigration status inhibited me from receiving government-funded assistance. As I look back on those times, I cannot imagine how we survived, but we did. It was only by some miracle that there was always food in the refrigerator and light that came on when we flipped the switch. We must have had an angel following us around all of those days.

During that time, I worked very hard to conceal my emotional distress from my daughter. I wanted to spare her the burden of worry and my continued anxiety over our financial matters. She was only a child and needed to be focused on her studies and her friends. When I sunk so deeply into depression that I was having difficulty functioning in daily life, I took antidepressants to help lift me out of the blackness that was clouding my entire outlook on life. But the doctor's visits and medication added more strain on our nearly non-existent budget.

When I had finally reached the end of my wits and there was nothing left in my control, I lifted my voice in prayer, crying out to God to help us out of the hole I had dug us into in London. The next day, I got a call from the agency that had originally offered me the teaching job in far-away Luton. I couldn't believe my luck when the agency representative told me that the position was open again and it was still for employment on a permanent basis. There was no hesitation on my part that time. I took the job immediately and praised God for His mercy.

The distance I would be commuting back and forth each day necessitated childcare for Jasmine. For the hours she would be out of school, and that I would be travelling on the train. God was again merciful in that situation, and I found a Jamaican lady named Afua, who had lived in the UK for some time but had outstayed her visa, so she couldn't obtain employment otherwise. Unfortunately, the arrangement didn't work out for long.

After the first two weeks, she seemed to have lost enthusiasm for the job and started showing up later and later each day. Abina had a job that was closer to our home, so on the days she could stay longer than me, she waited for the lady to show up and take charge of Jasmine, who needed to be escorted to her school. Finally, the morning came when Afua never showed up. I was on the train, on my way to Luton, when Abina called to tell me that Afua had called to say she wasn't coming in at all that day.

I didn't know what to do and I was in a panic. I was halfway to Luton already, and there was no way I could get back home to Jasmine before Abina needed to be at work. Abina could hear the distress in my voice and she told me that she would call in late for work and escort Jasmine to school. I was so grateful; she was an angel sent by God. But I was still left with the problem of finding reliable care for Jasmine during my workdays. Unfortunately, the challenge proved insurmountable and I had to resign from my position in Luton shortly after.

Meanwhile, the contentious relationship with my downstairs neighbours was still going on full force and escalating by the day. The week after I had given up my permanent position in Luton, I had one of my most frightening encounters with them. I had decorated the stairwell on my landing as an extended area of our home. Besides the several plants I had cultivated to give a fresh feel to the atmosphere, I had placed a picture of my dream car, a Ferrari, on the wall to serve as a motivator to keep up with the struggle of making a success out of my endeavours in that place. I had also put up a bright light so that we could see up the stairs when we came in at night.

The landing was a private area and was accessible only by a locked door, for which only Abina and I had the keys. When I arrived home late one night after running some errands, I found that there was no light in the stairwell leading up to my flat. It was pitch dark and I became very afraid, thinking of the neighbour's vicious dog. Maybe he was resting in the stairwell and would attack if I surprised him in the dark. I started up the stairs on tiptoe and was flooded with relief when I neared the landing without incident. However, I started to notice something coarse crunching beneath my feet.

I reached the door and fumbled to get my key in the lock in the darkness. When the door opened, I was able to see by the light on the landing that I was treading on smashed remains of the light bulb. The sight on the landing itself was even more sinister, though. The Ferrari picture had been obviously moved, the window that opened into my home was smashed, and all of my plants and pots were gone.

I was certain it was the neighbours, and I could not handle the harassment any longer. I thought of sinking to their level and calling on some friends of mine who lived in the roughest area of Brixton. I imagined these tough guys coming around to scare them into behaving. But that was a silly wish, and I knew I had to overcome the challenge that these people represented on my own.

I was now back to full-time job hunting and accepting any temporary position that came my way from the various agencies. The jobs I took ranged from a call centre representative to ironing and babysitting.

I knew one way out of the mess was to get more education for myself, so I took any savings I could scrape and enrolled in courses at a local college. The coursework was exciting, and I loved having something to stimulate my mind again. In fact, some of my fondest memories were made when Jasmine and I would spend our evenings together doing homework at the small dining room table in our little flat. I was determined to make our lives better, and I instilled the importance of education in my daughter so that she would never find herself in such a fix.

Despite the hardships facing you, being given a new day is a fresh canvas. Paint it beautifully.

CHAPTER 19: PENALTY

Someone else's errors can be the penalty of the innocent.

I was terribly distraught about having to quit my job because of my child's day care needs, and I was very angry with Afua for being so unreliable. I was tearing my hair out and cried until my head literally hurt. I punched my car door hard and wished I were in Jamaica so I could floor my accelerator. I needed a way to explode, but instead I felt trapped.

In my head, I blamed Afua for my dissatisfaction with my life, but I soon made a complete turn-around and started sending up prayers of thanks for her poor work ethic. She seemingly saved me from a disastrous situation that was brewing at the school in Luton where I used to work that I had been completely unaware of.

I realised that Afua's irresponsibility was really a blessing in disguise. God was looking out for me after all. All of my efforts to re-enter a teaching career could have been destroyed, and we would have been in an even worse position. Moreover, I had even been considering moving to Luton to be closer to the school, but would have wasted all the expense and effort and been left with no job. I had already put our flat on the market, and that at least, remained a good decision, because regardless of my job situation, we would be out from under the burden of a mortgage I could not afford, as renting was more affordable there.

I had to make a quick trip back to Jamaica to sort out some bits and pieces regarding our citizenship and residency status. I needed to apply for a new birth certificate, as there were some new movements in the Jamaican government system that necessitated re-issuance of old birth certificates.

On the second morning of my arrival, I woke early and left for the office of the registrar of births and deaths. My plan was to be first in line so that I could get my new birth certificate and be able to spend the rest of my time visiting family. Man, was I in for a big surprise! I was called forward by one of the first workers to open a window for service, and was greeted by a lovely lady who looked over my plain white paper certificate and directed me to enter the inner offices. I was so proud of my posh new British accent and the immaculate way I was dressed, thinking how it really was paying off in a professional setting and earning me better treatment.

I was taken into a secluded office, and to my surprise, met by the same woman, but then with a very stern look on her face. She informed me that I was in very serious trouble for trying to pass off a false document. I was totally confused, what did she mean by false document? I explained that I had that birth certificate from the time I was a teenager, when my parents had applied for an update regarding my father's name being listed on the certificate. She asked exactly where I had gotten the document I was trying to pass off. I told her that my parents had given it to me. She gave a slight smirk of disbelief, and I realised that there was a serious problem at hand.

I had never questioned the authenticity of that document. I had even used it to secure my visa to enter the UK and never had any trouble. The lady informed me in a very official tone that I was in possession of a false birth certificate and whipped out a large book filled with others that looked exactly like mine. She flipped from page to page, pointing at the signature line on each, and told me that the signature was falsified. I was in total shock. I again explained that my parents had obtained the certificate and given it to me when I was still a minor. I never would have questioned them. As a matter of fact, when it was given to me, I would not have even had the thought that they would have given me a fake birth certificate. I then asked how it could be such an obvious forgery, as she was suggesting, since I had used it to get my passport, my travel certificates, and my degrees—everything in my life that required an official governance approval.

Instead of answering me, she told me she had to call in the police. She said that was an offence that necessitated a criminal charge. I couldn't believe what I was hearing—the police? Was the woman mad? I had just come to get a new copy of my birth certificate, and now I was being threatened with handcuffs and a criminal charge. It was as if I had entered a nightmare. I had a flashback to the terrible juvenile detention facility where my sister had been held, and I knew that the Jamaican jails for adults were much, much worse. A wave of panic rose up in me. The lady told me to stay calm; she had already called the authorities. I was locked in the little room until they arrived, and those minutes were tortuous. I fretted over the confusing situation and how I had come to be in the midst of it. Surely, I thought, it was all a mistake. Or I would simply wake up safe in my bed and breathe a sigh of relief that it was all just a bad dream.

Finally, a group of men in uniform entered the room. They stated in official, barking tones that they were a special force from the fraud squad and were there to collect me on the charge of fraud. I couldn't even move to stand up from my seat. That was my first time being in such proximity to lawmen that were looking at me as a target. They firmly gripped my upper arms and helped me to my feet, escorting me directly out of the building and into the police car waiting outside. I was driven down to the fraud squad office, which was located in downtown Kingston.

I didn't utter a word for the entire drive, even though they kept throwing questions at me about how I had managed to get into the UK with a false document. All I could think about was being jailed and stuck in Jamaica awaiting a trial, unable to get back to my daughter, who would be thinking her mother had abandoned her. She would not understand what was happening. Luckily, the arrangement during this trip was for her to be with Tobore. That comforted me. I began thinking that I was actually getting a brusquer treatment than anyone else because of my British status.

I was taken into an office and a guard was placed outside while I waited for whatever my fate was to be. It was nearing noon, and I was hungry. The guard on duty checked in and said he would send someone to fetch some food for me. Finally, I was visited by the interrogators. They asked all the same questions that had been fired at me during the morning hours and repeated the same charges that were levied against me. I could only reiterate that I had nothing to do with it, that I was telling the truth about how I had come into possession of the document that had never before been questioned by any other governing body. But they weren't interested.

I was allowed one phone call, and I called my mum to ask her to come down to the station to help explain the situation—better yet, I said, please have my dad come. After all, he was much closer, since he still lived in Kingston. My mum said that she would come, but it would take some time, as she would be travelling from Saint Elizabeth. She also said that there was no way my dad would be coming. Apparently, he was too afraid to enter the police station and become entangled in that mess.

I found out later that my dad said he didn't feel any need to be involved, because he had only agreed to make his status official on my birth certificate. If I had known back then what the price of that small token of ownership would be, I would have opted to keep my mum's maiden name and would have happily maintained my outsider status.

My mum made the three-hour journey by bus, and when she arrived, she helped the police to coerce my dad to come in as well. I remember those phone calls vividly. The officers assured him they weren't going to arrest him because I was the one in custody. They finally convinced him to come in by telling him that all he needed to do was give a statement so they could determine what to do with me. I was sure my mum's cursing him to within an inch of his life also helped. I almost fell over with relief

Chapter 19: Penalty

when he finally made the twenty-minute trip from his house to the station. I realised that I might actually be released so that I could be allowed to go back to London to be with my daughter.

My mum and dad were interviewed in separate rooms to see if they would corroborate my story. I was petrified about what might be going on. Would they provide any new information? Would I be hauled off to jail? I was not in the room when my father finally gave his official statement, and the truth came out. He admitted that when he went to change my name on the birth certificate, he didn't go into the registrar's office. Instead, he gave my original certificate to one of his brothers who lived nearby, who knew someone that could get a *bandulu* (fraudulent) one for much less hassle and much less money. The bottom line was that he had produced a fraudulent document that I had been carrying around and showing off to all the governmental agencies since then.

The whole ordeal of my parents' interrogation took only about one hour, but it felt like an eternity to me. When the officers came back to the office where I was being held, they produced the written statements that my parents had given and told me to sign off on them. I was shaking with relief and my signature was a wobbly mess. The officer who took the papers from me said that I was one very lucky lady to have the opportunity to get out of there.

I wasn't sure what he meant, but it became clear when he explained that I now had to pay one hundred thousand Jamaican dollars to get free. Damn, that was more than my week's pay in the UK. It was all done under the table, as they say in Jamaica. I was furious! But I kept my outward calm, knowing that no misbehaviour would be tolerated in that situation, no matter how justified. I hadn't done anything wrong, but here I had to pay for a crime that my dad had committed and admitted to. As I gave up the money for my freedom, I steamed inside, thinking that if my dad had only claimed me from the time of my birth, it would never have happened.

Chapter 19: Penalty

I was finally allowed to leave the police station a free woman, but my day with the authorities was not over. I had to go back to the registrar's office, along with my dad, to get the situation completely cleared up. He was required to sign some official forms so that the name change could be officially approved.

I was still fuming from the unfairness of it all and demanded to see the head of the office, who came out and was delighted to hear that I had gotten it all cleared up. My joy did not equal hers, though, and I demanded to know why I was punished for something that could have been just as easily proven by a phone call from their offices. And I wanted to know why I was the one arrested when the people who had made my certificate without my knowledge were the wrongdoers. She listened to my rant and apologised, explaining that the office had to follow protocol, adding that there were many others just like me who were innocent participants in others' crimes. She even said that she was thinking of how the office could provide amnesty for these cases.

I was granted an expedited new birth certificate, and when I got it in my hands, I couldn't wait to hop on the next plane out of Jamaica. The love-hate relationship I had with Jamaica by now was a complex one. I have had so many traumatic experiences there, but it is the land of my birth. It's engrained in my DNA, but it has treated me roughly. I guess my relationship with Jamaica is like a tumultuous intimate relationship.

I returned safely to London, held my baby tight and told her how much I love her. As I explained the situation that had nearly kept me away from her forever, I was reminded of how quickly our ordered lives could spiral out of control. A deep-seated dislike towards my father blossomed that day, and I gained a greater respect for my mum.

I also arrived home to an offer on the flat and praised God for his mercy. I had even managed to make a small profit on the sale, which provided some security while I tried to figure out our next move. I was still convinced that purchasing a home was better than renting, so I looked for a house that was more in our budget and found one in Mitcham. This time it would just be Jasmine and me. While I waited for the sale to be approved, Jasmine and I had to move in with Tobore and his flat mates. Luckily, we lived nearby, and Jasmine had a more regular relationship with her father. He would pop up often around this period of our relationship.

We wound up staying for about six weeks, and the experience living with Tobore again under the same roof was strange, but not unpleasant.

The house they were in at the time had ample space, and Jasmine and I had our own room. In a way, it felt like our old life towards the end of our relationship, with us residing in separate rooms but getting along cordially in the common areas. I suppose our being back in a familial-type living situation stirred something in Jasmine's mind too. She had begun to recall our life in Jamaica, when we had lived in our dream home before that fateful night of the attack. She even started asking questions about what had happened to make us leave, which led to more pointed questions about strange men with guns and her other flashes of memory about that night.

I could not muster the courage within myself to revisit that painful memory, but I didn't know what else to do. If I had been in a more stable situation, I would have sought out intervention from a professional who deals with traumatic events, but I didn't.

We finally obtained the new house and were able to move in. I was so relieved to have a safe place away from the drug-addled neighbours and their vicious dog. In that home, we even had our own front door, with no communal space. Our new neighbours turned out to be absolutely lovely, and we settled in nicely. We even had a lovely garden space where Jasmine could play, and I could find some peace while toiling the soil by hand and planting flowers. I didn't mind that there was only a tiny bathroom and rather flimsy tub. The freedom I felt there was invaluable. I felt like my life was finally progressing, like I had begun to grow roots in that country and had found somewhere to live where I would no longer feel like a stranger.

I realised that having a house of my own was something that gave me a sense of security like nothing else did. Maybe it was because I grew up with my mum not having one for herself, or maybe it was the constant moving around that I did as a child. I always felt unsettled, but when I had a house, I felt like I was safe on my own, like I didn't need a man to provide for me.

My professional life was going steadily, and I had work daily. However, there was a strong governmental push at the time for teachers to have their Qualified Teachers Status, known in short as QTS. I sought to get the QTS certification, but I was lacking maths as a subject for my education degrees. In Jamaica, accounting was considered a math subject in college, and during my time in high school, our main math teacher had suffered from diabetes and was constantly on sick leave, so I graduated without that subject. I did get some math lessons, but they were few and far between. In addition, I wasn't the brightest student in the class, so I was always a challenge to the teacher, who chose to focus on the smarter students so she could catch up on all the lessons she'd missed while off work. The whole situation had made me hate math.

But that had become a problem. I couldn't get the QTS because of my missing math credits. I also didn't want to own up to anyone that I was so severely lacking in that subject. I was still expected to teach it. Sometimes, when I had to cover for a math lesson, I would sit and stare at the textbooks, terrified that the students would start asking me for detailed explanations. I couldn't tell a logarithm from an exponential, and the thought of having to discuss algebra frightened the life out of me.

I was so far behind in my math skills that no amount of studying would catch me up in time to achieve the necessary QTS. I conceded defeat and started looking for a way out of the teaching profession. I thought of the irony in the end of my teaching career. Originally, it was me who didn't like the field and thought it was beneath me, but in the end, I was not good enough to stay in it. That's not to say I was a bad teacher. I was actually very good in all the other subjects, and I genuinely cared for my students.

When the reality finally hit that I was no longer allowed to teach, I grieved as if I had lost something as important as my husband or my sister. It hurt just as much to be rejected by a system, as it had to be rejected by a loved one. I had given so much of my life to that career, and I experienced a real heartbreak when it was taken away from me. Here I was, a single mother in London with a new house, having to close another chapter of her life. What could possibly lay ahead?

> ***Heartbreaks are not always caused by people or intimate love gone wrong. They can come in unexpected forms, and I have had my fair share of all types.***

CHAPTER 20: PERMANENCE

Sometimes, just swimming into the waves is all you can do, letting the tide carry you to the destined place.

It was almost Easter 2007, and I was at my wit's end trying to find a job through the agencies. I was now regularised in the country and didn't need the schools for a visa, as I had received my highly skilled visa back in 2005. Without achieving the QTS, my opportunities for teaching had dwindled to nothing, but more worrisome was the fact that summer was nearly upon us, and the pool of job seekers would soon be flooded with fellow teachers who were unemployed between terms. I was back to taking any job offered so that I could ensure enough money came in to pay the mortgage.

I realised that a high-stress and unstable lifestyle was not sustainable long-term. So, I began to work towards completing my master's degree in business administration. My daily life was so full of activities chasing a paycheque that I had no social life to speak of. The thought of seeking out and finding a life partner hadn't even crossed my mind. Besides, if I was to be honest, I'd have to admit that I still considered Tobore to be the missing partner that completed our little family. So, in some ways, I didn't feel like I was missing anything.

I was still dealing with the persistent issues of having to keep my schedule flexible enough to be available for my child and to be ready for any situation that might arise with childcare. Every parent has had to deal with these issues, but they were even more of a burden when you were assigned as temporary staff. The administration was much less forgiving when hiccups arose in the daily schedule. I began to feel like I was giving

Chapter 20: Permanence

my own child the same instability that had marred my childhood, and that was the one thing I had promised myself I would never do.

I threw myself into the work of finding a stable, permanent job. Soon, I had applied for so many jobs that I couldn't even remember what I had applied for. When people called, I was completely confused about whether the job was temporary or permanent, what the job itself was, and how I should present myself to make the best impression. I was a mess, and finally I felt the burden of it all crushing my spirit.

I had managed to buy a small car in the previous year. There had been no getting around it; the available jobs were more widely scattered than was feasible to get to by the bus routes. One afternoon, I got into the car and drove to some nearby woods, where I hiked out into the field and sat down on the grass and cried. In my grief, I turned my face to the heavens and asked God to answer all of the blasphemous questions that had hung in the back of my mind for so long. Why was He punishing me? What had I done wrong that had attracted His wrath? Why did He give everyone else a smooth path in life, while He made me fight for every step along mine? Why did He stand by and allow me to be knocked back five steps for every one step I took forward?

No answers came booming down from the skies. I felt so alone and broken. I couldn't let my precious child see the utter distress I was feeling, so I pulled myself together and put on a calm and cheerful face to greet her at the end of her school day. I even took her on a quick jaunt to the park so that she could play and, for at least a while, feel the carefree spirit that I had never experienced.

In a way, being outside of the house was also an escape for me.

For a short while, I could clear my mind of the dreaded letters that were coming with bills I had no idea how I would pay. When we returned home that day, a pile of letters were waiting, just as I had feared. I took a deep breath and sorted through them. It was one after another with big red writing, signaling an overdue account and calling for immediate action. But one envelope in particular caught my eye. It looked like regular, non-threatening business mail. I selected that one to open and discarded the others in a heap on the table.

As I began to open it, I remembered all of the job applications I had put in and started to remind myself that it was probably just a run-of-the-mill rejection letter. To my surprise, it was a letter from a well-known supermarket chain inviting me to interview for their on-the-job graduate management programme! I didn't recognise the location where the programme was going to be held; some place called Erith that was southwest of London. That was no matter to me. I didn't care how far it was, I would drive there every day, if need be.

It looked like God was looking out for me after all. In my excitement, I went and purchased a cheap, but nice, power suit. On the day of the interview, I arrived at the site to find a slew of other applicants, all anxious and dressed professionally. We were a diverse group, each representing a different nationality and age. They put us all in a waiting room, and we sat in awkward silence for a few moments. It seemed that no one was willing to break the ice, so I took it upon myself to ease the tension in the room by engaging each person in a group conversation. Soon, we were getting a sense of where each of us came from and our current situations.

It was there that I met a man near my age named Tre. He was of German and Cameroonian descent, and I was instantly attracted to him. He was very GQ; gosh, he was beautifully dressed and so immaculate. He was the true epitome of a classy man, with grace and style. His dark suit was cut perfectly to fit his extremely tall and sinewy body, and the colour complimented his dark skin. I was smitten. We were called in for the interviews in turn, and the process was gruesome. But at the end I found out that I was among those selected to attend the second round of interviews. I overheard Tre getting the same news, and my heart leapt when I realised I would get the chance to see him again.

I had kept our chatty conversation going through that same waiting process, and by the end of the second interview, Tre and I had exchanged numbers. I was given the promise of a dinner date as well. But I did not get any news that day of an invite for the third interview session. I thought maybe they weren't letting people know directly that time and went home with a light heart from flirting with Tre.

When Tre and I met for dinner, however, I found out that he had received word about the third round shortly after the second interview. I went home and rummaged through all of the mail for a second and third time, hoping to find an envelope that I must have overlooked, but there was nothing. My heart sank. I really thought I had done a good job in the second interview, and it was the most promising career lead I'd had in a long time.

The next day, I resigned myself to the fact that I was going to be rejected from the programme, and I got myself ready to visit yet another employment agency to see what jobs might be coming up. As I was stepping out the door, my phone rang. It was the supermarket administration, and they were inviting me back for the third round of interviews. I was thrilled and determined to knock their socks off when they spoke to me next. The interview was to be held the next day at one of their stores that happened to be located very close to where I lived. I sent up a silent prayer of thanks to God. I couldn't believe I might land a job within a stone's throw of my home. That I might be able to stop the crazy commuting schedule that had me travelling from pillar to post all over London.

The third interview was even more intensive than the first two. I felt like I was on trial. I was re-entering the business world, and it was so different from the teaching system that I had been immersed in since my arrival in the UK. I had to refresh my communication skills, my ability to think on the spot, and think back to all the work I did in my dealer account role back in Jamaica and how great I was at that. This interview had to go well; I needed this job, so fierce Ava the survivor showed, and I

Chapter 20: Permanence

decided I was going to ace this. The interview consisted of cognitive skill tests as well as physical skill tests. I was given pallets to pull and pack. It was hard and heavy work.

I couldn't imagine that type of manual labour would be part of the role they were expecting me to fill, especially after all the administrative interview questions in the first two rounds. They had me count items on the shelves, work the cash register, and help with the end-of-day accounting and deposit of money into the safe. Basically, I had a go at every duty that any employee would perform in the store on a daily basis.

One of the hardest parts for me, however, was seeing all of the cash being counted at the end of the day. I was so envious. There I was, only barely making ends meet while working my butt off, and I couldn't imagine having that kind of income. It was a torturous test for my psyche, and I battled to not fall prey to my downtrodden emotions.

When the interview ended, I was sent home with no idea of where I stood or when they might contact me next. The pessimistic side of me thought that they hadn't given me an answer straightaway because I must have failed in one of the important tasks. Maybe I hadn't packed enough on the shelves or maybe I hadn't been fast enough on the tills? I began to lament that I was again back at square one. My nerves were frayed, and I went directly to my friend's house and cried my eyes out to her. She comforted me and reminded me of God's unfailing love, which I still doubted. She left me alone to think, and I wrote a prayer to the Lord:

Dear God, why have you given up on me? What sins have I committed that are so unforgivable? Why, regardless of how hard I try, does nothing seem to work out for me? Why don't you just take me in your protective arms and prevent me from going through all of this pain, suffering, and shame in front of my friends, my foes, and my child? Was running away from Jamaica not enough punishment? Was being held at gunpoint not a hard-enough experience to endure? What more shall I be required to go through, to give up, to be worthy in your eyes? God, please release my blessings. I am in need of a

Chapter 20: Permanence

miracle, right at this point in my life. My mortgage is due, and after I pay it, Jasmine and I will have no money left. My bank account is empty, the bills are piling up, and I have this beautiful and innocent child that I have to shelter and feed. Lord, remember that my family, especially my mum, still depends on me. Lord, please help me.

I left the prayer at my friend's house and headed home to face my mounting debts and the sadness that was threatening to take me over completely. I made dinner for Jasmine, tucked her into bed, and laid myself down to sleep. A week passed and I heard nothing from the supermarket, so I started reaching out to people around town for stints doing cleaning work. After two weeks of that, I couldn't take it anymore. The dust and cleaning solutions would cause such severe allergies that I would have asthma attacks. But there was nothing else, and I had to make money somehow.

As I finished a cleaning job in Shirley some weeks later, I decided to treat myself to a pint of lager. Jasmine was staying with a friend and I had the evening to myself. I pulled my car up and parked at a nearby pub garden where my friend said she would meet me. Right then, my mobile phone began to ring. The ringing of a phone had long since lost its appeal to me, as it was almost always a debt collector on the other end of the line. I was certainly in no mood to fend one of them off.

As the ringing continued, I began to worry that it was family back home calling, but that, too, turned me away from answering. More often than not, a call from Jamaica was only made to ask for money, or any contribution I could make, to cover school fees, medical expenses, or clothing. The requests seemed never-ending, especially since they thought I was living a rich life across the pond, no matter what I told them to the contrary. I thought of how my cupboards at home were empty. The money I had made that week from cleaning was barely enough to buy groceries for a few days and the car petrol was low. I reached over, switched the phone off, and headed inside to forget for just a moment that my life was so pathetic.

The alcohol did just the trick. It took away all my pain and eased the nagging worries that plagued my mind. I rarely ever drank, so I became quite tipsy rather quickly. When it was time to drive home, I didn't even care that I was still feeling so light-headed. As a matter of fact, a part of me wished that the journey home would end with me just being taken away by the angels; spirited away to a place where there was no hunger, no embarrassment, and no weight of responsibility on my shoulders. The life I led in London, hand to mouth, was slowly killing me.

When I finally reached home and parked the car in my driveway, I decided I was still numb enough from the alcohol to hear whatever stressful or bad news was left on my voicemail. I was shocked to hear a voice identifying itself as a caller from the supermarket chain letting me know that I had successfully passed the final interview and offering me the management job at the very store I had tested in on the last day. I was struck dumb. I couldn't believe the news I was hearing. I didn't even realise that tears were streaming down my face, unbidden. I must have sat in that car for more than thirty minutes, just crying and staring out into the darkness. Eventually I was able to move. I dropped forward onto my knees in that small space in front of the driver's seat and I sent up a heartfelt prayer of thanksgiving and worship.

When I gathered myself together, I made my way inside and had a dinner of baked beans and eggs on toast, and I saved a portion for Jasmine in case she was hungry when she got home. I called the friend whom Jasmine was visiting, to tell her that I was on my way to pick up my daughter. She instantly noticed the uplifted tone of my voice, but assumed it was due to my having found a man. No, I chuckled at her, there was no Mr. Right that was causing my euphoric state. I had found a permanent job, which was much better. Before I started driving, I made a call to Tre,

Chapter 20: Permanence

to see if he too had gotten the job offer. He hadn't, and my reward turned bittersweet.

The salary they offered was great, especially considering the pittance I had been working for, and the thought that it would arrive on a consistent schedule was almost too hard to believe. It had been more than four years since I had made a steady monthly salary, and part of this steady salary was owing to the fact I was now on my own visa. That freedom was blissful. The job was to start with a one-week training session that was scheduled at a location rather far away from my home. I was going to have to find someone to look after Jasmine, as her father had a job that was not conducive to the care she would need. I began to panic, thinking that childcare issues might again foil my chances of attaining stability in the workforce.

I finally decided to reach out to my sister Kem and ask her to stay with me again. Considering our difficult times in the past, she wasn't my first choice, but I couldn't think of anyone else who I would trust with Jasmine's care. In the time since we had lived together in that filthy little flat back when she had first arrived, she had birthed a daughter. Coming to stay with us now included her child, and I knew that ultimately represented a greater financial burden for me. Even though Kem was currently unemployed with very little support from her partner, it was not uncommon for me to always ensure she was paid to look after Jasmine for me while I was in the country or I was away.

With Kem and her daughter settled in to watch over Jasmine, I left for the week of training. I had begun to feel a little bit comfortable about my situation. For all the mistrust I'd had for Kem regarding our relationship, I did not fear that she would fail to take care of my child. I thought that situation might even work out in the long term, with her being home for Jasmine while I worked at the store near my home.

Unfortunately, I discovered rather quickly that I didn't like the job at all. The people who visited the store and the people who worked under my supervision were so rude, and there was nothing to be done about it. Every interaction had to end with me putting my tail between my legs and letting the other person feel like they had bested me. The job also included all of the physical duties that we had run through in that on-site interview. Apparently, there was nothing a store manager didn't have to do, from picking up trash in the car park, to cleaning up any mess in the aisles.

My workday didn't end after the store closed, either. In the after-hours, I was expected to fully wash the floors and lift heavy boxes for stocking. I realised my managerial job was really nothing more than a glorified cleaner/stocker. Yet, there wasn't much I could do about it. I needed the job desperately, and I would just have to suck it up.

I did have the responsibility of tallying up the sales at the end of the day and depositing the money in the safe, but I also had to work the registers and ring people up throughout the day. Rather soon after starting that job, I was transferred to another store that was a bit farther away and told that store was to be my "mother store." That meant it was the store where I was to stay for the duration of my tenure with the company. The hours remained long, and I found myself going to work before Jasmine had awoken in the mornings and coming home after she had gone to bed. I hardly saw her at all, and it was taking a toll on me. Kem told me that Jasmine was also pining for me, and that she wasn't happy.

Over the next few months I dated Tre, but things never turned serious with him. I soon found out that it was due to his womanizing ways. He had nine children with six different mothers. On top of that, he was legally married to one of them. He tried to explain to me that his wife was back in Germany and he needed women to comfort him in her absence. He told me he had women here, there, and everywhere and that I could be one of them. That offer did not appeal to me. He was far too carefree for my liking.

Chapter 20: Permanence

We managed to remain friends, even though deep down I was mad that he hadn't been the man I was hoping he was. He always made me feel special. When we walked down the road, girls would lap him up. It gave me a nice inner feeling that I was the one he had chosen to be with that night, and I would laugh privately with the knowledge that if they knew all his secrets like I did, they would probably turn him away too.

The job was beginning to take a toll on me, physically and emotionally. I found out that the other managers in that job had been there for years, yet they were still classified as deputy managers, so my coming in at that level made them a bit envious. It was blamed on company politics, and I was advised that the only way up was to keep your head down and your mouth shut. Kissing ass never hurt either. The way to help ensure a pay raise or promotion was to put in even more hours without any complaint. Asking for vacation time or sick leave would drop you back to the bottom of the pool. I felt trapped. To me, the more work you put in, the more they took advantage of you. I also realised rather quickly that I had significantly more real-life experience in the business world than the majority of the managers. That fact did not gain me any friends among the management staff, and I was viewed by many as a threat. I found out that all of the other managers, except the manager who was supervising my programme, were former cashiers. They weren't happy that I came in and started at the top while they had worked their asses off to get there.

The hostility manifested in our workplace. When new processes were introduced, or I found an old one that I was unclear on, I could never count on help from my colleagues who had an intimate understanding of the supermarket's inner workings due to their long history with the company. I whipped out my sales personality, hoping to charm my way into getting people to come to my aid, but that only ever worked with the cashiers and never with the managers. In many ways, the experience of working with these people was like being back in grade school. They would sabotage one another, making the tills short at the end of the day

Chapter 20: Permanence

or offering to help and then leaving things half done. Really, they would do anything they could to make each other look bad.

The challenges in the job extended beyond the management and cashier staff and went up to the executive level. The regulations that guided our workdays were proof of that. There was an unwritten rule that no one was to leave the premises during their lunch hour. Even the cashiers would quietly grumble that it was time they needed to go pay bills, make a doctor's visit, or deal with issues involving their children. It was apparent to all, however, that the reason for that practice was to keep the whole staff available for dealing with urgent matters as they arose, regardless of the fact that those urgent matters were usually the result of chronic understaffing.

At one point, I was even instructed on how to keep cashiers on shift who were trying to leave, regardless of them having completed their workday hours. And no consideration was given to the urgent need involving children that might have been calling them away. No cashier could leave their post until they were tallied up and cashed out by their manager. In my role as manager, I was told to simply ignore the cashiers' bell, which signaled their need for my services. I was told to busy myself with any mundane activity so that the cashier would have to stay on duty for as long as possible.

Leaving one's post before being cashed out was grounds for immediate sacking. The cashiers had no choice but to stay until I made my way over to tend to them. The thought of doing that to someone else, especially another parent whose child was waiting at home hungry or to be picked up from childcare or school, put my stomach in knots. I couldn't bring myself to do it. I marveled at the way other managers could simply ignore young mothers waiting at their registers and crying softly, torn between the needs of their awaiting children and the need to hold onto their jobs.

One of our star workers, a young single father named Elton, was a perfect example of that. Like all parents, he had childcare issues. But instead of being honoured for his stringent work ethic, he was routinely exploited for the good of the company. If he reported a potential upcoming conflict in his schedule, such as a parent-teacher conference that was scheduled before his shift that day that may make him slightly late, Elton's schedule would be restructured to completely obliterate that time off so that he would have to show up earlier than scheduled, miss his child's conference, and ensure that he would not miss one minute of work.

My refusal to play the corporate games earned me the mocking title of "softie manager" and scored me no points with my bosses. There was a rumour floating around that the company had already blackballed me from any type of promotion. I found myself once again stuck in a dead-end job and lacking momentum in my new career field. Was that to be my fate? I struggled so hard to find, a job and here I was on the verge of conflict that could possibly cost me the one secure thing in my life outside of Jasmine. I wished at this point that Tobore and I were together, as at least financially I would not have to struggle so hard; I missed my life in Jamaica, and this became a constant when I experienced struggles in the UK.

The unknown is wrapped in cycles of belief and only revealed to those dare to open the door of possibilities.

CHAPTER 21: REPUTATIONS

Reputations can attach themselves to us and become a permanent part of our person.

Things remained difficult at the supermarket, but I maintained my gratitude for the job and the opportunities it promised for a long-term career in administration. I had been there for almost seven months. But the longer I stayed, the more I became aware of the inner workings, or lack thereof. I became disillusioned with the managers who were supposed to be mentoring us as trainees.

Things really started to disintegrate for me over a three-week period. I struggled with making a simple request to be allowed time off work to meet in-person with my bank to rearrange my mortgage. I followed the company's policy for making such a request, yet each time I asked my direct supervisor, Sam, for an hour off during a single day of work, I received the clipped response, "Not today."

The deadline that had been set by my bank for completing the necessary paperwork was rapidly approaching. I was getting very anxious about how to resolve this conundrum and finally decided to take one of the days off owed to me, instead of pestering my supervisor anymore. Asking for time off presented its own challenges, particularly because that time was routinely denied under some vague explanation that involved an inaccurate overtime reporting scheme.

I knew that my daily overtime, like everyone else's, had not gone unnoticed by my colleagues and my manager, and I prayed that Sam would be fair when considering my request. I needed to prepare myself before approaching him. I first carefully checked the corporate schedule and that

Chapter 21: Reputations

of my local store to find a date when my absence would be least disruptive. The upcoming Friday looked perfect. Moreover, I decided to not simply take the day off, but instead request to exchange my rotation with that of another trainee manager, Emmanuel. That way, the other staff would not have to cover the duties of an absent trainee manager.

I showed up on Monday prepared to present my idea to Sam but found that he had taken a day off himself. I was not surprised to find that he had not made any attempt to cover his shift, and I felt good about myself for having enough respect for my colleagues to avoid the uproarious situation this always led to. As the day wore on, the staff encountered a few small situations in which we needed Sam's advice. I volunteered to make the call, thinking that I could be clever and use it to discuss my rotation exchange idea with him as well. However, as soon as I brought up the rotation exchange, Sam cut me off by saying, "There's never much to be done in the store, so don't worry about it." My heart sank when he hung up. I knew that statement didn't reflect the truth of our working conditions. There was a ton to do. The staff and I were living proof, as we were all scrambling to take over Sam's responsibilities in his absence. I knew I could never act so irresponsibly towards my coworkers.

On Tuesday, I again showed up ready to present my reasoned ideas for rotation exchange to Sam, but again I found out that he had just called in to take yet another day off. I checked Emmanuel's schedule and found out that he wasn't scheduled to be in again until the next day, so I would have to finalise my whole plan with both Sam and Emmanuel first thing the next morning. When I reported for work that Wednesday, the first person I met was Sam. We exchanged our normal friendly hellos at the canteen door and made our way inside to get ready for the day.

I had planned to lock my purse up in my employee locker and pop into Sam's office for a quick chat before either of us got overwhelmed with the daily routine. But as soon as we walked into the welfare area, a stocker named Kumar came up to us and started telling me that the employees from welfare had just been discussing the on-going problems with everyone getting their requests for days off approved. I felt a flicker of excitement, thinking to myself what perfect timing it was since Sam was still standing right next to me. Kumar went on to explain that another employee, Michelle, had suggested that a good way for the staff to get their time off was for them to accurately record all the hours they worked in a single day. She had even gone so far as to question the legality of the current practice of inaccurate recording the company used.

I could sense Sam's growing agitation. He had stayed silent so far, but it was time for him to stop the blasphemous talk once and for all. "We cannot do that. The district manager will go ballistic about it."

I was surprised at his strong tone of voice and tried to lighten the situation by telling Sam that I found it hard to believe the company did not want to obey. Sam simply shrugged and said that such topics of discussion were not for the day's start. He turned on his heel and beckoned me to follow.

I figured at that point there was nothing ventured if I didn't put my request to him at that time. I was relieved and a bit shocked when he merely sighed and gave me verbal approval for my time off that Friday, as well as for my exchange of rotation with Emmanuel. We even chitchatted a bit after that before I headed to the warehouse to start my workday in earnest.

A little over one hour had passed before I finished my immediate tasks. As I began to make my way to the main part of the store, I was delighted to see Emmanuel, and I waved to catch his attention. Before I could speak, though, he started yelling angrily at me, saying that someone had just told him that I had changed my shift with him without asking. I rushed to clarify the misunderstanding, telling him that I had only gotten permission from Sam to exchange shifts. I explained that I had been waiting for him to come into work that day so I could talk to him about it.

Chapter 21: Reputations

Emmanuel said that Sam had just told him the exchange was already complete. He was understandably angry with me, thinking that I had disrupted his schedule without any forewarning or consideration for his opinion on the matter. I couldn't get a word in edgewise, and before I knew it, he was pointing a finger at me, saying that since I had taken it upon myself to mess with his life, I would have to come in Friday night after closing to pick up the store keys to open on Saturday. I was a bit flustered at that point and stammered that I couldn't come in that late on Friday because my child would already be in bed. And besides, I wasn't scheduled to open the store on Saturday morning, Sam was. I asked if he could just give Sam the keys when their shift together ended on Friday night. But Emmanuel just glared at me and stormed off.

I went to see Sam straight away to get that messy situation resolved, but he was busy with the cleaning contractor and unavailable for a discussion right then. Emmanuel refused to even look at me, and I realised that the situation, though unintentional, had been unfair on him.

I needed to resolve it and take care of myself without involving him. I peeked back into Sam's office, but he was still with the contractor. He knew why I was seeking him out, and when he saw me, he simply pointed to the stack of rotation sheets for me to take and fill out. I changed Emmanuel's shift back to its original schedule and marked Friday as an off day for myself.

Not long after, Sam came storming out of his office, waving the rotation sheets in the air and yelling, "Come with me right now!"

I was shocked at his red-faced anger and said, "One moment, please, let me wrap things up."

He barked out, "I said come with me right now. What I have to say is more important than what you are doing."

He was bearing down on me, and I had a flash of the men who had attacked me back in Jamaica, waving their guns and coming at me with a similar cold look in their eyes. My first instinct was to cower, but within seconds, I found my voice and stood up for myself. I steadied my tone and said, "Please calm down, and please don't talk to me like that. We shouldn't yell at each other in the workplace."

That set him off. He shot forward and screamed in my face, "For fuck's sake! Come with me now!"

I steeled myself and stayed standing upright, staring directly into his eyes. I told him that I wasn't going anywhere with him until he calmed down and apologised for cursing at me.

He must have been dumbstruck by my unexpected refusal to cower to him because he stood motionless with his mouth hanging open. I took advantage of the moment and reminded him I had never been rude or disrespectful towards him and that I didn't appreciate his rudeness or his undermining approach. Not surprisingly, the ruckus had attracted the attention of all the nearby staff, who started edging away. Sam began to realise that all eyes were now on him.

He took a deep breath and stepped back from me, quietly saying a quick, "Sorry."

That was it? I thought. That whispered utterance was absolutely unacceptable as an apology. Before I knew it, I was telling him that he knew my name and that he needed to apologise to me properly. He set his lips in a hard line and gestured for me to follow him into the welfare area, where we would have some more privacy. Instead of getting the apology I was expecting, however, he turned on me and said firmly that it was his privilege as my manager to speak to me however he saw fit, and asked how I dare embarrass him in front of his other staff.

It was fortuitous that he had led us to the spot right in front of one of the corkboards with random company news, announcements, and policies tacked onto them. I immediately noticed one of the company's policy sheets and grabbed it down off the board, pointing to the paragraph that specifically addressed that exact situation. I reminded him that way of addressing me was considered harassment. He went back into his silent

Chapter 21: Reputations

mode and stared hard at me. As the moment of silence stretched on, I turned on my heel, gathered my belongings, and left the store.

As soon as I arrived at my home, I called our district manager, who was Sam's direct boss. He wasn't in, so I left a message telling him that I needed to speak with him urgently regarding an inappropriate and explosive situation at the store. He called back shortly, and I was able to tell him about what had just transpired. He agreed that Sam was out of bounds and that an employee should not be spoken to like that under any circumstances. He told me that he would start working on the situation.

About an hour later, the district manager rang back and asked if I felt I could work with Sam again. I replied that I could work with him again, thinking that time heals all wounds and sometime in the future we would likely cross paths, as our careers were parallel in that company.

To my surprise though, the district manager responded by telling me that he needed me to go back to working under Sam within the hour.

I nearly started crying when I explained to him that I didn't feel comfortable going back into the situation so quickly after what had just happened.

My breathing calmed down when he said that he understood my apprehension and asked if I felt that I could finish out that day's shift in another store instead.

When I agreed to his alternative plan, he said he would arrange something in the next hour. In the meantime, though, he wanted me to just drop by my home store and have a quick chat with Sam.

"It will be good for the relations of the store," he explained.

I reiterated that I didn't feel comfortable talking to Sam right away and said that I was happy to go, just on another day. I was shaken to my core, though, by his response.

He said, "Okay, Ava, you have left me with no choice but to start a formal investigation."

Chapter 21: Reputations

For the second time that day, I found myself stammering out an explanation to defend myself against an unfair attack. Sam had been so angry and so disrespectful. Having to interact with me right now because his boss was ordering it was unlikely to ease his anger. I didn't make any headway though, and the district manager told me he would have to figure out what to do from here that fit within company policy.

When he hung up, I rang my home store straight away. Sam answered, and as soon as I identified myself to him, he said that he was actually angry with me for four things that day, but I had not let him talk to me about them before I had chosen to leave the store in a huff. I had not expected that, and I could not imagine what these four things could be. After all, the day was still young, I hadn't even been at work that long before our situation exploded, and he hadn't seemed bothered by anything during our first morning chitchat session.

He began to tick them off, one by one. First, I was in the wrong for calling him to ask work-related questions on his days off. Second, I had been in the wrong when I had left a message for Emmanuel about wanting to talk on Wednesday when he came in (apparently, Emmanuel said my tone was abrasive). Third, I was in the wrong about an ordering mix-up, which actually had nothing to do with me, and I knew for a fact was his screw up. And, finally, that I was in the wrong for modifying the rotation on the scheduling sheets that he had pointed me to.

I immediately tried to defend myself, reminding Sam that he had told me to call him at home with work-related questions. It was a common practice among all the staff, as sometimes important items couldn't be found when he was gone, and we needed him to tell us where to locate them in his absence. My temper began to boil at the unfairness of it all. I justified my role in the situation involving Emmanuel, explaining that my intent was to protect my coworkers by having someone cover me when I was out so as not to be a burden.

I asked if he had listened to the message I left on Emmanuel's phone, and if he agreed with the assessment that I was rude. He said he didn't need to listen to anything, he already had the word of my coworker and that was all the information he needed. He then brought up the conversation in which I told Emmanuel I would not be able to pick up the keys on Friday night. When I started to speak, though, Sam cut me off and said that it didn't matter what my excuse was, I needed to make allowance for doing anything that anyone told me to, even another trainee manager. He ended the conversation by telling me not to waste my breath on explaining any of my actions or defending myself, he had already made a judgment on me and the case was closed.

I could not believe that in the end, I was the one who was going to be put at fault for the entire situation. I felt utterly used and disrespected. There was nothing more for me to do but wait to hear back from the district manager and learn my fate. When the call finally came, I was surprised to find out that I wasn't the one being transferred. It was Sam who had been reassigned to another store. There was a new manager by the name of Adelaide, and I was to report to her the next day.

When I showed up and introduced myself, it was evident that Adelaide had been briefed about me. The way she looked at me made me feel like there was a sign above my head that read *troublemaker*. The stress of the situation the day before still had me on edge. My asthma was acting up, but I felt there was no way that I could take a sick day with the previous day's events still so fresh in everyone's mind. I spent the morning wheezing and gasping for air as I pulled around the pallets of newly delivered vegetables and completed the stocking of the shelves. Adelaide noticed my struggles and inquired in a tight voice if I was okay. I told her that I wasn't feeling very well but she just gave a short "hmm," rolled her eyes, and went on with her business.

The other workers were more solicitous in their concerns for me, coming over to help me with the unpacking. One colleague even went to Adelaide and told her that my audible struggles to breathe were making him scared for my life, and he thought maybe I should go home early. That only earned him a loud rebuke in which she snapped at him and told him to stop being an "interfering git." She then called me over and told me in a low voice that she was on to me; she knew all about the tactics that staff would come up with to get out of putting in a good day's work, and she wasn't about to put up with any of it.

By that time, my breathing had become so ragged, and I was getting so little oxygen that I passed out. I could hear someone calling for an ambulance and felt myself being carried out to the car park into the fresh air. The ambulance turned up in no time and whisked me away to a nearby hospital. I found out later that as soon as the ambulance was called, Adelaide had started rushing around to act as though she had been concerned and that she had told as many staff as would listen that she had only leaned in to tell me to go home for the rest of the day but that I had turned her down and insisted on staying to work.

In the meantime, the hospital staff gave me a nebulizer, which immediately eased the constriction in my lungs. I was physically and emotionally exhausted by the time I was discharged to go home, with strict instructions for bed rest. The doctor had told me stress was the most likely trigger of my severe attack. He gave me a sick note to take a three-day break from work. In my time off over those next few days, I wrote a letter to the regional director, outlining what had really happened over the past week, and that morning with Adelaide. My hope was to somehow correct the injustice of the whole affair and regain my esteemed standing with the company.

Since I had witnesses who could attest to the truth in the matter, my complaint garnered a formal acknowledgment that Adelaide's behaviour had been inappropriate. I was disappointed that there was to be no consequence for Adelaide's actions, but when I returned, I found a new policy pinned to the corkboard that said any employee who was in physical distress should be dismissed to go home or to a doctor's office immediately. At least I was assured that the company hoped to avoid that situation happening again to any other employee.

I also found out when I returned to work that I was being immediately transferred to another store. The new store was farther away from home, but I was relieved, as I felt like my reputation was tainted at the present location. Now I would be given a chance to start afresh. However, I quickly came to realise that the spots on my professional persona extended company-wide. After one week at the new store, I still had not been entrusted with the duties involving cashing out or taking the cashiers' money to the safe. That was one of the key responsibilities of any mid- or senior-level manager, but my duties were kept to no more than those of a cashier. When I wasn't at the till, I was put on C-checking duty, a task that an entry-level employee would normally do, walking up and down the chillers, checking each stocked item to ensure that the sell-by date hadn't passed. It was that duty that made my demotion the most obvious.

Still, I didn't make any complaints and did everything I was told. My tactic for restoring my reputation was to be the perfect yes-man. However, after a month of that strategy, nothing had changed. I finally mustered up the courage to ask my manager if the job title I had been transferred under was different from the one I'd had at the last store, but he said that I was still a trainee manager. I wasn't sure how to respond, so I left the conversation and waited until I got home that evening to place a call asking him about the details of my upcoming schedule in compliance with my trainee managerial status. He was very congenial and said that I was set to start taking over cashing-out financial duties soon. He told me that anytime someone was transferred, it was company policy that they learnt the store's tills and stocking duties before they moved on to the administrative stuff. I had worked with plenty of transfer employees before, though, and I knew that wasn't the truth. I was a special case.

Exit strategies can creep upon us so secretly.

CHAPTER 22: THE CRUMBLE

Removing one brick from a stack can send walls crumbling down. Quickly escaping isn't always possible, so we sometimes get crushed.

At long last, I was given the cashing out and closing up responsibilities befitting my trainee manager status. I breathed a sigh of relief and thought for sure I had finally redeemed myself in the eyes of the upper management. That day, I was so proud when the money from the day's sales balanced with the money in the safe, and I held my head high as I prepped to lock up the store. I gathered my personal items together and went to reach for the store keys that I expected to find in my pocket, only to realise with a thrill of panic that I had not retrieved them from the manager's office before he left earlier that evening. I ran to the office, hoping against all odds that he had somehow forgotten to lock his office door, and I could sneak in and retrieve them without anyone being the wiser to my mistake, but there was no such luck that night.

I stood and pulled at the locked door for a full minute, even though I knew the door was locked tight. *Why? Why? Why?* I screamed in my head. My conscience taunted me with the answer: *you messed up! You are no good! They should have never trusted you!* I turned and fell back into the door and banged on it with my fist in frustration. "Damn!" I yelled out loud. The only way out of that mess would be to call the district manager, who had never forgiven me for my refusal to speak to Sam the afternoon of our frightening confrontation. Now I was going to prove him right in thinking I was a waste of the company's resources.

Chapter 22: The Crumble

I tried to steel myself for the phone call to him. His last words to me echoed in my head: "This company isn't for the weak hearted. We speak bluntly and we expect our employees to accept their lot without complaint." I knew that time I would be in for a particularly awful berating, and I just didn't think I had the fortitude to handle it. I started to cry but fought back the tears of self-pity. I paced the room and took deep, calming breaths. Finally, the panic and utter dismay started to dissipate, and I remembered that another manager had mentioned being in possession of an extra set of store keys due to a mix-up earlier in the week. I nearly collapsed with relief and felt the full weight of my anxiety lifted when she answered her phone and agreed to come down right away and bring me the keys.

I went home that night with a cry to God for His mercy but also with a plea in my heart for the tenuous situation I had found myself in to somehow be resolved. I knew that I could not survive under that type of stressful working environment for the rest of my life, especially when my efforts were leading nowhere, and I was killing myself to merely get back in the good graces of the bigwigs at the company.

That night, after I put Jasmine to bed and settled myself in, I took the time to reflect on my situation and to try and figure out a plan to get out of it. Writing in my diary had always helped me to organise my thoughts and gain clarity on anything troublesome that I was facing, and I was in need of such clarity. Jamaica seemed a good option, though I was terrified of my assailants. But I had to seriously consider it going forward.

April 2008

Dear diary,

Life here in London has been the most challenging I have experienced since my time at teachers' college back in 1993-1996.

At this particular moment, a number of factors are challenging me: my finances (I owe over seven thousand pounds on credit cards!), my job (I hate

Chapter 22: The Crumble

it!), and the way I am belittled and pushed around on a daily basis (I am the most qualified person in that stupid store, but I am treated like the biggest underdog!). Why is that, Lord?

I am disgusted by the people I work with. They are vipers, hypocrites, and ass-lickers. I am surrounded by the lowest of the low.

I am in the middle of doing a re-mortgage on my house, and that alone makes me have to hang in there and just take all the crap I am subjected to every day. I have no other source of income, so either I put up with everything that is sucking the life out of my soul and pay the bills, or I fight to save myself and lose my livelihood. Then the bank will reclaim the house, and I will lose everything that I sacrificed [for] in this fucking country.

If it was me alone, I might even consider giving up right now, but I have to keep a roof over Jasmine's head. God, and now my sister, and my niece are living here, too. Her help is invaluable, but the extra mouths to feed and board have exhausted all my resources.

So, really, I have no choice but to go back to work. Even though every morning starts with a panic attack and ends with another sleepless night as I toss and turn with the anxiety of what is to come when I enter that damn store's doors. If I do fall asleep, my dreams are all nightmares about what will happen if my alarm somehow fails, and I oversleep past the six a.m. opening time. Certainly, I would be fired. I know I am at my breaking point because I have started reliving my attack experience every time the alarm goes off, my mind tricking me into thinking it is the shot of a gun aimed right at my head.

I know that I am not eating well; the stress has just killed my appetite. No one needs to tell me that I am just going through the motions at work. I hate the lifting, the cleaning of the floor, and the packing of the shelves. My hands are so calloused that I am afraid to shake anybody's hand when I meet them.

My life has reached a stage where every time I compare it with what I left back in Jamaica, I cry. I really want to go back home, but Jasmine doesn't. She is ever so close to her dad and it would kill me to leave her here in London while I went back to Jamaica. I see no way for me to be able to go home. I just

Chapter 22: The Crumble

have to hang in there and put my desires beneath hers. I wish that there was some way both of us could be happy, but it's not possible at the moment. This is the harsh reality of motherhood; sometimes you have to sacrifice your own happiness for that of your child. Maybe my time to be happy will come when she grows up? Right now, though, she is all I have, and it would kill me to lose her. Tobore is still in the UK after all, and he now has his own new life and is doing very well. He stopped giving Jasmine support, and so I am now feeling like a new, hard journey is ahead.

To make matters worse, her uncle who had moved Tobore out of our marital home is also moving here, so she has one less tie back to Jamaica, and she will now want to go back even less for the holidays, which are the times I look forward to like a drowning man looks for a lifeline. As far as Jasmine is concerned, London is home.

I hate so many things about being in this dreary country. The cost of survival is far too high. I have to take every hour of work offered, even late at night, even when my daughter is home sick. It kills me to come home at one a.m. and find her homework left open on the kitchen table with a note to me asking for some clarification of something she doesn't understand, and knowing all I can do is write her a note back before I have to leave at five a.m. This is what our interactions have deteriorated to, notes written in the wee hours of the morning.

Tonight was an early night for me. I got home and was in bed right before midnight. I don't know if it's the exhaustion or my realizing the pathetic state of my life that is making me cry right now. It seems my prayers asking God why my life has turned out like this have only been met with a stone-cold silence.

I am sick of struggling! I want to be able to enter the grocery store and buy meat without having to sacrifice other items on my list. I want to not feel like an outsider anymore. I want to go home. Or find a way out of this constant cycle of working to near death and breathing a great sigh of relief every time a bill is paid. Please, God, hear my cry! Please help me!

I went to bed and hoped God had heard my cries that night. When I went to work the next day, I found that the new rotation had been posted. The last day for my having the safe responsibilities would be the day before inventory day, except I was scheduled to have that day off. I asked the manager about the discrepancy, but instead of switching my day off for another day, he asked me to come in on that day, even though I was not scheduled to be in the office. I had become so downtrodden that I simply agreed and went about my regular work duties.

That whole day, my heart bothered me. I needed a day off that week, as I had promised to take Jasmine out for the Easter holidays. I could not break another promise to her, as I was constantly making up broken promises to her. I went back to see the manager and asked him if we could please find a way to reorganise the schedule so that I wouldn't have to work an extra day that week. He told me not to worry and assured me I would get a day off as requested, but it would be the day after the inventory was completed. It was the best I was going to get, so I rescheduled everything with Jasmine and finished the week without a complaint.

The night after the inventory was completed, I received a call from the district manager, who asked if I could come in for a one-on-one meeting the following day. I explained that my rotation had been changed to provide for the day off that I'd had to miss to accommodate the inventory schedule. I also told him that I had rescheduled all the arrangements with my daughter to fit with the store's needs, and now those were set for the following day. I still remember the sneer in his voice when he said to me, "And you were very crafty in setting those plans to ensure that you had that day off. Well, it's not going to work." He told me I had better get busy changing my personal schedule around because it was not a request, but an order that I meet with the senior manager of operations that next morning. He ended the call by telling me not to worry too much; the meeting would be brief.

Chapter 22: The Crumble

Something in his voice put me on guard. An uneasy feeling grew inside of me. I began to wonder, had I done something terribly wrong at work that day? I wracked my brain for every movement I had made, every word I had spoken, but nothing stood out. Maybe he had found out about the key incident? A sick feeling churned in my stomach, and I realised I was afraid of that man. I was shaking so badly that I feared I would be ineffective in the meeting the next day. I called on my friend Shoa, whom I had known since my first teaching job here, and asked her to accompany me to the meeting for moral support. She immediately agreed.

When Jasmine awoke the next morning, I explained that we would have to move some things around and get a later start to our fun day than we had planned. She was disappointed once again, and as a nine-year-old, smart too. I could see in her eyes that she didn't trust me to come through with my promise to spend the day with her. I assured her that as soon as that one meeting was done, we would have the whole day together. When Shoa and I were walking out, though, I received a call telling me that the senior manager of operations was running late, and the meeting had been rescheduled for a few hours later in the day. It was just going to be too little time to leave the house to do anything and just enough time to make me have to break the promise I had just made to Jasmine.

When Shoa and I arrived at the office, the receptionist took one look at us and told me that I didn't need to bring any legal representation into the meeting. I explained that Shoa was just my friend, and the lady directed her to a seat in the waiting area and me into an inner office. As soon as I sat down in front of the district manager and the senior manager of operations, they handed me a letter and instructed me to go over its contents.

Even before I began to read, my heart sank. I was fired.

The two men were stiff and formal with me, simply dismissing me from the room. There were no false attempts at easing the pain of my being sacked. No one said, "Good job," or "You did try, but the fit just wasn't right." I returned to the waiting area in a daze and mumbled something to Shoa about being sacked. She immediately took over for where my spirit had shut down. She asked the two men who were hovering nearby what the reason was. To both of our surprise, they answered her directly but only said that because I hadn't yet worked there a full year, they were not obligated to provide any explanation. I felt the world unravel around me. The last glimpse I had of the district manager as Shoa took me gently by the arm to lead me out to the car park was of him slightly smirking. It was if he were saying to me, "Well, you got your day off."

Over the next few days, I began to realise the extent of planning that had gone into my sacking. Apparently, it came as no surprise to everyone else. They knew it was coming on that very day. I was the only one who was blindsided. I began to wonder how stupid I could have really been. How did I not see what was going on around me? However, I still could not get any concrete answers as to why I had been sacked. I met up with a few cashiers who I was close to, and the most I got was one of the cashiers suggesting that it was almost my one-year anniversary with the company, so that was their best time to part with me, as I was a troublemaker in their eyes. She said this was their strategy for those who didn't walk the straight and narrow. I wanted to get more information, so I went to my first store. It was uncomfortable and I had all sorts of feelings—what if I was seen by my old manager, what if they banned me. There were so many thoughts rushing through my mind, but I didn't care. I wanted answers, so I boldly went. I didn't actually get many answers, but I got a general sense of why. I was too bold, and I was seen as trouble. I understood it. Born in Jamaica, I didn't say, "I am afraid not," I said, "NO!"

After a year, sacking gets a lot trickier from a legal standpoint. And in management's opinion, I was going to be the manager that went against the fabric of what they stood for. I was being punished for being too nice to the staff. My consideration and Christianity were stumbling blocks, and I was too gentle with the female staff workers who were mothers. In fact, I was always saddened and would bring up the issue of having mothers on the cash registers when their children were left at school outside of regular school hours. Just because we didn't do a rotation with sufficient staff to cover the daily shifts. I got fed up at seeing grown women cry while my hands were tied, so I didn't fit into the culture of that organisation.

Even though my life had just taken the proverbial leap off the edge of a cliff, my dependents and family remained just as strongly reliant on me. I didn't know whether to cry or laugh when I received a letter from a friend back in Jamaica a few days after my sacking, asking me to give her an update on how I was coming along in collecting money to cover her university tuition and fees. I knew in my heart that I could do nothing for her, and it pained me to think about how that would be yet another person I loved whom I would be letting down. I would have rather just crumpled up the letter, thrown my phone into the river and pretended the request had never existed, but I couldn't do that. I sat down and put pen to paper:

My dearest Cassie,

I write to you this morning in one of the lowest states I have ever found myself in. My life just seems to be a series of low points. I am beginning to wonder if I have a personality disorder or if there is something wrong with me that attracts this kind of oppression. I am depressed beyond anything I have ever felt before. I don't even have the words to properly express what I am going through. When I am not numb, I am having a panic attack, and I feel like I am very near not being able to cope. Just the hustle of trying to stay on top of the most basic bills makes me miserable. Being on my own and with no one to help emotionally or financially is killing me.

Simply put, I am tired of life. I sit here typing and crying . . . and thinking how very tired I am of fighting this unwinnable battle that is my life. I want out of this rat race. If it weren't for Jasmine, I would probably be searching for a way to exit this life entirely, but I cannot pass my sorrow or burden on to her. I love her more than life itself. I have to hang on for her. But all she sees of me is the depression, which makes me impatient, short-tempered, insecure, and frustrated to distraction.

It was very hard for me to sit down and write this to you. I hate having to admit how much my life has regressed. I am so unhappy here in London, and I want desperately to return to my native Jamaica. However, Jasmine is now going on ten, and she doesn't want to leave. London is almost all she knows, and her dad lives here. All the jobs I have found here have been jobs of circumstance and nothing I would have chosen. The hours have prevented me from even being a mum properly.

I just received word that my mortgage has gone up due to the credit crunch. I have no idea how to pay it now that I am out of the job at the grocery store, but now to think that it is even higher than I expected, I really don't see how this will work out. I finally made an appointment to see a psychologist, and she agreed that I need to be under some attentive care, but where will I find the money to cover such an additional expense? I am nearing a breakdown . . .

How low can one get tossed before they just sink into nothingness?

CHAPTER 23: WEAKNESS

I think men become who we want them to be. They curve into the man that we expect them to be, and when we are no longer there, they become who they really are.

The day I lost my job, my house seemed lonelier than it had ever felt before. I sat alone in my room and cried. As I cradled my pillow for comfort, I remembered how so many times before, Tobore would have been the one snuggling next to me in bed. He would have been the one holding me while I wept into his shoulder, assuring me that however bleak the situation was, he would help see me through it. It broke my heart even more to think that I had lost that companionship, to know that I was really on my own against the world now.

Just days before, I had contemplated requesting that Tobore sign off his part of our house in Jamaica, so that it would be under my name solely. That would allow me to cut off my last tie to the one person who should have been my partner for life. Of course, I knew that was a foolish thought; he wouldn't do this, and selling at that time wouldn't make sense. The property needed work and we would not get much for it, so I discarded that idea.

Now, here I was with the weight of the world pressing even harder on my shoulders. I tried in vain to pull myself out of the emotional black hole that was consuming me, but even sleep proved to be another luxury denied me. I started using sleeping pills, but the few hours of pharmaceutically induced unconsciousness never left me feeling refreshed.

Before the sacking, I had been looking for other jobs. I had even had a few interviews (which I had secretly attended so as not to jeopardise my already tenuous position). My efforts had been rather weak and unsuccessful though, largely because of the extensive time demands from the store and my distraction with all the other pressures in my personal life. Now I was living in a constant state of needling anxiety and on the verge of completely losing my ability to function in even the simplest of daily tasks. When I sat down to take stock of my situation and come up with a productive plan, I started to feel the walls closing in on me, and the air became thick and hard to breathe. There was nothing that I wanted more than to run outside and escape everything that was constraining me.

I knew I couldn't go on like that, so I asked my general practitioner for a referral to a psychologist. Having a stranger to talk to seemed more effective at that time than leaning on my friends alone. They had their own issues, and I also didn't know who could handle the terrors in my past that I was still carrying around. I did consider calling on Tobore to make him my confidant. After all, we were on friendly terms with one another, and he already knew all of my past. Our wedding anniversary was coming up, and he had even called to ask if he could take me out for a private dinner that night. I had agreed because I was fairly certain that we would have no expectations of one another.

We had built a comfortable, platonic relationship, and it benefited Jasmine as much as it did Tobore and me. Gone were the days of angry glares across the table and screaming matches over the smallest of offences. We were able to do things together as a family in peace, like taking trips to animal parks and sharing holiday dinners. Tobore and I still supported each other financially, too. If he were ever in a bind, he knew he could come to me to borrow cash, and I knew I could count on him for the same. Unfortunately, neither of us had much to spare at any one time since coming to the UK.

I found out that the wait to get a psychologist appointment was months, so I decided to reach out to Tobore for some emotional support. Over the next weeks and months, I felt us really connecting in a meaningful way and thought maybe it was because we were building a friendship without the distraction of romantic involvement. We had even had several conversations where I shared with him my desire to find a man to share that physical side of life with, discussing my hopes for the occasional man I found attractive or with whom things could turn intimate. Little did I know that I was piercing his heart.

Tobore's silent torment finally came to my attention when something began to develop between him and a single parent from Jasmine's school. He began acting very strange and unnecessarily hostile around me, so I confronted him about it. I was not expecting what he told me next. He said that he still loved me with the same depth as when we'd conceived our daughter and told me that he couldn't ever love anyone else like that. He even told me that I was the only person he would ever consider having another child with and expressed the deepest regret for how far we had strayed from one another and all the things that had happened in the years we had been apart.

My heart melted. I began to think that somehow, after all we had gone through as a couple, we were both still subconsciously involved. Maybe, I wondered, nothing had worked out with other people because neither of us had ever really wanted to move on. We hadn't been intimate in a very long time, and the thought of it scared me. I had come to love and treasure our friendship, and I wasn't completely sure how I felt about abandoning that to enter into the tumult that we had left behind when we'd left each other's bed. The one thing I was sure of, though, was at that time in my life, I could not emotionally or mentally handle one more complication. I feared that chance at reconciliation might have to be delayed.

I had started submitting applications for work again, but nothing was panning out. One afternoon, after a particularly dismal interview, I was driving home and feeling so low that I was thinking how much better life would be if someone would just run a light so that I could be met by angels who would carry me off to heaven. I knew it was an insane thought, so I called Tobore and immediately started crying so hard that I could barely talk. He told me to pull off the road and compose myself, then to head straight home. He would be there shortly. I did so, taking only a few minutes to get my emotions under control and reaching the house only about five minutes later. As soon as I arrived, I sat down to wait for Tobore. While waiting, Kem and I fell into a conversation about my low mood. She offered to make me something to eat, but I declined because Tobore would be arriving at any moment and I wasn't hungry.

Before I knew it, two hours had elapsed. Tobore finally arrived, but he seemed in such a normal mood that I figured he had just been waylaid by something unimportant. He took me for a drive and we talked. He listened to all of my complaints and fears and gave all the right bolstering responses. By the time he dropped me off at home, I felt ready to go on with my life's battle. I was even able to make a few more appointments for potential job leads, one of which told me to come in right away. I grabbed my purse and was heading out the door when a call came from Jasmine's school. They needed me to bring her asthma medication because she was in the nurse's office with some worrying symptoms.

I cursed my luck. If I went, I would miss the meeting with the employment agency, but my child's health was much too important to be put second to anything else. I decided to call Tobore and ask him to help out once more today. Because he had just been so solicitous towards me, I was a bit surprised by his reticence to help out with that small situation, but there really was no time to dilly-dally. I told him that I would take care of it myself and not to worry.

I jumped in my car and drove to the school to drop off the medication. I called the employment agency and asked if I could be a few minutes late, but was told that their schedule wouldn't accommodate the delay. So, I drove home. Kem told me that Tobore had been at the house just a few minutes before I came back, but he had left when she'd told him I had already gone to make the delivery. Something in her voice made me

Chapter 23: Weakness

nervous and I asked her what she was holding back. She told me that he had come to the front door alone, but that she had seen someone else waiting for him in the car. A woman.

I rolled my eyes dismissively and told her that it was probably just some friend that needed a favour that day like I did. Her silence let me know that I was being a fool. She told me that it was clearly something else. The woman was very young and dressed like she was ready for a hot date, looking bored and very at home in the front passenger seat, with her feet propped up on the dashboard. She didn't need to say anything more about what she had seen. My heart recognised the truth of the matter.

I called Tobore to ask him about who the girl was that he was spending his day off with. He immediately went on the defensive and said it was none of my business. I told him that since he had just professed his undying love to me and opened the door to our reconciliation, it was most certainly my business. His tone turned very gruff and harsh, and he said that I was jumping to conclusions in my head about what he wanted of me. He said that our friendship was the end of whatever would be between us and that was where our relationship was and that was where it ended. I felt tricked and utterly betrayed. In an instant, all the trust and love that I felt for him disappeared with a finality that would affect the rest of our lives.

I knew that we would still have to interact with each other as Jasmine's parents, but I closed my heart to him beyond anything else. A week later, as I was continuing my job hunt around town, I got a call from Kem saying that Jasmine had been sent home from school with worsening symptoms, and she needed to get to a doctor right away. I was halfway across town and knew I couldn't get back home through traffic within the next hour. I moved my heart into professional mode, thinking that I would call Tobore as Jasmine's father to come and assist with his child getting to the hospital, since it was again his day off. He agreed and drove straight to my home, but quickly announced to Kem that he thought she looked fine. In his opinion, she didn't need a doctor. He said that there was nothing wrong with her that a nap wouldn't fix.

I found out later that he really was just anxious to get back to his girlfriend and had gone home grousing to a mutual friend that a visit to the doctor would have taken hours out of his day, just to possibly find out that she had a typical virus or something else common in kids. Back at home, though, Jasmine rapidly grew worse, and Kem became so frightened that she had me call another friend, who came over and immediately drove Jasmine to the closest hospital. Jasmine's state on arrival was so alarming that she was admitted and prepped for surgery to address an acute appendicitis.

The news shook me to my core. My baby was so sick that she needed to be cut open? My shock quickly switched to a seething anger towards Tobore. How dare he have been so flippant about our child's health? The doctor had told me on the phone that appendicitis could be deadly if left untreated. She could have died if we had ignored her symptoms.

If I had known then, the real reason Tobore had left (to cavort with his new paramour), I don't know what I would have done. I rushed to the hospital and found Tobore there at her bedside. My anger with him had only grown during the drive, and I flew into a rage at the sight of him. I literally chased him out of the room, screaming all sorts of accusations that he may have caused her death with his ignorant attitude.

I settled into the chair next to Jasmine's bed and refused to leave her for the night, even though the nurses advised me that visiting hours had ended. At around three a.m., a nurse came around to check in. I told her that Jasmine had kept telling me that her IV was hurting her, saying, "Mummy, it isn't comfy," while trying to pull on it. I asked the nurse to check it, and it was a good thing I did, because she discovered that the cannula had not been placed correctly. She said that they would try to replace it right away, but I stopped her and asked why she needed it. She said it was all part of the precaution to have her ready if they found out that she had appendicitis, and they needed to operate on her.

I was confused. From what I had understood, Jasmine had already been diagnosed. I asked the nurse to clarify everything and she said that they really didn't know what was wrong with my baby. They just suspected appendicitis, but the tests had all been inconclusive. I did not know very much about medicine or diseases such as appendicitis, but I was appalled that they were getting my daughter ready for surgery without really knowing what was wrong with her or what they needed to do. Surgery was so invasive and such a physical trauma. I didn't want her subjected to it on a suspicion. I demanded that they do more testing and get a better handle on what was really wrong. In the end, the nurse called the doctor and they acquiesced to me. Before noon, all of Jasmine's symptoms had resolved and she was released from the hospital. The test results came back and ruled out appendicitis. To this day no one knows what was wrong with her. I feel she was reacting to Dad's new partner and what may have felt to her like she was being replaced.

Over the next few weeks, Tobore's visits were very infrequent. Jasmine noticed and started complaining that he was neglecting her, so I doubled my efforts to keep them in contact in other ways. They would still get together on the weekends, only now he would just drop in for the minute it took to collect her and her things before they sped off in the car. Each time she came back from these visits, she would tell me about a girl that would stay with them for the whole weekend. I could tell that she was jealous of the attention he would shower on that woman, seeing it as time stolen away from her. Tobore was blind to that, though. Jasmine was demoted to the back seat of the car on journeys, even though it was an unspoken rule that she would never sit in the back of either of our cars. But the front seat was now occupied by Tobore's latest woman.

It all came to a head a short time later, when, one afternoon, I found Jasmine crying in the bedroom. She said that her daddy never paid attention to her anymore. It broke my heart to see her suffering like that, so I called Tobore to ask him to talk to her and to get his act together for her sake. He immediately flew into me. He told me that his personal life and his relationship with his daughter were none of my business. But, as every mother knows, anything that affects your child immediately becomes your business. I gave him a stern lecture and he agreed to speak to her about it.

I was afraid that Jasmine would get on the phone with Tobore and crumble into a frail little girl that gave up fighting for herself. I was filled with pride when she got on the phone and told him everything she had just told me. She asked him when she could see him next and they settled for Wednesday, his next day off. I drove her to his house on the appointed day, but asked her to first wait in the car while I had a quick talk with him. My intent was to stress to him the seriousness of the situation and that he couldn't merely dismiss her distress. However, what happened next would again change my life forever.

__Being totally broken and fragile can scare you forever,__
__if you let it.__

CHAPTER 24: LETTING GO

Letting go is sometimes hard, but a necessity in an effort to grow.

Tobore answered the door and silently invited me inside with a wave of his hand. We started talking about the situation, and he immediately became furious, yelling that I had no right to control his life. The personal attack took me off guard, but I got some clarity when he told me he thought my problem was that I didn't want him and didn't want him to be with anyone else either. The conversation became an all-out argument in each other's faces and screaming at the top of our lungs. He was angrier than I had ever seen him before.

His eyes had turned bloodshot red, and before I knew it, he lunged forward and grabbed me by the throat, squeezing so hard I choked for breath. I managed to bite his other hand so hard that he dropped his grasp on me. Before I could recover my wits, he had pushed me into the kitchen, and we were both striking at each other. I saw his fist coming hard at me, and I grabbed a knife from the counter. I didn't know what I was planning to do with it, but it didn't matter because he had already shoved me into the passage and slapped me across the face. I had dropped the knife in the melee, and in defence, kicked him hard in the leg. I sensed a hot wetness on my face and reached up to touch it, only to realise I was gushing blood from somewhere. I was filled with terror and looked at Tobore, only to see that he was bleeding too.

For some reason, that realisation set a fire in me. I reared back to fly at him with all my force, but he had grabbed a broom and used it to strike me across the face. The pain was tremendous and nothing like I had ever felt before. I was sure he had broken my nose, and I found myself flat on the floor. He was standing over me, screaming and cursing that I had rejected him and that it was his time to take out his revenge on me, once and for all. I will never forget the coldness in his voice when he said he had been waiting for that moment since before we'd left Jamaica. He said I had brought it on myself because I had cheated on him and made him look like a fool.

I was in total shock. A strange silence fell between us, and he finally grabbed me and pulled me up roughly, turning and shutting himself in a side room. I didn't know what to do. The whole scene felt like I had just experienced a nightmare and was merely waking from it. I started to come to my senses quickly and remembered that Jasmine was still sitting outside, waiting in the car. I grabbed at a curtain on the front window and wiped the blood from my face, thinking that I could simply walk out and pretend that nothing had happened. I didn't realise that I was covered in blood. As soon as Jasmine saw me, her eyes widened in shock, and she started crying.

I tried to calm her down and told her that I was going to be okay, but that I needed to call the police. She begged me not to, saying that she didn't want her dad to get into trouble. What was I to do? She was in hysterics at the thought of losing him. I started the car up and drove home. I finally got Jasmine to calm down by saying that adults, especially parents, sometimes have disagreements, and it was nothing for her to worry about. I began to try to figure out how to handle the situation. I decided to call Tobore's newest female friend, who had been spending a lot of time at his house. I had heard that she was a mother also, and I thought that maybe I could explain to her what I'd tried to explain to Tobore about Jasmine being upset with him for not spending enough quality time with her. My irrational hope was that she would pass on the message I had originally intended to get across before our altercation.

Chapter 24: Letting Go

I meant to only ask her to try to help Tobore understand how Jasmine was feeling and ask that she help him be a bit more sensible and conscious of his daughter's feelings. I ignorantly assumed that, as a female and a mother, she would be my ally and would understand how much girls want and need their dad's attention. After all, I was still legally married to him, and I also hoped she would respect that. I immediately found out how foolish I was being. As soon as I said hello and introduced myself, she laid into me. "Ey dutty gal, a long time me a wait pon you fi call me! Why the fuck you nuh left him alone and divorce him so him can be free to love who him want? Why the fuck you nuh get it that you and him over? Why you keep calling him to come around to your fucking yard? You nuh get it you a wife pon paper, but mi a him baby mother! Fuck off, gal. I am pregnant with his son. The one you could never give him."

I couldn't even speak. Instead, I just hung up the phone. Her words hurt me more than any of the blows that Tobore had rained down on me earlier that day. Clearly, she had been fed the idea that I was the one holding on to him, when in fact it was he who was holding on to me. Mainly because divorce would have ruined his chances to get his citizenship in the UK. The pregnancy also pierced me, and I understood why. During one of our last civil conversations just a few weeks before, Tobore and I had decided that if we were still estranged and not with anyone else by the time I turned thirty-five, we would come together and have a baby so that Jasmine would have a full sibling.

The conversation with that woman was not over yet, though. She must have used my phone number off the caller ID to start sending me abusive text messages, threatening my life, and calling me all sorts of despicable names. I began to put two and two together, remembering her from an earlier time with Tobore and how he had vehemently denied having any interest in her, saying that she was just some "ghetto gal" from his work. I should have just turned off my phone, but I was so incensed at the whole situation that I fell into a text battle with a person I didn't even know. I had no one to blame but myself for that event. Even though my inten-

Chapter 24: Letting Go

tions for contacting her had been good, I had opened the floodgates to set us on this hateful path.

I went outside to talk to my friend Norma on the phone and calm down. She tried to encourage me to delete the hateful texts, but I felt that I needed to keep them as evidence if things deteriorated further. The intensity of the situation exhausted me. I collapsed into a heap on the ground and buried my head in my hands. Just then, I heard a car stop and heavy footsteps come up the walkway. I lifted my head only slightly to see who was visiting me at that inopportune time and was confused to see three sets of shining black shoes. I lifted my head slowly, my gaze travelling up the legs of three sturdy police officers, their hands firmly on their truncheons. I instantly knew that they were here for me. Tobore must have called them to report me after I had left his house.

One of the officers calmly asked if I was Ava Brown and I told them yes. They beckoned me to get up off the ground and said that they needed me to come with them. I wasn't about to object. I cursed myself for not having called the police first and instead giving in to my young daughter's wishes of not wanting to cause Tobore any more trouble than we already had in our lives as immigrants. I told the men that I would come quietly, and they allowed me to first tell my sister that I would be out so that she could watch my daughter. If Jasmine asked where I was going, my plan was to tell her that I was just going out for a walk to clear my head.

However, Jasmine was the one who met me at the door, and I saw the extreme anguish on her face as she noticed the police standing in the background. Before anything else could happen, Jasmine began screaming and flailing, her heart tormented. She banged her head hard on the wall and fell. The police came rushing to help with the situation and when they persuaded her to take deep breaths, she calmed down to a miserable crying state. They tried to explain to her that they just wanted to take her mum somewhere quiet for a while so that we could have a talk, but my child was far too intelligent, and she knew better. In the end, I

Chapter 24: Letting Go

left with them, sitting like a scolded child in the back of the police car. Luckily, they spared me the handcuffs because I was being cooperative. My whole being was in shock; I couldn't even feel my heart beating and thought that maybe I had died, and my spirit was just somehow locked inside my body. I spoke up to make sure of the reality of the situation. I asked if I could use my phone to make a call. That was when they gave me the official word that I was under arrest. They then confiscated my phone, and they read me my rights.

We arrived at a police station in Norwood, drove up a back entrance, and straight to where the cells were. I had remained silent for the entire drive, but my mind was working overtime. I kept asking myself how someone who had once loved me so intensely, someone who had shared so many momentous events in my life, someone who relied on me as much as I did on him, could have done that to me. I was crying copiously and could hardly understand what was being said to me when the booking process began. I finally heard the charge against me: Tobore reported that I had come to his house and instigated a physical attack. I finally found my voice and tried to tell the police that they had it all wrong, but they were quite dismissive at that stage and said that they were just doing their jobs.

I realised that I had no advocate in that police station, so I decided that my best tactic was just to stay quiet. My God, I was shaking with fear! In no time, I was being led farther into the building. Someone removed my belt and took off all of my jewelry. A body search was then performed by a female officer, and in the background, I could hear another officer making account of my possessions. Finally, I was given one phone call, which I used to call home and talk to Jasmine to reassure her that I would be fine and home soon.

After the call, I was taken to be fingerprinted, to give a DNA sample (by mouth swab), and to have my mug shot taken. Everything they did was so invasive, on a physical and a spiritual level. I knew I was experi-

Chapter 24: Letting Go

encing what it was like to lose my freedom, and I flashed back to how awful the experience must have been for my little sister in those weeks before her death. The jail staff asked if I needed anything, and I requested to see a doctor and a solicitor. I still had open wounds from the earlier altercation with Tobore and I was afraid of infection or scarring if they were not attended to. They said that it was all in the process and ushered me down to a cell.

When I heard the heavy metal lock clank into place, I felt lower than I ever had in my entire life. The whole situation was surreal, almost as if I was suddenly in a TV show. Again, I started to think that maybe I was simply experiencing a very lucid stress nightmare on the eve before I was to confront Tobore about spending more one-on-one time with our daughter. Maybe I had fallen out of bed and was lying on the hard floor of my house. That must be the uncomfortable feeling under my back. But, no, it was really the hard bed in the cold cell I was occupying. I had to face the reality that I was in jail, placed there under the false accusations made by my husband. It was clear that he was at war with me, and I was losing the battle.

I started reflecting on our relationship from a more realistic perspective. One in which my heart was closed off and deadened to him. I realised how many mistakes I had made with him, especially in trusting him again after the first time he'd had a child with another woman. I had still allowed him to move to London with us. How foolish I had been to think that we could ever make anything out of the deteriorated shell of a marriage we had. I was shocked at how much he had changed as a person from the man I believed he was in those blissful first years we'd spent as a young couple while I was in teaching college. How could that loving young man be the same person who'd just sent the police to arrest me by using a blatant lie?

Even more troubling was the thought of how that man, who had changed so drastically, could still be a loving and cautious father with

Jasmine? Did he not think at all about how his false accusation against me would affect her emotional well-being and her livelihood? I remembered the status of my citizenship right then, and my body went numb again. How would an arrest affect that? And if my application was negatively affected, both his and Jasmine's would be in jeopardy as well. How could he have not thought about that?

I suppose he had reached a point where he just didn't care about any of it anymore. Something must have given him enough confidence in his own chances to feel like he could get citizenship without me. I realised that he must finally really see the end for us. There was no going back from that event. Our lives, even as parents of a shared child, were separated from one another from that moment on.

I didn't know what else to do. I was absolutely powerless to the forces shaping my life at that time. I closed my eyes and asked God to just give me the courage and strength to get out of the mess that my life had become since coming to London. I asked God to work a miracle so that I would somehow get released before nightfall. That way, I could be home before Jasmine fell asleep, and I could ease her fears. I lay there crying for who knows how long. I cried until my eyes hurt, and there were no more tears to come out of them. Each time the jailers passed by for a routine inspection, I would ask if my doctor or lawyer had arrived to see me yet. Each time, they told me no.

On the fourth pass, they asked if I wanted anything to eat. I had been so consumed with distress that the thought of food had never crossed my mind, even though I hadn't eaten since eight o'clock that morning, and it was now late afternoon. I merely mumbled that I wasn't hungry. There was a toilet in the cell, and although I wanted to pee, I just couldn't make myself use it, as the cell was open for all to see. I had been in the cell for around four hours when the doctor finally arrived. He made some sort of joke about the delay being caused by "London's Sunday service." I could only suppose that was his attempt to lighten my heavy mood, but it didn't

Chapter 24: Letting Go

work. His visit afforded me some freedom since I was taken out of my cell for the examination and treatment.

I stupidly thought that was my chance to finally be absolved of the false accusations. Certainly, the doctor would see that I was beaten up and call for my release. Instead, he simply went over me from head to toe, taking blood samples from the still open gashes on my lip and in my mouth, and made a report that confirmed that I had been badly beaten up. I remember him even noting the slap marks on my face, where the impact of Tobore's hand had broken the blood vessels under my skin. It made no difference. After he left, I was taken promptly back to my cell.

I began to have all kinds of panicked thoughts. What if I was never released? What if prison was my new home? What if social services took Jasmine away because I was an unfit mother locked up in jail? Or the lady with whom I had made hurried arrangements to watch her had to leave and couldn't stay there overnight. What would happen to my child then? Would she just be left at home alone? I just stared at the walls of the cell, and no answers came to my fearful questions. The ceiling and walls were covered with the names of all who "WUZ ERE," scratched into the plaster by countless hands. I had no interest in proudly claiming my residence in any jail.

Soon, though, I received word that my appointed lawyer had arrived, and I was escorted to the room where he and I were allowed to talk. I told him the truth of what had happened at Tobore's, leaving out no detail, not even the ones that made me look bad. He made only non-committal responses to all of my statements. Afterwards, I was taken to meet with another set of police officers in yet another room, where they had tape recording equipment. There, they made an official record of my statement.

The lawyer had accompanied me to make my statement, and I was glad he did, because it was clear from the first moment that the police thought I was lying. They tried to convince the lawyer that I was guilty, but he stood his ground defending me and continued to ask for proof of the accusations against me. After an interminable back-and-forth, the policewoman agreed with the lawyer and said that the information just wasn't strong enough to prove that Tobore was telling the truth in his accusation against me. Instead of being released immediately, I was placed back in my cell while they processed all the paperwork and made records in their database of the event, my statements, and all of my very personal information. I was finally released, with the knowledge that my fingerprints and DNA would be on file for six years before they would be deleted. I couldn't believe it. I was in the police database, all thanks to my husband.

As I gathered my belongings, the last policewoman who had been present for the debate with my lawyer came over and gave me a pep talk. She told me that I was lucky to be going home and reminded me that I needed to put everything with Tobore behind me and just focus on my child. She had a warm, almost motherly tone of voice when she told me to leave that man out of my life, that he didn't mean me any good, and I would be fighting a losing battle with him. She even told me that I had the right to go downstairs and make a report against him, based on the evidence of my bodily harm that was clear for all to see. But, without saying anything, we both knew that would only have stirred the hornet's nest. Besides, I was still struggling with the immense guilt of the damage I would cause to him by doing so. Even though he had just done the same horrible thing to me, I could not find it within myself to do it back to him.

At that point, I knew that I needed to go home to be with my child. I had no money, it was late, and I still needed to find a way to get there. I wasn't about to dawdle at the station. What if they changed their minds and tried to re-arrest me? I had run outside to the street and frantically waved down a cab. On my way to the house, I called my friend, who was still sitting for Jasmine, to ask if she had money on her. She said yes and I breathed a sigh of relief; something was finally going my way. When I got home, all I could do was grab ahold of Jasmine and hug her tight, like I was never going to let her go. We were both crying and clinging to each other for quite some time.

My friend who had come to watch Jasmine told me that after I had been picked up by the police, Tobore's brother had arrived and said that he was there to pick Jasmine up to stay with her father. Since I had told her the situation (and Jasmine had also told her of her own fright after seeing my substantial physical injuries), she knew better than to believe his ruse. There was no way she was going to give Jasmine to anyone in my absence. I thanked her profusely, and she headed home to her own waiting family. Jasmine fell asleep quickly. She was so exhausted after the stress of the day. I tossed and turned with fitful nightmares about the police coming back to get me again.

Our lives were never the same after that day. It was just another cruel reminder in my life that everything you know can be taken away in a moment. How your life's path can be changed drastically without your intent or input. The woman who was currently carrying Tobore's third child had started a campaign of hate against me—emails, letters, and phone calls. I was constantly bombarded. But my experience with the police after being arrested on false charges had frightened me so much that I did not trust them to help me with any situation. I was so traumatised by all of the events, I was unable to focus on the fact that I wasn't working and had no money coming in.

My friends in London rallied around me and Jasmine during that time and provided what little comfort and money they could to help us. Since Jasmine's birthday was coming up, my friend Norma invited us to her house for a celebration. Jasmine agreed to the plan right away because she had decided on her own that she didn't want to see her father anymore.

I finally felt free to file for divorce. There was nothing left tying us together. As soon as I was legally classified as a single mother, I qualified for social assistance and it provided a positive change in my life that I had never anticipated.

Chapter 24: Letting Go

The first thing I needed to do was get myself back together emotionally, and truthfully, that was one of the hardest things I had ever done. The experience of being arrested and locked up had affected my self-esteem in ways that I would have never imagined. I felt like society had labeled me as a criminal, and I lost all confidence in who I was. I no longer saw myself as an independent, tenacious woman, but as a shameful blot on society. It went against everything at my core. I knew that if I were to survive and be an effective mother for Jasmine, I would have to get back to who I had been before that unfair event took place.

Accepting that Tobore was not the man I'd thought he was proved to be just as hard. I relied heavily on my faith during that time and had begun to see God's hand in many of the events of the past years. In a way, He had continually shown me that Tobore was not the relationship for me, but I had been too strong-headed to recognise it. Serving the divorce papers to Tobore was yet another challenge. He had moved residence and I could not get anyone to divulge his location. All I found out was that he had moved in with the woman carrying his child and her family.

I finally discovered his whereabouts when one of my friends saw the two of them shopping at a grocery store near my house. I was shocked to find out that they lived relatively close to Jasmine and me, yet he had never once reached out to her since that fateful day, regardless of the fact that she didn't want to see him due to her hurt. She was a child and he was the adult—and he was her father. I was more heartbroken to learn that he was doing very well, both personally and financially. My friend said that he and the woman were laughing and joking like young lovers strolling through the store, with a whole trolley full of items. Meanwhile, Jasmine and I were wondering where our next meal was going to come from, since I had no money. We were hungry, and our cupboards were empty.

I went back to the same traumatised and fearful state that I had fallen into after the attack in Jamaica that had precipitated our move to London. Every time I heard a police car, I became nervous and agitated, thinking that Tobore was again exerting his revenge on me. Kem and her daughter were still living with us, but she was so displeased with the situation of me being jobless and so anxious, she decided to return to Jamaica with her daughter. Instead of being relieved that I would have two fewer people to be responsible for, I was heartbroken that I would be losing what little in-house support I had.

Our situation became more challenging over the next several weeks. Tobore finally reached out to start seeing Jasmine again, but he refused to let her go to his home or to see her inside of mine. Instead, he proposed that I should bring her to meet him on the street in a neutral area where he would park his car and they could spend a few minutes talking. Truthfully, I knew he wouldn't hurt her, and I wasn't fearful of him doing anything to her, but I felt that scenario was disrespectful to our daughter, so I turned down his offer. I told him that we needed to find a more suitable environment rather than a car on the side of the road for them to rebuild their father-daughter relationship. He responded by sending a letter through his solicitor that demanded visitation with Jasmine under any condition and accusing me of unlawful denial of contact with his child. To be frank, Jasmine did not want to see him, so I felt confused and trapped. By now I disliked anything to do with the law and almost panicked.

Besides that stress, I had started falling behind on my mortgage payments and I was then at risk of losing our home. Something had to change in our lives and soon. I had a long, serious talk with Jasmine, who was now ten, about our situation. I suggested that we might be in a better position if we were to quit London and go back to Jamaica for a while. Even though it broke my heart, I told her she had the option of staying in London with her dad, if she really wanted to. My sweet girl spared not one moment in declining the offer and saying that she wanted to come along with me, no matter where we went.

Chapter 24: Letting Go

I started planning for our move home. I put our house on the market, but quickly realised that we would fare better finding renters. I had to admit that there was a huge relief in preparing to go back to Jamaica. I had wanted out of London for a long time, but I had always consulted Tobore on it before. His response was always to dissuade me. He would tell me that I would mess up our immigration status and ruin everything I had worked so hard for already. Now, without him, the decision was completely up to me. I knew that my situation had become so dire that if I stayed in London, I would lose my house and my sanity.

As the day neared for us to return to our homeland, I blamed myself for the mess that had led all of us up to that moment. I blamed myself for bringing Tobore to London, and perhaps I was being selfish, but I brought him there with a view that I would have a husband and a family; that I wouldn't have to be alone and on my own. I felt used and questioned if he had used me to get there. I blamed myself for the deterioration of Jasmine and Tobore's relationship. And I blamed myself for all the hardships that we had endured as immigrants in a harsh new country. I had convinced myself that I was a complete failure in all aspects of my life: as a wife, as a mother, and as a career woman. It was in a fog of self-hate and depression that I booked our flights back to Jamaica. I would take my child back home to the land of her ancestors in the hopes of re-joining the well-worn path that they had forged from the slave ships to independence. After all, we were both born of their spirit of tenacity and resilience, and our paths still had many steps to go.

Life and revenge can be a very messy affair.

CHAPTER 25: HOME AT LAST

Reputations can attach themselves to us and become a permanent part of our person.

We landed in Jamaica, and man, it was far too hot. My friend Angel was there just to see that we landed safely. Of course, I was nervous about being there, but what choice did I now have? I had to put my big girl panties on and breathe in. I couldn't believe how much I felt the striking difference in the weather. Mind you, I had a terrible cold from the constant dampness in Britain and I could barely breathe. The extreme heat only made that worse. The flight back had been horrible. There were mostly Jamaicans on board the plane, and sadly, those Jamaicans lived up to the stereotypes. They really behaved like hooligans on the plane. They fought with the flight attendants and held parties at the back of the aircraft. The pilot had to announce that they were closing the bar, and that if the rowdy behaviour continued, he had no choice but to ask for police presence and arrests to be made when we landed at the Norman Manly Airport.

The main attendant said it was the worst flight she had seen in her twelve years. The travel was terrible for other reasons too: the food was awful, the service was under-catered, and the toilets didn't work. I felt like the airline had given us the worst conditions possible for our trip.

As a Jamaican, I felt deeply embarrassed that we had lowered ourselves to the expectations the whites had of us. How unfortunate that the good got categorised with the bad. I also felt embarrassed for my daughter, who had to endure such raucous behaviour by our own nationals. It was a good thing she didn't see her mum participating in any such brawls. We landed, and the crew gave no indication of what was to happen next.

We all became orderly and exited the plane. There were no police, thankfully, because we would have been delayed even further, and I wasn't in the mood, as I was frying. But what happened next was worse than being on an unruly flight. Immigration was good, but the baggage clearance could not have been more of a horror. The carousel area looked like a bombsite. Cases and bags were thrown around, stacked on each other, and there was utter confusion. Getting our bags was going to be a battle. I stood there looking at the chaos, and I realised that it was a vivid image of the country I called home. An accurate representation of what I had left Britain to come home to: utter confusion. To be honest, it was also representational of my life and where I was personally. As a matter of fact, "confused" was where I had been for a long time. I stood there taking in the scene, trying to manoeuvre my mind and my life out of the mess, when Jasmine saw that I had gone into my own world. Her gentle nudge in the side snapped me back from my dazed state. The child was my rock. She was always there to bring me back to reality in the sweetest way.

I took Jasmine across to a seat to stay with the laptop and the other items we had on hand, while I went to war to try to find our items of baggage. Mind you, it wasn't an easy road, but I managed to axe out our bags, and we headed to customs. I didn't have anything much to declare. I only brought back the items I needed most but couldn't afford in Jamaica. I had cereal and nuts mainly, and that "real" mayonnaise that I knew I couldn't afford to buy here. I also had the envied foil paper. Those items were luxuries for me. I paid merely one pound for each; a true bargain, I said to myself. There was the Wii video game for Aida, my goddaughter, and the wedding party clothing I was given to deliver as a favour for a friend. Hell, I wasn't going to pay for other peoples' stuff. When the customs officer asked what I had to declare, I said nothing. He said he wanted to open our cases and I invited him to. I was a little scared and nervous then, as I wasn't certain if I would be held for the wedding items and the Wii game. I had already decided I would leave them for the owners to clear if they became a problem. At Gatwick Airport, back in Britain, I had taken out the last two hundred pounds from my bank account to help pay Jasmine's school fee when we arrived back in Jamaica. I only had ninety-nine pence left in that account, so I knew I wasn't going to be able to spend any money. He asked me what my status was in Jamaica. I told him I was a returnee and went to London for a holiday and only brought back food to eat. I invited him to look as he was starting to get on my last set of nerves. Many people were getting on my nerves, I noticed lately. Presumably, it was because I was so alone and struggling, and sometimes I got worn out. But I knew I had to keep going, as I had a long way yet to go. I could not fail my daughter, so I kept going. He stamped our papers and told us to have a good day.

As we both got settled in Jamaica, my life seemed so overwhelming. There were school fees to pay, rent, as we were now in Kingston, over two hours away from our owned house, and the general getting on with life. Our home was empty of all vegetables and fruit. Of course, if I could have taken them back from London, I would have. They were far cheaper and seemingly better quality there. On rare occasions, I might have bought plums, pears, or apples. But these items were far too expensive to purchase regularly, and I had only bought kiwis once since I returned. Three for the price of two pounds, which was two hundred and forty Jamaican dollars—a luxury. But I must add that the Lord was good to us. Somehow, Jasmine's lunch box always had some fruit in it. I wished I could have gotten that girl to eat raisins as a snack. The child wasn't fussy, but her eating habits drove me up the wall sometimes. I wished she had grown up like I did. I knew hunger and appreciated anything I was able to get to eat.

Before leaving the UK, I had shipped several larger items of value. When the delivery arrived, they had forgotten my barrel containing many expensive items including a glass basin, which was worth close to one thousand pounds. While I waited at the wharf, I met the nicest old man.

Chapter 25: Home At Last

His name was Mr. Spence, and anyone would have loved him to be their dad. He worked at the wharf, and I learned he had recently had a stroke. In my mind he shouldn't have been working, but times were hard. He touched my heart. I guess sometimes I was just far too soft. Anyway, he promised to get the barrel to his office and then we could take it home from there.

I was hopeful that my friend Pete would lend me his truck to pick up the barrel, but I wasn't sure anymore. When I rang him to ask for his help, he suggested he call me back. He had told me his daughter had some school help project to attend, where she would be handing out "back to school supplies" to less unfortunate kids. I thought that was a brilliant idea, and I agreed to speak with him later. I thought he said he would drop the barrel off at half past eleven in the morning. But instead, he did not show until after three o'clock and spent all of ten minutes with me. It felt like a waste of time having waited for him, as his presence was of very little assistance.

Imagine Pete sent a friend to complete the job, rather than doing it for me as a friend who charged me over $3000 to move simple rubbish I could have moved myself. I felt ripped off. I felt so ripped off I wanted to cry. I wondered why everyone that heard my voice and my adopted British accent thought I had money. Or because I lived in a gated area, I must have been loaded with cash! If only they knew how I was completely broke and struggling. I told myself that was the last time I would ever be ripped off. From then on, I would choose who I asked for help, no more friends of friends. A lesson learnt and one to be remembered.

I was not going to allow these challenges to override the fact that I was enjoying Jamaica. The beautiful views of the countryside on my drives to see my mum, the neatly dressed school children in their uniforms, the ripe mangoes on the trees, ready to be picked. Knowing that their juice was sweet, and they were ripened naturally—oh, I had one hand in Heaven. The people smiling and saying good morning was so therapeutic, the sunshine kissing my face and waking me up in the mornings was priceless. The fact that I wasn't rushing around every day in the rat race was so good on one hand for my mental state. I felt like that was just what I needed. Jasmine and I needed that hibernating type of environment. At least, I felt I needed it in order to be my best self and to be the best mother I could be to her.

As the Jamaican heat was sweltering most days I went to bed most nights confused with my thoughts. The nights were so hot I couldn't clear my mind. Even though I had grown up here, I could not understand how people could live in this hot hell. I was also having difficulty breathing. I had a terrible stuffed nose due to the heat. We slept on the floor on an eight-inch- thick mattress that cost $7,500. In Jamaica, everything was thousands of dollars. Nothing was ever simple and inexpensive. Perhaps it was just me? Everyone else seemed to look at me strangely when I exclaimed how expensive everything was. Jasmine and I slept on the floor on the mattress, and we kept turning the air conditioning on and off trying to keep the room cool enough to sleep. I wished I could have kept it on all night, but I was too aware of the cost to run the thing. After all, in Jamaica, if you owed money to the utility company, they disconnected you. In England we were able to keep playing the game of "I will pay bit by bit" and wait until the final due notice to pay. I wasn't going take that risk in Jamaica. Moreover, the landlady informed me that the utility was in her name and if it got disconnected, she would not be happy. She basically told me to pay on time whether I had the money or not. I could not live in our home back in Montego Bay, as I did not want to be anywhere near that place. The memories were too dreadful, and I was already feeling close to a breakdown. Though money was tight, I was helped somewhat with the rent from the Jamaican property and help from social services back in the UK. As money was running out, I was hard on the job hunt, but that, too, was not going well. Tobore's family wasn't involved, so it was Jasmine and me soldering, and my focus was more on working on my mental state, keeping her in school, and general survival.

Chapter 25: Home At Last

One Sunday, I woke up at half past six because I couldn't sleep. It was far too hot. I tidied up the kitchen and tried as best as I could to set up some sort of a living room. It was slowly coming together. Since it was Sunday, we hurried to get showered and dressed because I was adamant that we were going to church. All my stresses and problems at the time were saying not to go, but I insisted, just as we would have done any other thing that needed doing. We went and it was such a blessing. I wore my Nigerian outfit and I felt so regal; Jasmine wore her Ghanaian dress kente cloth with a white crocheted cardigan. We found the Baptist church that adjoined her school, but I missed my friend Angel. She was a bit far for us to be seeing her daily but we kept in touch on the phone when we could. It wasn't the same without her hopping by to say good morning or sending us something nice to eat. She loved us with her sweet cooking. She was always sending Jasmine something especially nice to eat or drink—like her guava juice, so thick it filled you up—and every sip tasted amazing.

The pastor had spoken about being prepared for when our time comes. As I sat there in the congregation, I felt anxious and unsettled. I tried to keep calm. When the ushers came by to collect the offering, I put $1,000 in the bowl, but asked myself how it was so easy to have paid $2,500 to get cardboard boxes removed but I hesitated to give back to the Lord who blessed me through all my trials.

As the service continued, there was an elderly man in front of me who seemed to have collapsed. I initially thought he had died; perhaps it was the heat? He was whisked away by the elders and no sooner than five minutes later he was being rushed to the hospital. It was a poignant reminder of the pastor's sermon.

Later that evening as I was writing my thoughts, I had to pause because my daughter came in and asked me what I was doing. It was obvious that I was typing. I was doing about sixty words per minute, so I asked her, "Can't you see I am typing?" She pointed out to me that I had been snapping all week. I was aware of this but thought I had it under control. I was so stressed, and I thought I'd like to go down the road of oblivion and pretend everything would all be okay, sooner rather than later. I wanted to believe I had faith in God. Not as much as I would have liked, but enough faith. I felt I could get away with hoping that God would take care of the rent and all the lost bits would fall into place.

The next day, I woke up and called to check if the rent on my London flat had been paid into my account and found that wasn't done. I was furious because once again the estate agents hadn't set up the mandate, although that had been in place since July. I rang the estate agents, and their attitude was so disgusting, they basically said they didn't care. In the meantime, I was an ocean away and at their mercy to follow through with their responsibilities, and I desperately needed the money. All the other issues aside, Jamaica was in the middle of Hurricane Gustav. Can you imagine? I didn't just come home to Jamaica, I had chosen to come back during a hurricane! It would have been difficult enough to find a job there when the economy was stable, but it was nearly impossible during a major hurricane. Well, I remained hopeful. Through all of that, I was still hopeful, and infinite hope was my middle name.

> ***When life knocks you down, don't stay down—crawl your way out.***

CHAPTER 26: LANDLADY DRAMA

Money is the root of all evil, they say, yet it adds such comfort to life, one cannot ignore its power.

The landlady whom we were renting from was quite a piece of work. When I took the place, in her eyes I had no job and could not afford the rent. Fair enough. She said she generally only rented to companies, and I had arrived in Jamaica on my own. I had not worked since April of that year. She was more than correct. I was jobless in every sense of the word. My friend Pete had been able to arrange to get the house rented for me by pulling some strings. His company took the cash out of his salary, and I paid it back to him. So, the rent appeared to be paid monthly by a company. I thanked God for him in that case—he had served a purpose after all!

The landlady had been given a cheque for $120,000 for the August rent. Because I had taken the house on the tenth of August and she was insistent on collecting on the first day of each month, she needed to pro-rate that first month. I was waiting for her to refund me the prorated money. The woman had no respect for anyone's time. She had you wait on her and then did not show up. She didn't even have the decency to call to tell you she couldn't come. I had left many messages requesting the money. She kept telling me she would send it via her nephew. Needless to say, I never saw him.

I was still waiting for the money when one night she stood me up again. She had told me she would meet me at seven that evening. Jasmine and I got to the house on time. I rang her, and she told me she needed to call me back, but she didn't. I rang her again, and she told me she would call back, again she didn't. We waited for her until after eight o'clock. My

God, she didn't even care. We had gone back to our apartment when she rang to say she was now in Cherry Gardens and could I come to collect the money there? She said she had been decking a house (making the roof out of pure cement and mortar). I wondered who the hell she thought she was. Not only didn't she have any regard for my time, she wanted me to kiss her kitty. I was having none of that. Yes, I was renting her house, but I had two of my own. One in London and one here in Jamaica. I wasn't renting because I was someone who didn't know what it was like to own their own place. I was renting because I couldn't live in my own house for love nor money. Anyway, she didn't bother to show again, and I wasn't going to chase her. I had a discussion with my close friend and confidant, Norma Jean, and I informed Tobore via email that I was looking to get the house valued with the view of selling it. He replied telling me to do what I wanted with it. Meaning if I wanted to sell, I should go ahead.

I went for an interview on the following Wednesday with a company called GeofoTek, when Jasmine rang to tell me that our power company had disconnected the light in the communal areas. *Damn*, I thought, *how could our landlady do that?* The utilities were in her name. She came across so diligent with things like that. She apparently had not paid the bill. So now we had no washer and dryer, not that I could afford to use them. She made us buy tokens from her to wash and dry our clothes. They cost about five pounds each, so nearly five hundred Jamaican dollars. Our dirty clothes were piling up. That day, I knocked on the neighbour's door and she told me that having the utilities shut off wasn't normal. I took solace in that, and I went back indoors. About twenty minutes later the neighbour rang the door to tell me the landlady had told her that she was going to fix it, and the lights would be back on soon.

At about half past eight that night, the landlady came around with her brother, and she went into my kitchen and started eating my genip fruit. I found that incredibly distasteful but said nothing. Her brother tried to look at the cooker to see if he could hook it up because I had been waiting on that as well. It appeared that all that time the place was wired for 110 amps, and there I was with a 220 cooker from London. Never mind that, it was set up for gas and electric, so I could have used the gas, but the lease agreement insisted that you used electric! So, since I moved in, I had not been able to cook a single meal. My last option was to cook some tikka masala rice in the microwave. And I attempted to cook rice and chicken in my vegetable steamer, but that took hours. They left and she never mentioned my money at all, and I was too afraid to ask.

My sister Sheena came to stay with me for a bit. She was twenty-two and had no job; in fact had never worked as far as I can recall. While she was with us, she drove me mad. She wanted everything in my closet, ate all the food in the wink of an eye, and was too quick to stamp her ownership on my belongings. I was surprised she was still so naïve and had to ask myself if that was how I would have been if I had lived with my mum all this time. She was as unexposed as I had been. Even so, I was glad she was there, as this gave me a sense of family and Jasmine had someone to play with other than me. Her visit made me glad Jasmine was very exposed to an international lifestyle, but more so that she was a sensible and clever child.

Despite the hurricane still bearing down on the island, Jasmine and I went to Mandeville to meet up with my mum. She insisted on taking me to see her pastor because she was worried about the path my life had been taking. She wanted me to see a spiritual man. I was scared but trusted my mum. Thankfully it was nothing like I had envisioned, and it was, in fact, a true pastor and a church. Before we parted, I asked my mum for some lotion and she whipped out a black roll-on bottle that looked like deodorant. Jasmine and I looked at each other in shock, and we retorted, "No, Mama, we said lotion."

"Hold your horses," she said, "it's lotion." My mum had taken out the marble-like section of the roll-on and poured lotion into the bottle. I couldn't help myself. I had to laugh. My God, she was resourceful. It went a long way to explain to me how they survived their living conditions.

Although it killed me each time to see where they lived, they seemed to be content with it. Even then, the lotion had a lovely smell. One that I would have taken even if it was in a roll-on bottle any day.

We headed to the Mandeville market. At the mouth of the market there were police officers threatening to close the market hall down because of the ferocious hurricane. In spite of that, everyone went about their shopping. I really would have thought that I was pregnant had I been sexually active because I desperately wanted a cow's head to make a traditional Jamaican meal that evening, but there was no cow's head to be found. In the end, we purchased all sorts of fruit and vegetables. Pumpkin, Jasmine's favourite, spring onions, callaloo, yams, cucumbers, and bumpy bananas. These saved our lives when we came to a tollgate, which was a long drive away from our final destination. Unfortunately, all the shops were closed, and we had to settle with the fruits as our evening meal. Anyway, that was all I could afford because our funds were running low.

Being a mum was still at the forefront of my life regardless of the turmoil. Reading stories to Jasmine was very important, especially with trying to keep her sane and in a routine, as much as I could in our current situation. One night at about half past nine I had read Jasmine a story and tucked her into bed when I realised why God only gave me one child. Perhaps with more than one I wouldn't have been able to cope! She took so much of my time but was such a blessing.

She was eleven years old and in year six at school, and I didn't remember having so many books growing up. Of course, I didn't have the money to buy them, so I didn't have them. I felt so sorry for her because she had to take roughly fifteen books to school every day. The kids piled their books into pulley trolleys on wheels, similar to the ones taken to the supermarket in London by the older women, who filled them with their food shopping. I personally didn't like it, but it seemed to be the in thing in Jamaica at the time. It was painful seeing those little kids pulling what looked like suitcases for travel to school full of their required books.

Jasmine had a male teacher for the first time in her life that year. It had not gone down so well. You see, some teachers in Jamaica were a bit reserved with positive words. I wanted to compare it with the UK, but quickly reminded myself that the UK is more checks and balances. A number of teachers in the UK used positive words to students, simply in an effort to meet OFSTED standards. I had to teach Jasmine to understand the differences in teaching methods. She gave me one prime example where a pupil didn't know something, and the teacher told her she should have known that by then. "Sir, I don't understand how to do this math's problem," said Serita. "You are not serious, Serita? You are in grade eight; you should know this from grade five," said Mr. Jackson. Serita sat at her desk with her head bowed in tears while Mr. Jackson got on with the rest of the class.

I had to talk to Mr. Jackson, Jasmine's teacher, about how he spoke to the kids in the classroom. He tried to tell me that I babied Jasmine too much. He told me I needed to let her grow up and to give her space. If only he knew the life she had led.

We knew in the UK it would have been said in a more positive way even though it meant the same thing. I felt as if I were back in school because it seems like when your child is in school, you are also in school full time. There was much more parental involvement needed in Jamaica versus the UK for sure. We were still facing lots of adjustments but were spending much more time together. It was lovely, and Jasmine seemed to be coping. She had been hard on herself. She got eighty-eight percent in math and that wasn't good enough! Jasmine was not happy, and it was evident. "What is wrong, Jasmine?" I asked.

"Mum, how can I have worked so hard, studying late into the night, missing playtime, and only get eighty-eight percent?" She walked off in tears and closed her door. I followed and knocked on the door, trying to comfort her. She said she wanted to be left alone, so I went back to the kitchen where I was busy making dinner.

"What did I do wrong, Lord? Would she be better in the UK? I am here now, so this must work, Lord, and I just have to accept our fate. We are in Jamaica now, and she will cope."

I prayed for her to be able to handle all the adjustments, although to be fair, she was doing well. Perhaps better than I was. She had met a girl, also in year six, who had lived in Clapham Junction, about twenty minutes from our home in the UK. That was refreshing for Jasmine. She needed to make friends; it was necessary.

I had also met another parent, one from Texas, who had taken her two sons and moved to Jamaica. I felt blessed when I found out that the woman didn't even have a car, and she had to travel with the kids in a taxi for miles. Luckily, she was moving closer to me, and I offered to help her settle in while I was trying to do the same thing myself. When she told me her story, I realised again that in many ways I was truly blessed. At that point her kids' school fees had not been paid. She wanted to pay via credit card and that wasn't possible. I said a prayer for her. In the end, she revealed that her move to Jamaica was for self-preservation. She needed to or else she would have gone mad! She had an ex-husband who was literally driving her nuts, and her sanity and ability to care for her kids could only be saved by her move to Jamaica. I knew about the need to escape. That night after I placed Jasmine into bed, I wrote an email to a few of my friends I left behind in the UK.

Hi, guys . . . life is really settling in and I have two interviews next week. . . took the adventurous bus ride to downtown Kingston . . . Welcome to jam rock, I guess. It was an interesting ride. I have to point at everything, as despite my efforts everything seems to cost me more . . . and they claim I have an accent. All aside, I am coping, and I am enjoying Jamaica. God has been truly good to us. Jasmine had a blessed week. She ended with a 95% average and we are truly glad.

Chapter 26: Landlady Drama

We are happier than we have been in a few years. I feel God's promise that I will get a job in the near future. Despite missing you all, I know you are just a phone call away and we are accessible to each other.

Once again, thanks for helping to keep me sane during my most testing times . . . I love you all so much and appreciate you all.

Here is my home number: XXXX area code 1876; please do not give it to anyone!

Guys, I am knackered and am going to go now. I need to sleep. BTW we have also found a church . . . it's at Jasmine's school . . . so that is perfect for us. We fellowshipped there last Sunday . . . hope to go again this Sunday.

Miss you all. Love you all. Love, Ava and Jasmine Sept 5th

Journal entry

September seventh. Today was a very sad and melancholy day. I felt so ill I could've been pregnant. If I didn't know better, I would have thought I was. Of course, I wasn't. It has been ages since I was last with a man. Still, I was in and out of bed all day with a bad stomach. Jasmine had come home from school the day before with rashes in the palms of her hands. I didn't take it too seriously at first, but when she took hours to complete her homework, I became concerned. That night, I decided her rash wasn't getting any better and I took her to Andrew's Memorial Hospital. They told me she had scabies. That explained the itching I had been having since last week. I thought it was because I had changed brands of my feminine pads. The change was for no other reason but cost, as I couldn't afford my preferred brand anymore. But, I too, seemed to have scabies in my vaginal area of all places (of course it was never tested and how I contracted it was uncertain). I couldn't sleep all night. Jasmine was itching. I was itching. It wasn't a lovely feeling. Goodness, I itched until that area was sore. I was relieved that there wasn't anyone going there.

As the days went by and the scabies died down, we tried to go back to some form of normality. I was so exhausted. Every day Jasmine had homework

Chapter 26: Landlady Drama

I needed to be involved with. I didn't even have time to watch the news anymore. It was almost as if I was back in school. I had to admit that half the time I didn't have a clue with some of what she was learning. Thank God for math sessions online; they were most helpful.

I had had numerous interviews since I returned home, yet no job offers. I even contacted my former companies, but they all said no vacancies were on at that time. I dug into every contact I still had left but "No" was a familiar word and a full sentence in this scenario. I was getting terribly frustrated by it all. I had one more interview set up all the way in Spanish Town. I hoped it would be the one to change my life in Jamaica. I realised I needed to pay for the valuation report on my marital home in Anchovy. That was going to cost me all of $36,000, which I would have to find all by myself—some sort of loan hopefully. I could take the cost out of the sale whenever that happened. I asked God to help me.

I sat reading the elements of my journal or whatever it is that I was jotting on paper as I journeyed. I felt like a total failure.

It seemed that my having nowhere to live was part and parcel of who I was becoming. Tobore had been living in Havendale, just a few roads down from where I was living with Jasmine in my womb. As I drove through that neighbourhood I had to wonder if God was taking me back to face those gremlins. While Tobore and Colette were warm and safe in their big house, I had to seek refuge with a friend, Jen, and share a room with her child, Dani. Jen was good to me; I thanked God for that. She took me in while I was pregnant with Jasmine.

It seemed that Tobore's family wanted to fight me for possession of Jasmine. Audriana, Colette's daughter, rang to ask Jasmine when she could come by their house. Jasmine told them to ask me. Colette rang back to tell Jasmine that she was old enough to decide for herself who she wanted to see and when. She asked Jasmine to have me call her, but if this was an effort to cause a confrontation, I wasn't interested. It was their way of telling me that they refused to ask my permission. They had decided to see Jasmine as an adult who could decide what to do on her own.

Jasmine got to the point where she didn't want to call them or talk to them at all. When they called, they drilled her and asked her the same questions over and over despite already knowing the answers. "When are you coming to visit? Why are you not calling your father?"

I found it all a bit hypocritical. She had seen and heard enough. I was sorry she had to deal with this and yet, in some respect, I helped to cause her that pain. But she needed to just be a child and not be stuck in the middle. Sadly, I thought coming home would have helped us both, but there we were with all sorts of predators prowling around.

Jasmine was in school a lot. She was completing her final primary school year, and the move from London to Jamaica meant she had a lot of adjustments to make. That meant late evenings at school and extra lessons on Saturdays. All we had together was Sundays, and church was a big part of our lives. It had to be; I needed something to keep me sane. But, of course, Colette wouldn't give me the opportunity to explain that to her. I am certain she thought I was simply keeping Jasmine from them. She was too bitter and had too much hatred for me where Jasmine was concerned. I was certain they sat there crucifying me for keeping her away, not realising that there were other reasons. Would they have ever cared to ask what my reasons were? Of course not, so then why would I bother or care about them? She was the same child they nearly drove me to abort. They had treated me like such shit. I had gone for the abortion, and while I was sitting in the GP's chair stirrups, something in my mind screamed, "No!" That may have been the single best decision I had ever made in my life.

I took some time out of my writing. Although cathartic, it was becoming a challenge. I was depressed and alone, reminding myself of hardships I've suffered.

Here is a diary entry from that time:

Chapter 26: Landlady Drama

I haven't written in a while due to many factors. I have been really downtrodden, but more so, wondering what's going on in my life. I decided to stop applying for jobs because I have applied and sent my CV to more than three hundred places in Jamaica. Okay, that may be exaggerated, but it's quite a lot, and so far, nothing has happened.

I had just settled in to lying low and trying to figure out what was happening, when unexpectedly, my sister Babs came to see us, and it was so refreshing. I loved every minute of her visit. In that moment, I realised how much living in the UK took me away from having my family's company and laughter, regardless of how hard times were. In spite of everything, I was thankful to be home where there was laughter.

Sometimes all we want to do is shove the past in a room and lock the door, but we just can't.

CHAPTER 27: HEADING BACK TO LONDON

Removing one brick from a stack can send walls crumbling down quickly. Escaping isn't always possible, so we sometimes get crushed.

Before I knew it, it was December and Christmas. A period I had hated since I was a child. We were heading back to the UK, and I had all sorts of emotions in my stomach. But we still maintained a home there, and there were things that needed tending to. It had been a long time since I had written anything in my diary, but I wanted to get some of my thoughts down.

We have been back in Jamaica for a while, but nothing seems to be happening for me in relation to jobs. It's rough, but through it all, I have managed to find myself and meet some wonderful people along the way.

I call them my gems: Angie, and more importantly, Jegs and Auds. I will talk about them later. It's bumpy, but we are surviving.

As I am writing now, we are in South Bermondsey in South-East London. We travelled to London to take care of some necessities. I was apprehensive and fearful about undertaking the trip. But it was here, in London, I got my first taste of Iylana Vanzant. Her amazing book—Yesterday I Cried—*given to me by my friend Jegs, helped prepare my mind.*

Yesterday I Cried is about authentic power that has influenced me ever since reading it.

And here I am in a box room with a single bed, hardly able to hold Jasmine and myself. But hey, I will roll with the punches.

We had come back to the UK to apply for my citizenship as I wasn't sure where I wanted to be planted permanently at this stage of the game.

Chapter 27: Heading Back To London

On arrival, we were met at Gatwick Airport by Rafel, my new love interest. I paid all of fifty-one pounds for a taxi from the airport to my friend Hanna's house.

We disembarked in the parking lot and hoped Hanna was home. Luck would have it that although they weren't in, the door to the building was accidentally left open. Then again, I believe nothing happens by coincidence. I climbed the stairs and left my four suitcases at her front door. I knew they had no space. They lived there with their three kids. God, I felt helpless. But I knew they wouldn't turn me away. With that faith in our friendship, I went to visit my old house, a five-minute walk away, while Jasmine stayed with an old school friend of hers.

I was crestfallen by the condition of my front garden. The tenants had just left it to the ravages of the weather and environment. It was filthy. Even though the garbage truck had come, the garbage men didn't pick up the rubbish because it wasn't properly packed. I knocked, or rather rang the doorbell, but no one answered. I went to our neighbour, my dearest Ross. He was in and delighted to see me.

It was good. At least someone was happy to see us. I begged him for a phone call, and we called Tobore to tell him Jasmine was in London. Tobore seemingly already knew we would be there, and that's another mystery. I chatted some more with Ross. I told him how I felt, seeing my place had been poorly kept. We caught up a little more and then I went downstairs to see my back garden. I was sad; the tenants had scraped up my strawberry patch, along with every plant in the back garden, and they had thrown them out with the rubbish.

Finally, someone opened the conservatory door and inquired as to who I was. That must be Len, the tenant, I thought. Len pulled back a terrible velvet curtain, which had been kept in the shed, and peered out. He was about to throw us out when I explained who we were. When I went inside the house, I could not believe my eyes. Everything was in shambles. Such a mess, and there were many more people living there than I remembered

Chapter 27: Heading Back To London

renting the house to. My mind was in turmoil, but I tried to compose myself. The trouble was I had lived there, so I knew what it should have looked like. I had to restrain myself and reflect upon the mortgage they were paying and the fact that I couldn't afford to lose them at that moment. I wasn't working, and things were rough with me. I looked at the man that I came to see and talked with him about the house in general.

Before I left, I collected the post that had been accumulating in the months since my departure. My creditors were all after me. I knew I was in trouble. When I left the UK to go back to Jamaica, I couldn't afford to pay even half of my bills. I had lost my job and didn't know any way out. I had simply buried my head in the sand. I ignored the onslaught of past due bills. I had never been in such a position, so I didn't know what to do. Once again, I reminded myself of the purpose of my trip. I thanked the tenant and promised to get the insurance company involved with the damp in the house.

I left and tried to find the library. To my surprise, our library in Pollards Hill was being refurbished. The work had apparently started since our leaving, so I couldn't have known. I left and went to the Mitcham Library, a short distance away, after which I went back to Hanna's flat and sat there until Jasmine was ready for her GP visit. Jasmine needed asthma pumps, and I knew I needed to stock up on them because I couldn't afford them in Jamaica. Rafel and I arranged to meet later that day, and I took Jasmine to the GP before dropping her off with my friend Joy.

Joy was taking Jasmine out shopping to keep her busy and so she wouldn't feel displaced. However, Joy called to say Jasmine had a headache, and she needed to bring her back to me. Once Joy had dropped Jasmine off and I tended to her headache, we were off to my friend Shoa's home. Shoa had always been good to me, and she had been a source of strength ever since we first landed in London, almost seven years before. While Jasmine was still with my friend Hanna, I met up with Rafel.

Chapter 27: Heading Back To London

At midday the next day, I picked Jasmine up, even though I didn't know where we were going to sleep that night, but there was too much to do before I had that worry. I rushed to Croydon to get my bank statements from my vault, so I would have them with me when I went to submit my citizenship application at the registry office. That chore took longer than I expected. I was late in picking up Jasmine for her eye appointment; thankfully she was still at Hanna's house and I knew she would be ok.

In a fluster, I called Shoa and asked her to book me a taxi for midday because I was on the number 60 bus, coming in that way, and I would not have time to wait on one.

When I got to Shoa's, the taxi hadn't arrived yet and we had already missed one eye appointment scheduled on the day we landed. I called the office to say I was running late but needed them to see us that day.

I was told to not be more than five minutes late. We were already ten minutes late. Eventually, we got there, and she was seen. Luckily, there were nice people in the office we had dealt with before. Jasmine got her eyes tested and was given a new prescription. I was hoping she didn't need other glasses, but I knew she had become used to her specs and she also wanted to choose a new style. She ended up choosing a green pair, and once again, I paid for it all myself. I had paid for the first, and now the second pair, and her dad had not contributed a penny.

I was happy; that was one less thing for me to worry about. I needed to find somewhere to sleep that night, as I needed to leave Hanna's house now that I had used up enough help. The entire trip had been a struggle, but I was handling it better than I thought I would. Somehow, I had gained strength from somewhere. I ended up sleeping at a guesthouse, and that was another thing to handle. It felt so strange. I was so close to my own home, but I couldn't walk to the front door and put a key in the lock. It was not my house to live in; it was merely rented property.

Chapter 27: Heading Back To London

Life has many cycles, and I think I have been through all of them. I went to pick Jasmine up from Shoa's, but we didn't have anywhere to go immediately after.

We were to go back to Hanna's house, but she hadn't yet come home from church. I lounged around at Shoa's, waiting. I really felt out of place, but I had learned to respond rather than react. I wanted to scream and shout and cry and maybe even lash out, but I breathed, focused my mind in a positive space, reminded myself why I came here, and accepted that this was temporary. I wanted to call Hanna and remind her I was there, but I was a beggar not a chooser; I needed to be still and wait.

We eventually headed to Hanna's place, and she was there. Later that day, after stopping in at my friend Temi's, we went to meet Rafel's family.

Afterwards, we attempted to look for a room. I was very aware that Jasmine and I needed to find some place to stay. We were going to be here for a few weeks, so it was a temporary discomfort.

Hanna's place was too cramped. She had been so hospitable to us, but our welcome was overstayed—it was far too crowded, I could tell. I looked for a place all that Sunday to no avail, so we had to stay with Hanna.

The next day, I woke up ready to apply for my citizenship. I had caught the number 118 bus, but doing London by train and bus was proving a bit difficult for me. I was out of practice with the big city and its climate. The temperatures were so low, being December, I couldn't feel my feet at some points of my journey.

I got to Morden, where the bus terminated, and ran to a parked black cab. I was certain I was going to be taken, but he said he wasn't working. I wasn't sure if it was fact or fiction, but I didn't bother debating it; I had no time to spare. I ran towards the mini cab station, and just my luck, there was not a single cab in house. The operator sensed my agitation, and I told him my dilemma. He wasn't certain what time he would have a cab but said that I could take the number 93 bus. I went to the bus stop and was angry for being late on such a day, but I contained myself. Any other time, I would have just burst. While I waited at the bus stop, I sent Jasmine to tell the cab operator that I was there, and if a cab came, he was to send it to us directly.

Before Jasmine even got to the door, a cab driver turned up. I praised God, and we went with him. The drive was only about five minutes, but it was so bitterly cold, it would have been a very difficult walk.

We got there and I apologised profusely to the registry people for being late, but they were pleasant, and my fears were unfounded. I learnt a lesson—not to work myself up for no reason. I was seen but told that the forms I used had been revised, and the woman helping me was certain the home office wouldn't take them. She made me pay in advance and told me to return with the new forms signed up by my references I was pissed off but told myself that God was in control.

Next, I had a meeting with my divorce solicitor, so I rushed there and managed to sign the affidavit for my divorce and decree nisi. In only six weeks my divorce would become final and the decree absolute.

I really wanted to be free from Tobore. While at the solicitor, Tobore called and asked where we could meet. He wanted to see Jasmine. I told him to meet us at the library in Pollards Hill because I didn't want him to get wind that we had no stable place to stay. After I hung up the phone, the solicitor told me I needed to visit another independent solicitor's office to get the affidavit witnessed. I got nervous. Was there no one in her office who could bear witness? So, I went to another office down the street on the corner, and guess what, there was no solicitor in house. I ran farther up the road and thankfully found one in. I got the document signed.

I was overcome with emotion. Part of me wanted out, and part of me wasn't ready yet. I quickly reminded myself of the jail and the room I was put in, and who it was that put me there. So, I snapped out of it quickly. Back at my solicitor's office, we wrapped up our meeting with the financial agreement. We decided I was going to go after his pension, and I told

Chapter 27: Heading Back To London

the solicitor I wanted it immediately. I didn't want to wait until he was old before seeing any of that money. I needed that money right there and then; after all, I was broke and needed to care for his child. She also said we would go after sixty percent of the Jamaica house and that he should maintain me until I remarried. I could just imagine his face turning pink when he heard that!

He was going to be mad, but I didn't care. I felt that was revenge, and I wanted it badly.

I left the solicitor's office and called him to tell him to meet me at the HSBC Bank at Mitcham instead. I felt riled up to see him. After all, I had just signed my revenge on him. I felt good. As we arrived at Mitcham, we crossed the road, and I let Jasmine post a letter. I saw him waiting with "her" in their new CRV. Seeing them together, I didn't know what I felt. I can't explain, but it was very strange.

He hadn't seen us and called to ask where at the HSBC he was to meet us. I told him we were waiting in the back for him. He took ages to arrive where we were. It was as though they were planning something in the car before he walked over to us. As we waited, fear set in and I wondered if he was bringing the police with him. I had nightmares that he would try to take away my child. I would sometimes ask myself if I was being fair, but she was all I had. He came, and I felt nothing. No hatred, no contempt, nothing. He knelt at Jasmine's feet as she sat on a chair in the bank, and he told her how happy he was to see her. She said to him, "Dad, if Agnes is there, I don't want to go to your house." He told her she didn't have to see Agnes, his girlfriend. He told her that he didn't know what the plan was for that afternoon, but I was relieved that I had some "me" time after all. We had a brief discussion around him helping with Jasmine's maintenance, and he agreed to help, though it wasn't much. It was more than I had at the time. What position was I in to argue?

I told him that he could have her from one in the afternoon to six o'clock. I am certain that shocked him. I knew it was the last thing he expected to hear from me. I didn't want to be predictable to him anymore.

They left, and I went to sort out my business at the Department of Social Services. They had written to me many times, and I had missed my six-month review with them because I was in Jamaica. That wasn't good, as that was my only source of income. That was how we were able to live. But before that, I needed to go to the library to use their computers. I had to find someplace to live. I logged on to Gumtree and finally found a place to rent for a few weeks while we were in the UK—it was all the way in Bermondsey. It was a small box room, the size of my closet in Jamaica, and that wasn't an exaggeration. It was seventy-nine pounds a night, but quickly went up because I had Jasmine, which meant two people. Oh, how I have had to pay my way with that child of mine, but I love her unconditionally and I wouldn't have had it any other way. I went to the place and paid the deposit. I was shocked when I asked to use the toilet and was told I could wash my hands in the kitchen sink. I decided I wasn't going to do any cooking there. How I would survive was another thing entirely. I left without the keys and unsure if I could trust those people. But I left in good faith. She gave me a receipt for my deposit and told me I could pick up the keys on Wednesday. That wouldn't be long; after all it was already Monday. The room was the smallest I had ever lived in, but I had no choice. I needed to be out of Hanna's place.

Lack can bring such desperation that even your body will give way.

CHAPTER 28: DISPLACED IN LONDON IN DECEMBER

Living in a country where there is government help can be the best buffer one can have in desperation.

I finally went to get my review done at the Department of Social Services. I was so nervous; the last thing you wanted to do in London was to get in trouble with the state. I was told I couldn't just walk in. I had to ring the person I was to meet with, and she gave me an appointment for Tuesday. I agreed because I needed to get that resolved. I needed to pay Jasmine's school fee for January, a new term back in Jamaica, and I had no other means. Her dad had already decided he wasn't going to give us any more money than he already was. I had decided too that I would not ask him for more.

I knew somehow, I would cope. I felt I was doing the best I knew how to do.

Kem had come through for me, though, which I considered to be about time as she offered to keep Jasmine.

I needed her, and I was on my way with Jasmine. Along the way, I managed to fit in a hairdresser's appointment, which was such a success. They did my hair beautifully, and I felt proud. We left for Luton, and Kem's home. I was a bit hesitant on the train because I didn't trust men around my child. Especially men I did not think had the correct values. But I reassured myself that I had taught her well and Jasmine was sensible enough to know when someone was trying to take advantage of her. I called Kem from the train and asked if she had food in the house. She snapped at me, and I almost turned back. But I had to remind myself I had nowhere to go. I needed someone to leave Jasmine with.

We got to Luton and it felt like the coldest day that had ever been. We took the number 10 bus, and Kem and her daughter Beatrice met us. It was a happy moment.

I had never been so happy to see Kem in my entire life. I wasn't sure at first if it was that I missed her, or if it was seeing Beatrice again, or just that I felt really stuck. I realised I really missed them terribly. Kem was family and she loved Jasmine deeply, and I loved Beatrice. We ran to each other and hugged. Sometimes I wished we were not living in two separate countries, and that this was us returning to London to live, versus a short trip that would see us leave in a few weeks.

I kissed them, and we just held each other: all four of us. We hurried ourselves to her place. We sat and chatted and caught up. After some time, I ate a quick meal of spaghetti and left for the station to meet up with Rafel. I walked to the bus stop and saw a cab waiting and asked if he could take me. He said no because he was booked by someone else. The lady who called the cab arrived and decided I could share the ride with her, the long and short of it was she knew my sister and ended up paying my way to the train station. How funny life can be and how small the world is? I met Rafel at the station and we went to London to enjoy the evening together. It was an okay evening and one that certainly shifted my attention from all the stress I was going through. We went to see a film, and he wanted to be all mushy, holding hands and caressing in the cinema. I wasn't at that place. While I enjoyed his company, it wasn't where I wanted to end up, at least not amid the mess I was currently in. We parted ways, and I ended up sleeping in a guesthouse, as I dreaded going back to the cramped space at Hanna's. I needed my own sense of independence and privacy. The next day I went to the pharmacy to collect a prescription. I also picked up Jasmine's nice, new, green glasses. She would get them when she got back from my sister's. I picked up my keys for the rental and took along my stuff from Hanna's place. Rafel came with me. He had proven to be such a supportive help for me since I had been there. If only I felt for him in the same way he felt for me, we could have made Heaven come to Earth. Alas, I didn't.

I felt displaced in the room, but just had to deal with it. I had made my bed. That evening, and I was settled in the room, a Korean girl called out to ask why I broke the door. I thought, how could I? I had to explain to her that we came in and shut the door carefully and nothing broke. This was utter madness. It seemed that she wanted to scam me into paying for what I didn't damage, and I was not going to have any of it. I'd had enough of people taking advantage of us.

For about thirty minutes we were locked in the house. It was a fire hazard and completely unacceptable. I told her that she should call the landlord to get it fixed. She said we should all put in together to pay for it because the landlord was so far away. That said to me she was cunning and perhaps not to be trusted. Then she suggested we could walk through the living room of one of the other tenants, a Japanese guy who lived there, and try the door, as it opened from the outside. The door opened, of course, and that was the end of that discussion. She quickly apologized and we laid that to bed.

Was she trying to make a quick buck from me, or what? I didn't know, and I didn't care.

I needed to get food. I went to the corner shop, and Rafel met me there, where I bought some supplies. Fruits and vegetables, drinks, and necessities to prepare meals. I had planned to spend only twenty pounds, but that didn't work out. I couldn't stand the thought of using the utensils they supplied, remembering I had been told to wash my hands in the kitchen sink after using the bathroom. So, I also bought plates and cups along with spoons. As Jasmine was not with me in the room for some of the trip, Rafel wanted to take up permanent residence I had told Rafel I wanted to be alone that night, so I took the bus back alone. I wasn't certain of how I would manage with six carrier bags by myself, but I did. I exhaled a sigh of relief when I arrived. I unpacked the bags and organised myself. I had a bath and slept like a baby. I wasn't in the mood to talk to anyone. I wanted to be alone to sleep and boy, it did me good.

I woke up the next morning and knew I needed to get Jasmine from Kem. My life was like that, one task after another. It came with ups and downs and I had to roll with it. I was supposed to meet Kem at the station, but after waiting for a while I decided to get a duvet from my favourite store, Primark, which was nearby. It was too cold in the box room and the heat came on for only two hours a night. In the middle of winter, that was harsh. I also needed to sleep with one of the windows open because I didn't do well with carpets on the floors due to allergies. I met up with Kem and wished we were staying with them. I needed a sense of family, but every time I got to that point, I reminded myself I needed to make my own family. We said our goodbyes, and I took Jasmine to see our room. She seemed disappointed but tried not to show it. I did the best I could in the situation, gave her a hug, and reminded her it was temporary.

The London trip was something else. We ended up spending Christmas with my friend Emma, her daughter, and their friends. These were people we didn't know, but it felt like we were all one family. They were such lovely people; we couldn't help but notice. However, that highlighted even more the fact that I was alone. I really didn't have any true family of my own except Jasmine. Granted, had I been back in Jamaica, I would have certainly been welcomed into my mum's humble abode.

Jasmine had seen her dad only twice while we were in London. Can you imagine, after all that time away, he couldn't have made more time for her? He didn't even give her as much as five pounds to use as spending money. Instead, he took her shopping for perfume for his girlfriend. The child had taken him into a Clarks shop with the hope of getting some school shoes. He quickly told her he had no money. Right after that, he went and spent eighty pounds on perfume for his secret obsession. She reported asking for a bear as they passed the Build-A-Bear store. She was presumptuous enough to ask for a fifteen-pound bear. Of course, she didn't get that either.

Once again, I felt as though I were starting over and was really stuck. That was a feeling I got a lot in my life, and it seemed I could not escape it. I began thinking that perhaps there was something I was simply not doing right. I spent most of my time alone in the small box room in Bermondsey. I didn't feel that was a good place for Jasmine to be. She only stayed there when we needed to take care of matters involving the doctors and the opticians. These were luxuries we couldn't afford in Jamaica. Otherwise I sent her off to visit friends. All in all, our tasks were accomplished to some extent.

While staying in London, I didn't have a clean place to wash my clothes or cook while renting the box room. I found myself waking to piles of dirty clothes, hoping that whichever friend I was to visit that day would be kind enough to let me wash my things there. Sometimes I was lucky, sometimes not. I called a friend, Ajua, and asked if we could stay with her, as I was now ready to leave that box room. She agreed, and I was grateful.

The feeling of being neglected was gone. Jasmine and I stayed with her together. She gave up her warm, cosy bed to accommodate us. Her house was our house and she didn't make us feel in the way. I remember when I went to move out of the box room, my friend Tim was a Godsend. He borrowed an old van from his boss and helped me move.

When I arrived at Ajua's house, she didn't ask why I had brought so many bags to her house. Instead, she was gentle and decent about it. I was certain in her heart she must have felt fear and confusion, but given her nature she just reassured me it was okay. She helped me to unpack and was such a sweetheart. We were like one happy family. She is Jamaican, and that is just part of what makes us an amazing community, though we were only staying a few days, so she wouldn't have to be inconvenienced for too long.

Chapter 28: Displaced In London In December

I remember on New Year's Eve, Jasmine and I were walking back to Ajua's house, and although I didn't have much money, we stopped at an off-licence liquor store and bought her a nice bottle of wine. It was costly, but I thought Ajua deserved it. New Year's Eve caught us as lonely souls. No party invites and no one to take us out. But I knew we would be on our way back to Jamaica in less than ten hours. So, we drank some wine and toasted the New Year. After that, I packed. I had all four cases filled once more, as I had offered to take back wedding clothes for a friend of Ajua's. It was the least I could do after she accommodated us. It felt like I was giving something back to her. The morning came quickly. I had not gone to bed until about half past three and the cab was coming for us at half past five, so I had very little time to even take a nap.

I was uncertain if I really wanted to go back to Jamaica. At least in Jamaica I had a lovely, large, warm house waiting for me. That fact was reassuring irrespective of what else was going on at home, and I took comfort in that. I didn't want to be in London anymore. I felt entirely displaced, but I needed my citizenship to be able to return when I wanted to, so securing that was key for me, especially for Jasmine's future. The fact was, regardless of what else was going on, her father lived there. I didn't want to close that gate. The displacement wasn't just about me, it was more about my child. I didn't like having her feel uncomfortable.

I picked my thoughts up and continued readying myself. I quickly showered, trying not to wake up Ajua's partner, which was almost impossible because it was a small flat. I got dressed and made the dangerous choice of wearing flip flops, forgetting that it was four degrees outside. I was already packed and the one pair of boots I had were unfit to wear, so I left them to go into the trash. I had packed a suitcase with some clothes I intended to leave in London, as I knew we would return sometime. After all, we had not severed all ties with the place. A hard part of leaving Ajua was leaving dirty clothes behind, which I had to ask her to wash. She didn't object, but within me, I felt sad.

I woke Jasmine and she got dressed. We were organised and ready to leave. Ajua helped me with the cases down the stairs. We were so loud, we must have woken up all their neighbours. I was not happy about that but could not do anything about it. I had to rationalise within myself that it was okay.

The cab came soon after that, and I was absolutely livid. The taxi driver told me it would cost much more than I had bargained to go to Gatwick and my money was tight. I put on my regular brave face and asked him to explain why. After much haggling, he called his operation room and said he was ready to leave. I had to come to terms with it and agree to the rate. Now be mindful, I was already spending double seeing it was New Year's Day. But the driver turned out to be a lovely person and we chatted all the way to the airport. He even told me I could have checked in the previous night for my flight; little did I know.

I arrived at Gatwick and needed one pound to pay for the trolleys. By that time, I was solid broke. Recession had reached me on New Year's Day. With not even a penny from her dad, Jasmine could not be of any help to me. The cab driver graciously paid for my trolleys and I thanked him for his kindness. Pushing the trolleys was difficult, but like always, we managed. The lines at the airport were crazy. I had not imagined there would be so many people there at that time in the morning. All I could think was that they must have slept there. Our luggage and hampers were offloaded from the trolleys within minutes, and we had ample time to scout around. James, Rafel's friend, was in the North Terminal because his mum was leaving for Nigeria that same day. We went over to pay our regards, then came back to "lay," as we say in Jamaica, until it was time to board.

While there in the airport we stopped at a WH Smith and I picked up the book of the moment to read on the plane, *Dreams of my Father* by President Barack Obama. I used up the last of my UK credit card allowance, but I needed to read something to inspire me. Jasmine got herself some books and I also got a stamp. I needed to post a letter to the Educational Welfare Office regarding withdrawing Jasmine from the school registers in London, and I needed to ensure I posted that letter from within London.

Jasmine found a five-pound note in an old purse she had tucked away in a bag she was taking with her. We felt we could part with this, so I bought a Girls Aloud CD to take back with us to Jamaica. We went to sit in the airport chairs in the waiting area. The flight seemed to take ages to board, or was it simply because we had checked in early? Even after boarding the flight, there were still people checking in. It was going to be a long day.

Sometimes just letting your hair out and breathing deeply can be the best therapy ever recommended.

CHAPTER 29: HOMEBOUND

Home, regardless of the state of play, is the only place I feel at peace.

Angel picked us up at the airport. After three weeks of standing in the cold at the various bus and train stops in London, the sight of my own car was so delightful. I almost jumped out of my body to tell Angel that I wanted to drive as she pulled up beside the curb. As though she had read my mind, she told me I needed to drive. *Phew! What a relief,* I thought.

I got behind the steering wheel and once again felt like I was somebody. London had all but stripped me of my sense of importance and the security of the things I had built. I felt almost the same way I did when I had gone to Britain the first time. Stripped of all my pride, hard work, and dignity.

Well, there I was, gaining some of my independence back.

In some ways it was ironic. You see, I had gone to a land I thought was better. But no matter what the situation, I should not have felt that way. Now I was back in the land that was my own, and there I felt much more relief than in the place I had called home for more than six years. As we drove away, I felt that I was leaving all that baggage behind. But then I was even more confused. How could coming home to Jamaica bring such relief? There was comfort in my own bed and the ability to cook for myself. I loved my food. When you looked at me, you could tell I lived near my kitchen. Having the ability to move around a house instead of being confined to a single room no bigger than my Jamaican closet was pure heaven.

Chapter 29: Homebound

We stopped at Angel's for a quick dinner of stewed peas with pigs' tail and rice. Oh, that was exactly what we needed. Angel updated us about what was going on in Jamaica as we gulped the good food down. Soon after that, I raided her pantry. Angel ran an old Jewish home, which housed three Jewish people, and the remaining rooms were let to university students. She always had food. And she was always so generous to us, we felt blessed having her in our lives.

As I arrived home the joy of pressing that remote buzzer as we approached our gate was exhilarating. I drove into the parking lot and sat in the car, appreciating the fact that I had a beautiful place to live in, even though at times in my life, affording it was a heavy weight in itself. At that moment, I had even forgotten it was only rented, but it was home and mine. I quickly unloaded all our stuff and headed for bed. Oh, how I missed my king size bed. Jasmine and I hugged in our bed for a long time, and the next thing I knew we fell asleep.

I was gradually able to get back into the rhythm of things. I needed to sort out Jasmine's uniforms and school things and get unpacked. I had brought back something for almost everyone. My mum, my stepdad, my brothers and sisters, my sisters' kids, a neighbour in my mum's village, the head teacher at Jasmine's school, her teacher, another two teachers, and two parents, Angie and Jem, Angel of course, Auds, her kids, Jegs and her kids. I was blessed to have been able to touch the lives of so many people, although I went to London and came back with little or no money. Thank God for Primark.

In Jamaica it's just expected that when you travel you are to come back bearing gifts for everyone. Unfair though it may have seemed, it was a part of our culture, and you felt empty and worthless coming back empty-handed.

I thought to myself, the next time I travel, I am going to break that spell because I really put myself out on a limb each time. I was again worried about pleasing everyone else. I hardly purchased anything for

295

Chapter 29: Homebound

myself. Just a few pairs of shoes and a bag. Not that I needed them, but to be frank, I felt better buying something for me. I guess it spoke to the void inside me that I still struggled with all the time. I had a weakness for handbags, clothes, and shoes. Irrespective of how many of those items I bought, I still felt the void. I realised that the items I was hoarding wouldn't help. But I wasn't ready to come out of denial then, and for the moment it felt good. I wanted to stay in that bubble. It was one I had come to feel safe in; one that I wouldn't let anyone else know existed. Just me, myself, and I. Sometimes I did wonder if people around me knew. Then again, I didn't really give a damn . . . or so I thought.

I had an interview with a food company in Jamaica. Although jet-lagged, I went to it anyway. I was so tired I was hardly able to walk in the black heels I had bought in Peckham. Nice, sexy velvet at the back, with open toes. I wondered if they were too much. It was Jamaica, not the UK! I also didn't wear the traditional suit. I opted instead for a black corduroy waistcoat, some grey trousers, and a pale greyish-blue shirt. In my mind, I looked good and felt good.

The interviewer was a young girl who had an easy manner and was nice enough to talk to. We spent hours chatting. She had a brother in Austria, and she told me how she had been to Germany. We talked for three hours after the interview had finished. I thought to myself: *Don't be fooled; I know well I haven't got the job, but the girl was pleasant to talk with.* You may wonder why I even bothered to waste my time, but I knew that life had more span to it. I was just relaxing and being human. I left the interview and went back to Auds and Jegs's place. We hung out for a while and then I left to go home.

I stopped at the supermarket to get a few bits and bobs. My friends had gone to Coronation Street to get me some fresh fruit and vegetables. With huge bravado I asked them how much I owed, knowing if they told me even ten dollars, I would not be able to pay. Like the standup people they were, they said I owed them nothing. Then again, I had done enough

Chapter 29: Homebound

over time for them to warrant some fruit and vegetables. I had driven them many places for free because I had a car. I am not complaining, but we seemed to play what I call "quits," meaning we would be even on what we had done for each other, so no charge—we did "quits" every so often.

The opening of the new school term was near, and I went home that weekend and tried to rest. The days ahead would be challenging, I knew that and didn't have any clear vision of how I would overcome it. We went to church that Sunday at Boulevard Baptist Church.

Monday came and I took Jasmine to school, after which I went with Auds to pay the school fees. After I gave the guy all of $37,000, I had no money left. I felt bewildered. I took the bank slip to school and just continued like nothing had happened. After that, we went back to Auds's house to chill because that was what most days were like. Since I had moved to Havendale and found her, that had pretty much become my ritual. One of dropping Jasmine at school, then running to the safe haven of Auds's home. Some days I did my other hobby of going to interviews.

My life had been like that of late, with no job since I went back to Jamaica in 2008. I had fallen into a painful, voluntary life of luxury. I didn't like it but sometimes I didn't mind it. I had the time when needed, to do what I wanted, when I wanted. Other times when I needed money for extra lessons, or the light bills, or even the food bills, I hated it. I found that my entire life was totally centred on Jasmine. From dropping her at school, to going to her quiz matches, to being her chauffeur and picking her up, to getting her supplies. I had no existence of my own. There were days when I just wanted to go shopping or have a cup of tea, but those were luxuries I could not afford. In London, I could get a cuppa for fifty pence or even go to Primark and treat myself to a pair of shoes for three pounds or so. But here, I was barely able to buy mere essentials, and at times I was unable to even buy meat to go with dinner.

At least I hadn't felt as depressed as I had when I was in London. There was something about being in Jamaica that was comforting amidst the hardship. I had the feeling that someone would catch me if I fell. In London I felt total despair. I felt as though I were totally alone always. Truth be told, I was alone. Tobore had proven he wasn't who I felt he was, my sister couldn't be relied on, and my friends were typical Londoners doing their own thing.

Auds and I had met at the school. Her kids were new to Quest preparatory school but not new to Jamaica. She had recently moved to my side of the island. She thought the school would be better. She was also running away from some other things that are not for me to talk about, but that girl did give me some insight into internally dealing with problems.

As the days in Jamaica went on, the hardships heightened. Before we left for London, I had been buying burgers for $280, and just before a month or so later the cost was up more than $300. I couldn't afford to buy them anymore. In my fridge were some chicken feet—it was the only meat. I simply had no means of buying anything else. Jasmine and I tried to live with what we could afford. One decision I took to heart after I came back from London was to pack her lunch instead of her buying it. Not that I didn't want the freedom of not having to worry about what to put in her lunch box each day, but I simply couldn't afford to pay the $650 per week. So instead, I sat her down and had the painful conversation that her mum really couldn't afford to pay for her lunches anymore, so from then on, she would be taking packed lunches. I promised her I would try to ensure they were healthy and tasty. In my mind, I knew how difficult that would be, seeing as I had limited resources of money.

That's what we did after we got back from London, and she was so good about it. She ate whatever I provided and never once complained. There were some Saturday extra lesson classes when I dropped her at school and all I could afford to pack in her bag was a banana, an apple, some cheese, a tangerine, and a drink. Maybe some water and a crisp pack as a snack. The norm was for them to buy lunch on Saturdays. We talked that morning and I told her it was either I pay for lunch, or I could pay Mr. Good for extra lessons. I knew she would rather I was able to do both, but she said: "Mom, I will take a packed lunch." As for paying Mr. Good, I had exchanged ten pounds I had in my purse, but it yielded only $1126, which was not enough because his fee was $1200. I needed to find a little under $100 more before Monday. I placed my trust in God that it would appear. At the same time my car's fuel tank was on empty as it had been for many days now. I had not been able to purchase more than $500 of petrol since I came back. You see the London trip was way more than $100,000, and that left me broke. Plus, my benefits from the Department of Social Services had been cut. They had wanted to see me last October for my interview. Because I was a no show, at least until December, they had cut my benefits to a meagre twelve pounds per week. Still, I would say God bless England, because at least we were receiving something.

Where we lived, I had to buy tokens to do our laundry; I hadn't bought any since last October due to the lack of funds. I had been hand washing all our things and I could feel the effects on my back. I went to my friends' places to do my dirty linen every now and then. However, I was uncomfortable asking them repeatedly, so I tried not to do it too often, and when I did, I took my own detergent and fabric softener. They insisted I didn't need to; but I felt that I was scrounging enough, so that was the least I could do. There were times I had laundry waiting to be done, but I literally didn't have the strength to deal with it.

I had been tempted to go and cash in a policy I had taken out for Jasmine years ago. I needed money to pay my rent for February, and I wanted to fix up the house in Montego Bay, as the tenant had made some repair demands. I had it on the market for sale, so the tenant's demands were not senseless. Giving it a once-over would make it more sellable. The real estate market was soft at the time, and even though I had an offer, I didn't know if the sale would go through. The offer was for eight million Jamaican dollars, but I knew the house's value was much more than that, and I was not going to give it away. I travelled to Montego Bay and got the house painted so that it could be rented out. Whether it rented for long term or short term did not matter; we needed money coming in. I knew the painting was going to cost me money I didn't have. I emailed Tobore to ask for his help, but of course you can imagine what he said. He said no, and I left it at that. It was clearly a dead-end.

I was going to spend some time with Keri, my friend who I met in London the previous year. She was there studying to become a marine pilot. Here in Jamaica, she lived in Port Royal. I was so impressed with what that girl had sacrificed for her career. She put marriage and having kids on hold, giving up on the man she loved whom she met back in London, since she was bonded by her contract in Jamaica and had gone to the UK on a scholarship from her company. Perhaps if I hadn't had Jasmine so young, I would have been more ambitious. I still felt tempted to complete my law degree. That had always been my passion, but my motivation was low, and I felt so tired. I slept more than I did anything else, apart from eating. I hardly played with Jasmine either. For one thing, she had grown a bit more independent of me. There were times I would go into hiding in my own little world. Thankfully, she was so occupied with her end of primary school exams—her GSATS—she hardly even noticed.

I had plans to go back to London in July, but until then I was depending on an investment I had of $500,000, which was due to mature, to help us get by. Hopefully, I would gather all of it and to be able to pay the rent for the rest of the year. I was still looking for a job, but parts of me felt like it was a waste of time. The economy was bad, and I was not motivated. It was going to take lots of intrinsic motivation to get me back on board. I was lost, so lost, it was shocking.

Feelings of frustration, anger, and bemusement hung over me as I reflected on where I was. I seemed to have no one to turn to. My siblings still had great expectations of my ability to help them. My brother was even looking for sheets to make his bed at a nearby construction site. His request turned into a heated conversation on the phone, and I hung up. Something I was doing a lot more of lately—hanging up when I got frustrated. It was easier than arguing, or so I thought. Surely, it was easier than having long conversations I didn't want to have. It was my way of coping.

I felt hurt after that call. I had helped my mum's kids, and they blew it all and asked for more. Now that I was the one on my face, I was not asking for help, I just wanted to be left alone. I was frustrated with them all. Who was there to help me, now that I was down? I had fallen and fallen hard. The trouble with my family was they never believed I didn't have any money, even when I was starving. I was the educated one, and they thought that education equaled money. They could not fathom the possibility that I had none. They felt I should always have plenty to give. But at that point all my reserves had dried up and I was the one who needed help. I needed reassurance that it would get better.

I wondered who could identify with me? Who could relate? Certainly, my own family were too self-absorbed to realise my own fall from grace. I called my mum and my friend Keri to come around, as I needed some support. Mum came, and all I could do was place my head in her lap and weep. As I cried, all my life came spinning before me. It was as though I had just landed off a flight and was disorientated. Like a vulnerable baby, here I was alone in the world with very few to care, and those who should care could not see past what they thought I was worth. Keri stayed the night and we watched TV and ate jerk pork and crab. It was like food was my best comforter then. Luckily Keri paid for that too, which made the evening better. Keri left the next morning, and life went back to my school run routine. I had to work through my emotions, as the call from my brother made me depressed. I put on a Lisa Nichols tape and heard her say, "When all is said and done, it's always going to be okay!" In that moment I turned to one of my favorite stress reliefs—cleaning. I started cleaning the already clean house, for therapy of course, with some good Bob Marley in the sunshine, reminding me not to worry, as everything would be all right. I called Rafel and he was also supportive. We had been on the phone daily since I left London, with him even promising to visit

Jamaica. I realised in that moment that no one had what I needed to fix my shit. Instead, all I needed was inside of me. So, I started digging more inward and decided to build my mental strength to cope better.

Little did I know how much I would need that strength for what awaited me back in London.

In the words of Lisa Nichols, my hero:" I am my own rescue."

CHAPTER 30: THE JOURNEY OF AN UNKNOWN VISA GIRL

You can be caught in spider webs even with your eyes wide open. It's not being caught that matters, but it's deciding that this is the last web.

When July came, I returned with Jasmine to London to settle yet again as I hadn't yet received my immigration status and was not going to risk losing it after struggling for so long to get it. No sensible person migrates and leaves their papers/passport when it was possible. As a result, I was now saner and more determined to return to London. Moreover funds were now dried up and my ability to get gainful employment in Jamaica was taking its toll. The first thing on my mind was to get a job in order to sustain myself and so the moment I landed, applications were being sent left, right and centre.

There, Rafel's presence in my life, which had been irregular, began to grow.

I met Rafel shortly after I had the "bust up" with Tobore in London. I hadn't been involved with men very much after that final breakup with Tobore. In fact, I hardly went anywhere, and the few times I went out, I don't think I saw anyone who piqued my interest. This could have been due to the fact that I was still going through the healing process from my divorce, so meeting a man wasn't at the top of my list.

However, I liked men. And I missed having one near for sex and companionship. I missed having someone who would share my struggles and help out with things like paying bills and looking after Jasmine. I couldn't depend on Tobore anymore, or even Kem. I felt very alone.

Then I met Rafel.

He was from West Africa, and it amazes me now that I eventually fell for him as hard as I did because when I met him, he possessed nothing that I'd generally go for in a man.

He had so many uncultured ways—he didn't know how to use a knife and fork, he was always walking like a mountain climber, his dress sense turned me off, and I can't remember smelling perfume on him ever. He wasn't a good looker, either. He had never been to the dentist, and that turned me off, big time. The guy was truly not what I had imaged or like anyone I had ever dated before.

Also, he had never married or had kids, he had no car, no secure job, no house, nothing. He was a dead-broke man. I, meanwhile, had been the owner of two houses in London, had a degree and an MBA, and owned part of a house in Jamaica with my ex-husband. I was his age, and I had been on my own since I was a child. I had been married and almost divorced and had raised a child all by myself for nine years, and what had he done with his life?

I even wondered if he was just using me get a visa and regularize his status in the UK. I didn't trust him one bit.

So how did we end up together? It all happened at the same time I landed a job in sales, something I was familiar with. This gave me some stability and life was slowly taking back shape in London, back to good old Blighty.

To begin with, he pursued me hard. Even though I took time to warm up to him, he was dedicated, persistent and he took a cultured interest in my daughter. This happened when my sense of self-worth had been very shaken by Tobore's cheating, and my struggles trying to find a job and look after Jasmine. Rafel's constant, adoring attention was just what I needed, and it snuck past my caution. I lapped it up.

He seemed to care for my wellbeing. I kept asking to visit his place, but he wouldn't let me. He said that I, as a teacher, couldn't visit him because he lived with drug dealers and he didn't want me to lose my job.

He also earned my deep feelings by telling me his mother died, and he was raped by his aunt at twelve. The stories were so close to mine that I soon feel like I had found my soul mate.

And there was one more element. He had this medicine—his awesome lovemaking. It was a pacifier each time. Regardless of what wrongs he did me, he would show up at my home and stay a few days and the medicine fixed me.

All these things came together for me when I came back to London this time with Jasmine, and before I knew it, I was in love. This was when the real trouble started.

I started wanting more, and he kept saying he needed time. This only increased my need for him. We were now in role reversal. I was starting to feel I was losing control because he started monitoring my friends and, in his view, every man wanted to sleep with me.

Before I realised it, I was pregnant . . . and found out he was living with another woman. This was the reason he hadn't let me visit him at his home. I was about to lose my mind because not only did I feel the fool, I had been played by him, and his friends and family I had never met. Most of them had popped into my life through phone calls to him every now and then when he was around. I'd had no clue of what was being said as they spoke in their African vernacular. They had all known what he was doing, but he had led me to believe that I was his everything.

I felt trapped.

I finally invited him to come and discuss our choices. Of course, he was reluctant at first and when he did come to see me, he asked me what I thought his friends and family would think when they found out I was pregnant with his child. He said it with such disdain. The rest of that saga ended up with him walking away from me the same day he found out that I was pregnant. I ran him down crying and begging him to stay. The next day he came back saying he was immature and made a mistake and he was sorry and wanted us to take this seriously. Of course, fool that I was, I made love to him there and then and felt my world was finally on the right path . . . until I got dressed and he told me he wanted us to do things the right way, and that's why he wanted me to have an abortion. The moment I said no, he vanished.

For five whole months I carried that child in me, and I almost literally lost my mind. I was lost. The job was hard with the pregnancy; it was on the line, and I couldn't cope. I was shocked, depressed, and maybe even suicidal. I didn't want to have another child on my own. My daughter was eleven, and I certainly didn't want another child like this. This sudden tragedy, as I called it, saw me broke and abandoned. Life was so hard one of my friends dropped one hundred pounds on me every time I visited her. I was the scum of the earth, begging not to live. I ended up on the dole, ashamed and wanting to die, not wanting this baby inside of me, but knowing I could not get rid of it as part of me hoped Rafel would have come back. My moral compass also taunted me. Life dragged by, and I felt I was in prison, tormented. I had dreadlocks, and in the interest of passing time, I sat down and used a pin to remove every piece of my locks. What I was left with was an afro on my head, looking every bit the mess, I was in. Days seemed like years and years a whole lifetime. I locked myself away and found myself almost among the walking dead, rejected by a man who, when I'd met him, hadn't been to the dentist once in his life and was wearing and owned dirty Primark underwear. Yet there I was, pregnant with his seed and dumped by him. But I had to live. There was my daughter who needed me, and so I had to go on.

One day I saw Rafel on the bus not far from where I was living. I was huge, about five months gone, and the man didn't even look at me twice. I ended up losing the baby and I must say I felt relieved. RIP, Matthew Josiah Brown. I loved you, baby. Sorry for everything.

Chapter 30: The Journey Of An Unknown Visa Girl

Immediately after this, Rafel came looking for me, apologising and saying he was having dreams that he needed to come back to me. He said he was sorry. He cried, and he knelt down and asked me to forgive him.

I now believe he returned because he heard I was no longer pregnant, but I did not think that at the time. I believed him and thought he had just grown up. So, I took him back. He had hooked me so well that even after lying to me, abandoning me when I got pregnant with his child, ignoring me, then crawling back with lies and more lies, I was so caught that I could not see my way out.

You see, limited vision and fear and a lack of self-esteem can cripple you. You can easily stay in a relationship that is abusive. I couldn't see my way out, so I stayed. I heard the critical self-talk of a single mother with two failed relationships: "It's all your fault." Fear, the most subtle and destructive of all human diseases, took me over. At my age, fear held me back from doing what I knew was right. It paralysed me and placed me in a hypnotic spell. I gave up on me.

Even so, what happened next should have been enough to awaken me, yet I slept on in fear.

I fell pregnant again by him.

This time Rafel didn't run away, so I was hopeful. After we went for our first scan, he and I went into Primark to shop for clothing, as I was getting very big really fast. He picked up every piece of maternity clothing on the racks, but as soon as we approached the cashier, he stood at the entrance of the payment line and left me alone. At that moment, I saw clearly that this man never had anything to give but was always ready to take.

I think, if I am honest, a part of me left him emotionally then, but physically and in a deep, needy place inside me, I was tied to him.

Rafel left that day and went to his place. Yes, he still kept a room for himself. His excuse had been that, as an African man, he needed to do our relationship the correct way! He said that meant he had to be able to provide a home and living for his family before we all lived together. This did not make sense, as he was able to provide sex but not the responsibilities of what it came with. In hindsight I should have realised that this was evidence of someone who was never committed, but I didn't understand that then.

After that first day clothes shopping, Rafel was mostly gone for my pregnancy. He claimed to have lost his father. But since I had never met his father, I had no way to check if what Rafel told me was true. I don't know if the lady I met was his stepmother. Nothing was for sure. It was all a blur, and now I don't give a toss what the truth is anymore.

I remember one morning when I was pregnant, I went to his house on my way to work and what I saw nearly sent me into early labour. I was just in time to see him getting ready for an outing with a middle-aged woman in her car. To him, I was invisible, although I was heavily pregnant. I was broken-hearted, and I can't say if it was the reality of what was in front of me or the fact that I was carrying his child that made me so angry. I was fuming. He later told me that the lady was his aunt who had raped him. Yeah, right!

In the same period, I was fool enough to visit him and give him some money. He wanted a loan to help with his ticket and other expenses to return to his country to bury his father. Remember he never had any money. Years later, I realised I was merely his ATM and he wasn't in fact as broke as he proclaimed he was.

He used me in so many ways, but I was too blind at the time to see it. Our relationship was a mixture of quarrels, fights, and arguments, constantly. I couldn't understand the contentious type of relationship we were having. It was as though a malevolent spirit lived in our relationship, stirring it up like some form of voodoo.

When our son, Brad, was finally born, Rafel wasn't around. In fact, my mother, who was in the UK for Brad's birth, called Rafel that day only to have a woman answer his phone and say he was in the shower. Need I say any more? Did he live in one room in a shared house? Can you imagine what happened before he went in the shower on the eve of his son's birth?

The week that followed my son's birth is one I can never forget. When I gave birth at the hospital by C-section, there was no one at the hospital to collect me and take me home because Rafel was not there and my mother couldn't drive. It was my young daughter who took a cab home with me, a lonely journey. I cried privately on my way. The fairytale I had was cast off. There was no loving husband to help me. And though the doctors said no driving for weeks after I got home, I had to get into my jeep to get a car seat and pushchair for the baby. It was hard, only two days after Brad's delivery, but what choice did I have?

On my way back from that trip, my daughter called me in tears. I could feel my stitches tingling as she told me the girl who had answered Rafel's phone to tell my mum Rafel was in the shower had called our house. She had threatened to throw acid on us—the kids and me. She told my daughter she knew where I lived, and I was to leave her man alone. I hurriedly drove back home only to find my mother at the gate with a knife waiting for me to come home. Now get this—Mum was visiting from Jamaica, it was her first visit, and she was jolted with fear for me. I got home and called Rafel, but of course he lied, as always, telling me it wasn't his ex, and blah blah. It was not until I told him I was calling the police that he admitted she *was* his ex.

Eventually, Rafel decided he was going to come and visit our son.

I didn't believe him, but he pleaded and promised, softening me up so he could come over. Believe it or not, he was late. And had he been collecting items like diapers and such for his son? No. He turned up with a peacock bag with four pieces of clothing for his son that didn't fit because Brad was a big baby. Of course, Rafel couldn't know this because he had been absent. Before long, though, he charmed my mother, and he and I were at it again. Rafel was extra nice and promised that he really wanted a family and was glad God had blessed us not just with a child, but a son. We had to get married.

It all had happened so fast and even with the warning signs I saw then, I felt trapped and in so deep that I couldn't turn back. Have you ever felt like you were getting into something even though there were warning signs that it was a really bad idea?

Here were some of the signs that should have warned me off marrying Rafel:

- The night before we got married, he slept in his room and was on the phone with his acid-threatening ex.
- He lied that he had lost his job, but in fact he was fired.
- He wasn't providing for his infant son.

The day of the wedding, if I said I was happy to be there, I would be lying.

I didn't want to go; I felt heavy and knew I was making a big mistake this time. My first marriage wasn't a mistake, but this one had red flags posted all over it.

I have never seen Rafel early for anything, but he was on time for the wedding, and what was very interesting for me was the sign that was revealed to me in the registrar's office.

We had to meet and go over some paper details and a part of this process meant we needed to pay for the certificates. Well, what do you know, I was thinking marriage, so I had money for two licenses and brought that out, but he only had had money for one? If that wasn't a sign to run, nothing else was.

The wedding went ahead, and it was a dark day. There was no help and care. He had done nothing. I did all the work.

I realise now that I was the worker bee for this man. The day ended and life went back to normal as he went back to his room and me to my house. I felt like I had been sold to the lowest bidder.

Things started going further downhill once we got married. We had constant arguments, and he started treating me as though he owned me. Not in a respectful way, but more like, "I have the keys now, so you can sit and not move until I open the door." There was something in my heart telling me there was more to this than I understood. My intuition was telling me to wake up and listen.

I wish I had known better how to listen.

Exit strategies can creep upon us so unknowingly.

CHAPTER 31: THE WOMAN MADE OF STEEL AND STONE

The strength you possess seemingly only truly gets found when your back is braced hard against the wall.

I was tired of us living apart, so I gave Rafel an ultimatum: we needed to be living together or it was over. I was now totally fed up of this arrangement I didn't sign up for. He agreed, and with my friend Annie's help, I started looking at apartments online. I was willing to move myself and my kids out of the home I found comfortable into a new place to please this man.

But when we found a new home at last, he tried to stop me from signing the papers. I didn't know why at first, but I eventually found out. Remember that I had written to the Home Office many times about this, expressing my concern that Rafel might just be using me to get his visa. They never responded. And whenever I asked Rafel if he had gotten any word on his visa, he would say, "God will take care of it." When I finally called the Home Office, they requested I send a letter outlining my previous queries. I was alarmed when they informed me that they had already given him his visa. They even gave me the reference number showing this had happened a *month* ago—and he never told me.

This was why he objected to me moving us to a new house: I was listed as his visa sponsor at my current address!

Before I discovered all of this, we continued to maintain two separate houses, with Rafel being a visiting husband, living in the same borough literally a fifteen-minute drive away. His actions were haphazard, inconsistent, and most importantly unreliable.

There was one particular incident when he left the iron switched on, on the floor still hot. When I spoke to him about it, I reminded him that the baby was now crawling. This ended in a very huge argument, and I asked him to leave the house because I felt it wasn't the best idea that he stayed the night. He refused and became aggressive. He grabbed my right arm in an effort to take away my keys. I had to call the police, who then came and told him to leave my house and go to his own.

Another incident was the night before my son Brad was blessed. We had a discussion in a car park in Purley Way and we had a difference of opinion on what the word *suburban* meant. He was someone who couldn't stand not being right and he started shouting and swearing in front of the kids. I told him to get out of my car because I didn't appreciate anyone swearing in front of my kids. He refused to leave the car and I felt threatened, so I had to call the police again. They spoke to him on my mobile and asked him to leave. He told them I was his wife and he wouldn't leave. The police asked whose car it was and determined that if it was mine, he needed to leave. The police hung up and promised to come soon after that. He got out of my car and I drove off, taking my kids home and leaving him there. Can you believe it? He didn't show up for his son's christening the next day?

Once, we went to Elephant and Castle to eat in a Nigerian restaurant and our son was acting up. His dad got really embarrassed and started saying I wasn't raising him right, because African kids didn't behave like that. A disagreement ensued, and to my surprise I discovered Brad was soiled and had been acting up because he was in discomfort. We went to the car park, changed Brad's clothes, and I asked his dad if he could feed him while I attempted to drive home. He refused to feed his own child because he said he was disobedient, and when Brad called him Dad, he didn't answer.

I tried to tell Rafel that we didn't live in Africa and he shouldn't feel embarrassed because of what people thought of his two-year-old child.

Chapter 31: The Woman Made Of Steel And Stone

He started shouting abuse at me and it was difficult to focus on the dual carriageway from Elephant and Castle driving towards Croydon. I pulled up on the curb and asked him to get out, and he told me not even the police could get him out. It became a very heated quarrel with his shouts and screaming almost shaking the car, so I drove to the Brixton Police Station, and it was only then that I was able to get him out.

It was a tumultuous relationship of break up/make up. The pattern of abuse he inflicted on me was not often physical, but emotional, leveraging the fear of my being a single mum again and the underlying threat of him taking away my son. Rafel told me very subtle stories of how many women who crossed Nigerian men lost their kids. He joked about how he could take Brad, and I would never be able to find him.

That threat became apparent when Rafel came to the house under the pretense of taking Brad swimming. As any mother would, I went to check his bag with the simple intent of making sure he had all he needed. To my surprise, a bag was packed, with all Brad's clothes and many items Brad would need, without my knowledge. When I asked Rafel about it, he threw his regular shouting match and told me he was Brad's dad too. I reminded him that the child didn't live with him; so taking him without my consent did not make any sense. When I asked him when he planned to tell me, he said he was going to call me later that day. He finally just left. So, Brad didn't get to go swimming, but maybe avoided losing his mother forever.

Time passed, and as always, Rafel and I ended up back together. It was part of our very sick, tumultuous relationship. I felt trapped and knew it wasn't good for any of us, even the kids involved, but I didn't know how to walk way.

Still, the next incident that happened made me grateful for the first and maybe only time that Rafel was in my life. There is always a silver lining, I tell you.

Shortly after we reunited this last time, I had an incident with my daughter whereby social services got involved and I spent a night in jail. Jasmine was placed in Tobore's care for a month.

I genuinely cannot expound on this right now for legal reasons. As mentioned, Rafel and I were once again back together, and so he was staying at my home with Brad when I was arrested. The next day I was sent home and social services came around and interviewed him. They asked him in front of me if he had any concerns with me as the mother of his son. He told them none whatsoever.

Rafel's endorsement of my mothering was soon to change, though I only learned about it later in court documents.

The change happened during two trips I took abroad. One to Germany, and the other to Jamaica, to promote my first book, *Bamboo & Fern*, which is now combined into *The Mango Girl*, which you are reading. The extended version of my memoir. I have been writing this book since I was about twelve and my mother gave me a great beating for asking who my father was. It was then that I started making pen and paper my best friend. I first published it in 2014 after I was featured in *The Financial Times* here in the UK as part of a case study from my university. It came out of my writing a piece about myself, and the rest is history.

Anyway, Rafel was aware of both trips and was supposed to help. This discussion had happened before he tried to take Brad without my consent. I expressed to a few friends that I felt uncomfortable leaving Brad with him after that incident. They both agreed, and so I left Brad with a friend who kept him from time to time, and I likewise cared for her kids in exchange.

On the second leg of my book promotion in Jamaica, I took Brad with me because I needed to feel he was safe It was a weeklong visit. Whereas the trip to Germany had only been three days, taking Brad to Jamaica took much longer but meant he would get to see my home and some of my family.

Chapter 31: The Woman Made Of Steel And Stone

Rafel knew I was taking Brad because this was discussed before the trip. You can imagine my shock when I learnt later of his complaint, outlined in court documents, showing he had called social services claiming he didn't know where Brad was. I had emails that were sent to him from Jamaica informing him that my flight had been cancelled. This proved the deceptive person he was because he knew I would be none the wiser that he had called social services to report me for abduction.

Before I learned of those complaints, before the issues in court, I still thought we would be moving in together at last. To help look after my kids until that happened, I got an au pair from Spain. She turned out to be far too intense in the way she handled Brad and Jasmine, but I believed she would only be temporary.

And other good things were happening that maybe made me overlook the bad. I was nominated for London's Leadership Peace Awards, Women for Africa Award, Diva of Colours Awards, and more importantly, I was asked to be the guest speaker at the Merton Young People Awards ceremony. This was my first paid speaking gig, and I was totally excited. I would be addressing three hundred people, including parents and dignitaries. I was over the moon. I invited my friends Sher and Annie, as well as my husband. To my surprise, Rafel said he couldn't come because he had work. Maybe?

Now be mindful, I had never heard of the Merton Young People Awards before the day the email came into my inbox. But they wanted me to be their guest speaker, so I needed to deliver. I recall sending various emails back and forth asking questions like how many people would be there and what age groups, etc.

I needed to be great because this was what I wanted to do for the rest of my life.

I spoke at the awards ceremony and got a brilliant reception. I even ran into former colleagues from my teaching days who were attending. I can't forget one girl named Dee, a teacher with whom I worked, asking me what I was doing there. I told her I was one of the guests. I didn't say guest speaker to be honest, as she was one of the white teachers that made me feel unworthy back in my teaching days. As I walked away from her, I went to sit in the reserved seat left for me right in the second row. Wow, my friends and I were sitting right behind the dignitaries. I had a little tear in my eye, and I pinched myself privately.

In the midst of all this good feeling, back in 2014, I bought Rafel his first car. He was chuffed. He had also agreed to see a therapist as we worked on our marriage. My hopes were foolishly high.

Soon after that, I was invited to speak in Ireland during Africa Black History month, at the store where my book was to be launched as well. I was delighted that Tobore's cousin, my beloved Norma Jean, had arranged this for me. I was so happy to be getting international exposure, and I jumped at the opportunity. Rafel was meant to pay for all of us to attend, and to be honest this wasn't going to cost more than £700, but he wasn't able to find it. Without him or our children coming, I asked my very good friend Voneta to accompany me.

I was all packed for Ireland. Jasmine would be staying with Tobore. Then Rafel offered to stay at my house with the au pair to help ensure Brad was okay. I had no issue and thought it was great. He was, if for no other reason, almost forced by default to look after his child, and so I was happy. Are you recognising the pattern of him pretending things were fine as he plotted his next move? Later, I found out that he took this opportunity of being in the house without me to scour through my documents, stealing all he needed of my private papers.

Just before I went to Ireland, he kept telling me that his office was giving him issues over his visa and he was inadvertently loading more pressure on my shoulders, worrying about his visa application. I did not yet know that his visa had already been approved, which made this another lie. And it happened through my letterbox without my knowledge.

While in Ireland, I sent him pictures of the event, trying to encourage him to be a part of my world, yet he was very distant. Something wasn't right.

Now don't get me wrong, he was never a very mushy person, at least not to me and the kids, but I had a need for some more warmth. He barely responded. It was like flat Coke: no fizz. I recall something in my spirit telling me things weren't right back home with him and the au pair, so I sat on the hotel bed and called home. Though it was not even eight in the evening, no one answered. The au pair's mobile went unanswered. His mobile and the house phone rang out. My heart and head were uneasy. I knew something about that night wasn't right. I got the au pair after many attempts. She came on the phone and the first thing she said in a sleepy voice was that he was sleeping. I will leave the rest for you to make of it what you desire.

Things were clearly not getting better between us after all.

I came back from Ireland, and we were very civil with each other. We even made love on my return. But I couldn't go to work because I now had no childcare. I got rid of the au pair because I could no longer tolerate her. I was working in shipping, and as Jasmine was still with Tobore, I had no one to look after Brad, so I asked Rafel to collect him from the nursery.

His response was to complain that when I came in, I hadn't said hello. I tried to talk to him about getting childcare so that I could go to work, and he flew off the handle, shouting, screaming, and getting so angry he couldn't calm himself down. He threatened to finish me off, said that I was treating him like a dog, that I hadn't said hello, and I showed no gratitude for him picking up his son from the nursery. I had to point out to him that picking up and dropping off Brad was my daily routine, so he wasn't doing me any favours. He shouted and told me he would deal with me. He would teach me a lesson because I was disrespectful and didn't understand that he was the man. He repeatedly said he would destroy me, as though he needed to get my attention. He said I seemed to feel that because the papers and radio stations were showing me some attention, I was all that was important. I told him to leave my home because he was shouting, and our son was covering his ears. He told me to call the police, and I told him I wasn't afraid to do so.

He told me, as he left reluctantly, that he would ensure I paid for this and that he would not stop until he destroyed me.

Purging is absolutely necessary at different phases of our lives, but purging only becomes effective if you truly grasp why you are being purged.

CHAPTER 32: WHY THIS CAGED BIRD SANG

Storms don't always kill you; they toss you about and give you resilient muscles that make you "rare metal." They teach you to dig deeper for stuff you never knew you possessed.

The true beginning of the end went like this:

Rafel had been treating me like I was nothing, as if I didn't exist. He came to my house, ate the largest plates of food that he didn't provide. I was caring for his son and myself, which were his responsibilities. I was at the end of my tether. My health was waning. I had high blood pressure. I was worn out mentally, emotionally, and physically. And I was fed up with him having sex with me in my sleep, basically raping me, as I obviously did not consent to this. He disgraced me, cursed me, and had no regard for me.

And still the sickness of the abused woman prevailed. I didn't call the police. I still believed we could make things work.

So, I sent him several text messages saying that had he been a more responsible father, I wouldn't be suffering like this. Had he taken his responsibility seriously as a husband, I wouldn't be in such a bind and be so stressed. Also, I sent him an email outlining how I felt.

Unfortunately, the email went to his entire department at work.

The truth was, I was venting to him and it wasn't my intention for it to go to his team. This happened because I had an opened email that he sent me before and copied to his team. That said, many men who loved their wife or their child would be mad if something like this happened, but they would smooth things over with their office and deal with it calmly. Not Rafel. He went to the police!

I later realized that it was because his girlfriend worked in the same office. He was more embarrassed about living a double life that I think only he and maybe a few of his close friends knew about. Most of his colleagues didn't know about me and didn't even know he was married.

He already had a plan in place, and naïve as I was, I didn't know he was already talking with a lawyer about divorce, planning his escape agenda, and I played right into his hands. He needed an escape and a woman was waiting. A woman who was not just waiting, but waiting in his office. I didn't know this. I didn't know that even though Rafel was still married to me, he was preparing to be wed in his culture, with a real wedding, a traditional African ceremony. The one his customs and tradition respected. This woman he wanted to marry had no British residency visa, I was told, so I guess I could understand the urgency. After all, she had been in waiting for so long, she needed to get the golden prize.

Before I knew it, I received a court order for non-molestation and other orders including a Prohibited Step order meaning I could not move Brad from the UK to live anywhere else. The accompanying documents said I was mentally unwell and a bad mother.

Rafel had used documents like Jasmine's and Brad's birth certificates that he could only have snuck out of my house when I was off in Ireland. It was evident to me that he had been planning this for a while.

This was also when I finally saw the number of times he had reported me to the police station over the years—even while staying in my bed and supposedly both trying to work on our marriage.

It also became very clear I was right in my earlier fears that he was just using me for his visa regularisation. He never meant to be with me. After I had called his bluff by insisting on him moving in with us, which he couldn't do because of his other woman, he executed his Plan B and used Brad, our son, to access and regularise his papers. He told me many stories of how silly we European women were because "Nigerian men" knew the loopholes to jump through to achieve what they needed.

Chapter 32: Why This Caged Bird Sang

My pastor, who had been determined to save our marriage, said he was happy to testify on my behalf. Everyone around me pointed out how many hundreds and thousands of women and men in this country are exploited like this daily, how a simple sperm donation, without the responsibilities, gives you the right to act irresponsibly and then claim the rights of a UK citizen.

Of course, Rafel had already told me that he no longer needed to exploit me to get his papers because now he could just exploit our son and the UK law would protect him. Even that I might have forgiven, but I had a problem with the lengths he had chosen to go to discredit me. I wanted the court to see him as a lying witness, and also as someone who was deceptive, a thief, and unsuitable to look after my son.

I wanted him to have supervised visits in a contact centre and the molestation order to be contested by my solicitors, as well as the allegations to be verified and proven, and the bans on my actions lifted because they had no credibility. Rafel had a visa agenda, and this needed to be highlighted to the courts. I also wanted to check if he had a Nigerian passport in my son's name, and for him to tell the court the truth if he had committed bigamy.

Some part of my abused-spouse sickness made me still feel we could make our marriage work. Maybe it was low self-esteem, fear of being alone with two kids, fear of having Brad stolen from me, or just perhaps feeling like a failure with yet another marriage. I don't know how, but it somehow felt like love to me.

But I was still going to fight.

What followed can only be summarized by telling you that I spent the next four years in court. I became totally broke with bailiffs constantly at my door for my unpaid debts. I went without even having lunch at work, and the list goes on.

I sank into a place that had me unwashed for five days. I stank, I became a zombie, and my two kids saw me in a state no child should see their parents. We went through moments of being unable to find food as I struggled to pay the barristers' fees.

I had to stop paying my mortgage, which landed me in arrears, and I lost my house in the process. I fell deeply into debt that saw my utility bills unpaid. I was unable to buy petrol in the winter, and I had to wrap my son in a blanket as I dropped him off to school.

What was most heartbreaking was that what my husband did caused me to be unable to pay his son's nursery fees for six months. My son nearly lost his place, and I begged on bended knees to the council for a payment plan.

It broke me, and broke the spirit and wellbeing of my kids. I struggled between dislike, indifference, and pain.

There were even times when I thought about reconciling with Rafel, if for some strange reason, he was open to it. That's how broken I was.

But as more and more of his deceptions came out, I finally moved from dislike, hurt, and pain, towards recovery. I pushed my way through the birth canal and came out with greater purpose.

I recall one day, I shocked even myself as I sat at home just about to appear on a radio interview. The tears streamed down my face in between the interview questions. But believe me, I pushed through, and that pain gradually became anger, and the anger became a determination to use all of this to make better relationship judgments, to make Brad a better man to women he comes into intimate contact with, to love myself more.

And above all, to not to let Rafel win.

The battle took me to both criminal court and family court. In criminal court, after I was found guilty of harassment, I appealed, and I won. The judge was shocked and saddened that Rafel had done such things. He saw through the case quickly.

In family court, Rafel turned up with a Jamaican barrister, which maybe he thought would give him an edge over me? This from a man who

Chapter 32: Why This Caged Bird Sang

didn't have money to even top up his oyster card, the card used for transportation here in the UK. Rafel had been using my money all this time so he could save enough of his own to take me to court.

I was mortified and fainted from shock in the court bathroom. This was the man who, five weeks prior, accepted his first car, bought by me. This was the man who, five weeks earlier, was in my bedroom making love with me.

I finally came to realise that our relationship had been doomed to failure before we started. He always had a hidden agenda. And there was always at least one other woman in the background, and maybe three more.

I won't lament it anymore but to say that in the end, Rafel hardly saw his son. Part of the reason he didn't fight hard for Brad may have been that the judge said if Rafel got custody, he'd have to tell me where he lived. But I think the real reason was that Rafel didn't care enough. Brad was at primary school and his father didn't know the name of his school, the name of his teacher, when he was ill, where he played rugby, or who his friends were. When the judge found that Rafel had not seen his son for three months, he asked Rafel when he would see him next. Rafel said in a month's time. To top it off, he said he couldn't pay the twenty pounds per month that it would take.

Parts of me thought good riddance, but the sad part of me thought about my darling son. He deserved better, but I couldn't be his dad and mum combined. I could only be the best version of a mother I could be.

The bottom line is that Rafel accepted in court to only see his son twelve times per year. It is still my hope that when he truly decides to love his son like a father should love his child, he may decide to get involved. I am leaving the door wide open for my son's sake.

I walked away from court and thanked God, for that part of the journey was over. I was singing in my head one of my favourite poems—Maya Angelou's "Caged Bird."

Today, I have come to a place of ease, contentment, and thankfulness. I have forgiven Rafel, and I needed to. Because by not forgiving him, I would be holding myself prisoner.

You see, what he meant to be my *bad* has become my best *good*. He left me, dumped me, and abandoned me, but God took me up. More importantly, ever since I released Rafel in forgiveness, the sunrays have come, and that has been the best thing of all.

I may never talk to him again, but we share a son, and for that reason, and that reason alone, I will say I wish him well.

Overall, I went through hell throughout my life, but this one floored me. I was convicted of harassment, but I appealed and won. I was meant to die. This man I fell in love with wanted to see me dead. However, I have come to learn that the woman I am today has been elevated by what caused me extreme pain. And today I walk in my God-given assignment, thanking my ex for leaving me, because that has resulted in my becoming a better woman and mother, one who has decided not to be anyone's footstool, but to see the signs and refuse to ignore them at the onset.

I've shared stages with great speakers such as Eric Thomas, Nick Vujicic, and Lisa Nichols, and I have a feature film that is being produced about my life.

I have learnt to be patient, more forgiving, not to settle, and to walk patiently, knowing the man who was made to love me will come. He will honour and respect me, as I will adore and honour him.

Whatever opens you up is never as important as what it opens. The field that is open is what truly matters.

They say the truth shall vindicate you. Sometimes your vindication takes more time than you think, but don't get impatient; it does come.

CHAPTER 33: MY FULL CIRCLE

There is a cleansing that only comes from revisiting the things that caused you pain and held you captive.

A few years later after all the mess with Rafel, life in general, and my journey so far, I was sitting in the Marriott Hotel in Warsaw, Poland, waiting to have dinner with someone who was going to help shape my life and give me yet another quantum leap forward. He flew me to Warsaw to discuss my book, which was at the time optioned to become a feature film. He wanted to translate it into Polish.

Now forgive me for thinking small for a moment because I never envisaged that my book would even be translated into Spanish, the language that I was more intimate with, having grown up next door to Cuba, let alone an Eastern European language. Never, never, never, and I daresay never, meaning not even in my wildest dreams, did I see that coming. I was not only going to have my book translated but I was invited to speak in front of over 15000 to share my story. This was huge and in Poland at that!

I look over my life, and I must say it's been tumultuous. I seem to have made some of the same mistakes far too often, and I had to come to a place of awakening.

That awakening came in 2013, despite the court, the drama, and the tosses and turns. It was on that journey that I encountered five human beings in the personal development space that truly woke me up. They came in the form of Lisa Nichols (I call her my "shero"), Eric Thomas, Nick Vijicic, Steve Harvey, and Abraham Hicks. There have been others, but these five played a huge part in how I crawled my way out.

Chapter 33: My Full Circle

I first came upon the Steve Harvey story about how he had hit rock bottom and was sleeping in his car, and how he turned his life around. Lisa Nichols couldn't buy diapers for her son, so she used towels to hold him together. Eric Thomas was a high school dropout who became homeless. Nick Vijicic was born without arms and legs. All four of these incredible global people have decided that their personal circumstances would not stop them. Instead, they have used their deficiencies and made them proficiencies. They have all refused to accept the life they have been given, and through their walk, they have been able to touch millions globally.

Abraham (Esther) Hicks's teachings as a mindset and spiritual teacher have totally transformed my mind-set, vibration, and life. Little did I know that I would get the chance to meet all but one of these five individuals in less than two years. I spoke on stage with Nick Vijicic and Eric Thomas, and most recently, spent a weekend with Steve Harvey in Atlanta. Lisa and I are working on a project together, and she has done the foreword for a book I was instrumental in compiling.

I had started working on *The Mango Girl* movie project, which saw the team (myself, the line producer, assistant producer, and two executive producers) visiting the American Film Market in Los Angeles. We attended many meetings around movies, and my life was truly taking a very hectic, but enjoyable, journey. I was scared and excited at the same time.

I was involved with hosting Eric Thomas in London, and the event was beyond our wildest expectations. There were more than two thousand people from thirteen different countries. Because of that event, I was invited to Poland, and I spoke in front of more than 10,000 people, sharing my story of pain, anguish, poverty, incest, lack, resilience, tenacity, courage under fire, and purpose.

It was an exhilarating experience, as I also got to take my kids with me. They were so proud of their mother. I recall my daughter coming backstage and crying. My son stood on stage with me, listening to a Polish song that we both didn't understand, but the atmosphere was so charged it didn't matter. As I stood on that stage, in front of all those people, I was overwhelmed. Little ol' me, the girl still going through the stresses of life, the court cases, the childcare challenges. God has truly blessed me, as here I was, being treated like a queen in a foreign land. If anyone had told me I would be doing that while I was selling mangoes in Jamaica, I would have laughed at them.

Yet, here I was living it. I was picked up at the airport and dropped at a five-star hotel. My room was one of the most beautiful suites I have ever seen, and there was more than enough space for my kids. As I practiced my speech, I was overcome with pride to see Eric Thomas—the man whose words "Pain is temporary," got me out of my own rut—clapping and saying I was doing a great job.

I knew that I was on to something special. I knew that I was born to heal lives. I knew God was going to use me in a big way. I didn't know what the rest of the journey would look like, but I did know that it would happen. My wings had just opened, and I was ready to fly.

After that trip to Poland, life was never the same.

I then realized that my thoughts were becoming things, and the Bible verse that states, "As a man thinketh in his heart, so is he," came to mind. What I was thinking and preaching were now manifesting in my own life.

Things moved fast, and the next thing I knew, I was in dialogue with The Jamaica Tourist Board and The Film Commissioner of Jamaica, with a view of visiting with the team to do a location scout for the movie (looking at the scenery and locations that will be involved in the film).

It all happened so fast, and before I knew it, I was on a flight headed to Jamaica with two people from the team who had worked in the movie industry for years. It was a very weird feeling as I do go home often, but this trip was very different.

I wasn't just going to my home or my mum's home, I was going to a hotel already paid for, with a driver waiting at the airport. Part of it felt surreal, and I shivered at the thought as my son and I sat on the plane.

The flight was rather enjoyable. One of the team members who was much older, treated my son like his own grandson. It was so refreshing to watch, as not only was it a great experience for my son, it was for me, too. I have never had that experience. In that moment, my son and I had a similar experience at the same time. We landed in Jamaica in what seemed like the shortest flight I have ever taken home, and it sure felt bittersweet. You see, I was the girl who fled Jamaica almost in shame, after being held at gunpoint and nearly having a nervous breakdown. So, to be going home in this fashion was a big deal. To some, it might be nothing, but if this is all that will ever happen, if the movie never gets made, this right here, was a big deal.

The plane landed, and we seemed to have taken London with us. It was the first time in sixteen years that I landed in Jamaica on a wet tarmac. There was a downpour, and in my head, the gods were cleansing and washing all those demons from me, and refreshing, as well as renewing, my path.

We sat in the plane on the tarmac for more than twenty minutes. Though not happy, I knew it was unavoidable. We eventually disembarked, and what happened next was something I see only as a scene in the movies.

Before we even took one step off the plane, there was a representative at the door of the plane sent by the Jamaica Tourist Board. We were walked down through the other passengers and whisked to the middle of that walkway where she was waiting from Jampro.

It all happened so quickly, and all I know is that within minutes, we were at the front of the queue, being rushed through immigration and outside where my mum was waiting for us.

There was a bit of wondering where I should go first. Jampro needed to talk to me; Mum needed to see me as well. So, I decided to greet Mum and give her my son so she could love on him while I spoke to Jampro. I settled the team in the beautiful car Jampro had sent to pick us up. We

Chapter 33: My Full Circle

were given our itineraries at the airport, and I was reminded that this was a business trip. It wasn't a fun, family, and home trip.

We all got in the car, Mum included, and we headed for Kingston. It was late at night, and we were exhausted. The driver took us on a new highway I didn't even know about, and this halved the journey. We arrived in Kingston at about eleven p.m., and the former director of tourism was waiting on us in the five-star hotel that was booked for us. After the introductions were done, we were all given gift bags with memorabilia and ushered to our rooms.

Can I just be a bit ghetto here? I was overwhelmed by my room. The hotel suite was almost the size of my London home, and that's no joke. My bed, in comparison to my London bed, was a tennis court. You see, London has an issue with space for the most part, so a house could cost £300,000, but it's a small home compared to a house in some parts of Jamaica.

I have become so used to small beds and bedrooms. Needless to say, I have a king-size bed in the UK, but this one was not a bed, it was something else. I missed Jamaica for things like that, and as for most people, a big bed is the norm back there. Once I crawled out of my poverty in Jamaica and became an adult, I only slept in HUGE beds; Tobore and I had a king size bed that could fit six people at one go. I was reminiscing in this moment in this bed. I had to snap out of it, as it was no longer my reality.

My mother was blown away by the entire suite. She didn't want to sit down on the sofa; she didn't want to disturb it. Mama has a sofa, granted, but that was different. She walked around the suite, captivated by the sight of each item, and staring in admiration at me, wondering in her mind where her daughter had got to. Granted, she was now living in a home I had built her. It was not lavish but a step up from our one-room shack.

Though, in my mind, I was nowhere as elevated as others were feeling I was at this point in my life. I was shattered, so I jumped in the shower and was ready to hit the sheets. I was feeling and hearing the bed calling me so powerfully. For the first time in more than two years, I didn't need to worry about my son's wellbeing. His Nan was there. She had taken over the shift, and for that, I was at peace.

Mama and my son slept on the tennis-court bed, and I slept in the living room, on the luxury of that also felt like a California King…oh boy Jamaica was nice.. I was out before you knew it, and the hot Caribbean air caressed my face. The top floor was where I felt safer; you see Jamaica will always have that reside of fear for me because of my attack I shared earlier. We all fell asleep rather quickly. In that California king bed I was engulfed in the arms of home regardless of where I roamed. My DNA was planted here. I always feel more connected to Jamaica than any other part of the globe regardless of what I had experienced prior to leaving my beautiful island.

I even slept with the balcony double glass doors open, it felt peaceful and I was so torn in moments such as this.

The next day, bright and early, Mum took my son and disappeared to Saint Elizabeth where we are from. My heart was beating fast while worrying about the awful driving that goes on in Jamaica, worrying about accidents on the road, but then I went back into my vortex and was content that he was okay. I called them every hour until he was safe in my mum's home. I could hear his aunties, cousins, and family members that he had never met hanging around him, and in that moment, I knew I had made the right choice to take him with me to Jamaica. He was getting a better education by seeing family he has never met than by sitting in a classroom in the winter in the UK.

That day, we had breakfast and started working from our itinerary. It was time to get rolling. Needless to say, my entire body wanted to sleep and just glide into the sunset, as I would do had I been on holiday.

We set off and walked to the Jampro head office, which was a few blocks away. Although midway through the ten-minute walk there was a

Chapter 33: My Full Circle

car to pick us up. The meeting went well, and while there, we were put on the radio for a quick interview.

Our days were packed with location visits, and eating the local fruits, some of which were new to me. The crew said they had never seen such variety of fruits. One of our location scouts took us to Spanish Town Market where we got mangoes. Oh, la la, I sank my teeth in and forgot where I was or who I was.

You see, once I see a mango, my name is called. I want to just grab it and start ravaging it. I totally savoured each bite, and the juices that ran down my hands. Nothing tastes as good as a well-ripened mango that was left in the sun to mature.

Our scouting took us to schools, churches, homes, and all that we needed for the pictures or exterior of the film. My days were packed with scouting and poolside meetings with directors, producers, and in general, Jamaicans in the creative industry. All meetings were arranged by Jampro.

There were moments when I wished, rather than sipping fruit punch and Red Stripe beer at the poolside in a meeting, I was sitting at a jerk spot in Port Royal over a fish and festival.

Days went by quickly, and it was almost time to go. I had eaten so much food and felt fatter than when I arrived. Between the patties, coconut water, jerk of all sorts, and red pea soup, Jamaica was my food place, and the team was truly having a ball. Often, you would hear them say that they have never been anywhere where the spirit of the people was so vibrant, and these men have travelled extensively.

We visited the Coronation Market, not just because I love the place and it is a business area, but because it was potentially one of the sights to be used in the film.

The trip was a buzz, I must say, but it all came crashing down when the Jamaica Railway Corporation arranged for me to visit one of the actual trains I used to sell mangoes on as a child. It was all going well, and

Chapter 33: My Full Circle

nostalgia was in the air until one of the crew members asked me, while inside the actual train, if that was how it seemed when I was selling on it.

Now, for the life of me, I cannot tell you why, but tears started streaming down my face. In that moment, I started seeing the little girl on the train en route to Cambridge St James, Jamaica, calling out, "Mangoes, mangoes, anyone wants mangoes!" and the faces of the people who pitied her were all in sight. The ones buying to be kind, the sexual encounter with her father, the gun barrel in her face, the living with someone else while Tobore stayed in his nice house, the migration to London. The tearing apart of my soul. All the times I was rejected, the smell of urine at my mum's house, and all those experiences that were bad. Note, only the bad ones came crashing in, and next thing I knew I was on the floor in an almost foetal position.

Thankfully, I was only with the men, and they seemed not to know what to do or how to handle the situation. They decided I needed to be alone, so they walked off and left me to feel the moment. I suppose it cleansed my soul. I can't explain why it happened. It was a simple question that just blew open the floodgates.

What I do know, however, is that it was necessary. I needed it. For the first time, I felt free.

The trip ended, and I had one more stop to make. To visit where I actually sold mangoes but first, we had to take make a stop at Sarah's home. My heart was racing, as I had never really been back in that area since I ran away from Sarah's home. The team wanted to see the actual community where this warrior was born.

We also needed to pick up an important person. My son. Can you believe it? My son, yes, my five-year-old Brad, who was only about four years or so younger than I was when I was selling mangoes. I have never been away from him without worrying, but I had not spoken to him for days, as each time I called, he was too busy to talk to me. He was having fun roaming in the community that I grew up in, visiting some of the

Chapter 33: My Full Circle

same places that had been important to me. This was such a moment for me, truthfully, as I knew that week he spent in that poor part of my world and community was a stark comparison to his concrete jungle "better life" in London. When I am in London, I am never given a breather with my son. I have no one to help me, and just to have had that respite, I relished it and my soul was able to relax for a week. He was safe and in the best hands apart from mine, as I know my mum wouldn't allow a fly to land on him.

Our driver picked us up early to make the meandering drive to Mile Gully. The journey was filled with mixed emotions. There was anxiety, excitement, flashbacks, and just wanting to get there and see the place one more time—or maybe I didn't want to see it at all. Like I said, I was a bundle of emotions.

We got there after a two-hour drive, and on the way, for the first time, I realized that Jamaica had pockets of rainforest. Yes, I studied geography, but it wasn't my focus at the time. It was a beautiful country, with some interesting inland attractions to be seen. Balaclava looks so different. In fact, as an adult it didn't seem like the places I saw as a child. You see, all buildings seemed amplified through my child's eyes. The plazas I sold mangoes on were all still there, but they were so small. It didn't seem to make sense. The platforms were almost gone, as the trains were no longer working.

I ran into an old man who remembered me, funnily enough, and as I stood there, I was proud of the skills I had honed at that spot: survival, tenacity, and resilience. We drove to my community, and after saying hello to a few people, we arrived at the first place I can recall being home. I saw some regular faces, and they were all excited to see me. They pondered why I had two white (Caucasian) men with me. I told them why I was there, and they all became excited. I took the team to my old home, and it all looked the same. Nothing had changed. I hadn't been to that particular house in many years, but there I was, standing on the very spot I ate,

Chapter 33: My Full Circle

showered, slept, and got some good old beatings from Mama, though our relationship was a better one now, and more affectionate. The team was shocked at what they saw. That one-room shack, to them, represented so much more of who I BE in the world. And yes, I said "BE" for emphasis, though grammatically incorrect. They finally got the entire movie just by being there in that moment. They were ready to leave and they got it. You see, like a book, you sometimes read three hundred pages to get one lesson, and that one lesson could write a new book. That was what happened to the team at that moment. They saw my place of entry into the world, and that wrote or tweaked the entire script.

We were headed to pick up my son when one of the team members laid his hand on my shoulder in the jeep and told me that he now got me. He got my assertiveness, my resilience, my courage. He got who I became, and why. He saw where the fire in my belly came from. It came from the fight to escape that childhood. I know he meant it in a good way, and at that moment, he told me he had all he needed to tweak the script, because he saw far more than the book had in it.

He said, "We need to go darker with the script, Ava."

I was happy that he saw it and realized that the trip was worth it, as sometimes we need to be at that moment to create amazingness. We got to my mum's home (sadly my stepfather was at his farm so we missed him), and she was finally living in her own home for the first time. I had finally placed her under her own roof. Yes, she was now turning keys to her own home, one that I managed to build for her. It wasn't a mansion, but it was hers and not dilapidated. She had a cooker, fridge, inside bathroom, and even her own sofa. Mama was comfy by many standards of comparison.

Most of my siblings were away, and I saw very few family members. Parts of me were torn to not have seen them, but others were not. Just before that trip, I was cursed out by some of them, telling me I didn't do anything for them or my mum. I was tired and somewhat detached from

Chapter 33: My Full Circle

some of my siblings. That said, it would have been nice to see them, but I had no choice in the matter. We were on schedule, and the driver had strict instructions.

Mum had all things you could think of ready for me. Cereasse (a leaf tea), yam, breadfruit, you name it. She didn't have a mango. I realized my son was out of sight, and when I questioned this, I was told he was hiding in the back, and he didn't want to come with me. He loved the outdoors and wanted to stay more in Jamaica, especially with his Nana and all the many cousins and friends he had made. You see, back in London, he had very few friends. None on our street, for example, and the way I juggle life makes it hard to answer all his play needs, though I try very hard. I had to tear him out of his grandma's hands to get him to come with us, and he cried awfully. My heart broke as I was reminded how far apart we all were, how many family members I had in Jamaica, and how non-existent that was for me in the UK. I was heartbroken by the fact that the Home Office refused my mum a visa so often, though she has been there before with no violation. At least then my mum would get to see us, and we could feel a sense of support, and my kids could get some from their Nana. We drove off, with the image of Mama and I in a close embrace, one like we have never had before. You see, Mama isn't the mushy type, so I had to steal that one.

We drove to Montego Bay to revisit the house where I got held up at gunpoint, our marital home, and that was easier than I thought it would be. I no longer felt the emotions. I blocked them out. The house was looking good, and I felt I should be upset that I lost it, but I absolutely wasn't. I felt relieved not to be associated with it. The team took pictures of what they needed, and we left to settle into our hotel to sleep before our flight the next day.

On the plane back to London, I felt sad that I was leaving Jamaica. I had fallen in love with the place all over again. It felt as though all the disasters that forced me out had dissipated, and I was set free by the trip.

My demons no longer existed. There was so much to why I fell in love. There were gorgeous men who weren't afraid to tell you they were keen to get to know you. Now don't be fooled, they may not all qualify, but it was better than what happened in London. While I was there, I tell you, I literally had to pray because I was tempted. I had to remind myself of what I promised myself and my new partner, the one I was waiting on to show up in my life: That I was saving myself for someone who truly deserved me.

I valued my body and respected my kids and didn't want another disastrous relationship. I also knew it was temptation because of how long I have been alone. Thank God, He held me close as I came back to London.

I also fell in love with how free life in Jamaica is. The people just smiled all day. I missed the food, the sunshine, and more so, my family. Regardless of our relationship, all families have ups and downs.

As we sat on the tarmac, I felt torn between my new place where I live in London, and my home, the land of my birth, Jamaica. My DNA stretched between two worlds, and in that moment, I wished I was on the plane, but I had to snap back to reality as my teenager was in the UK, missing us like crazy. I put on my big girl panties, wiped the teardrop from my face, and started thinking of life back in the UK.

The flight took off, and whether I wanted to stay or not, I had no choice. We landed at Gatwick airport, and I realized I was going to miss the crew. We'd had a great time. We said our goodbyes, and the cold of three degrees snapped me back to reality. I hailed a cab and headed home, wanting just to curl up and cry. I opened my door and went to my daughter's bedroom. She was sleeping, and I had to kiss her softly on her cheeks, reflecting on our journeys and how we have soldiered on to this place. She was a stronger girl than either of us realized, and while from my struggles she bears the scars of mental health issues, she was my first baby, and seeing her safe in her bed made my heart proud that despite all of the shit, I did my best by her. I gave her a tight hug, and her brother

Chapter 33: My Full Circle

crawled into her bed, and they both went to sleep. My bed was filled with one of my adopted daughters and her daughter, who I consider my granddaughter (my daughter's friends), so I went downstairs to the sofa and went to sleep.

I didn't want to be sleeping in London, but here I was. We had work to do on the script, and I was now ready to focus on making *The Mango Girl* movie a reality. I wanted to help others see that where you are from doesn't determine where you end up. I don't know what God has planned for me, but it's my hope that somewhere in there, he has a Jamaican king, preferably in the UK, who desires a queen and wants to live back home. I sure would like that very much.

I went through the rest of January just using that Jamaica trip to hold me together while I planned for the event that came out of my awakening, called *Purposewalk*. An event I do annually now because I do believe through our experiences most of us find our true purpose. I certainly found my purpose through my struggles.

As I reflect on my journey, I am thankful that my kids came into my world. Yes, there were points when their being in my life made it hard financially, and in terms of some opportunities, but I chose them every time. I am not as rich as I should have been, not done half of the things I could have done, but I was there as a mama, I cooked for them and was there when they were hurting.

My journey has been a hard one. Some of it based on poor choices, poor insight, and perhaps loneliness. I have come to realise that my childhood continues to leave me with remnants of loss, and I'm constantly trying to work on my confidence and self-esteem, but I am a work in progress.

I know I will not stop making mistakes until I die. What I hope, however, is that I avoid repeating the same mistakes and instead learn from them.

Chapter 33: My Full Circle

As I close this chapter of my life, which is to be continued in a different form, I woke up this morning truly rested and reflective on my journey so far. Here it is from my view in summary:

I realise how resilient I am, how packed with steel and stone I am. Below is a snippet of what I have so far undergone in my short-lived life.

- ✓ Having seen the barrel of a gun ****
- ✓ Raped in front of my two-year-old daughter ****
- ✓ Both of us left for dead on a beach****
- ✓ Been homeless as a teenager*****
- ✓ Not one, but two failed marriages (not proud, but it's my reality****. Hence, I stay single now to be more discerning) *****
- ✓ Not to mention the monies I have lost*****
- ✓ The personal family issues I have endured ****
- ✓ The things I now go through that I will speak out on one day****
- ✓ Spent a night in jail here in the UK******
- ✓ Being convicted innocently then appealed and won*****
- ✓ Survived a forty-eight-months court battle with my ex*****

I smiled as I reminded myself that if those things didn't tear me apart, then my GOD must have me preserved for a purpose.

Be encouraged in understanding that you are made of steel and stone and God has a plan for your life, hence He puts you through the fire. Without the mess, there is no message.

Stay resilient, tenacious, embrace courage under fire, as you always will rise.

As you chose to read my book and share on my journey, I want to thank you all for coming along on this path with me. Please stay focused on appreciating the little things in life, as there is abundance even in your circumstance.

Chapter 33: My Full Circle

Please don't forget to love daily, forgive often, and speak your truth.

Love,

Ava

Everything has a way of coming full circle in our lives. I feel like I have journeyed the world, and Jamaica is where that full circle comes together for me.

CPSIA information can be obtained
at www.ICGtesting.com
Printed in the USA
BVHW090812030521
606328BV00012B/527

9 781628 657210